"This book offers a clinical approach to non-neurotic phenomena and unrepresented mental states that emphasizes representation, not as a given but as 'a developmental achievement through which previously unbound or inchoate forces become bound and contained in the psyche."
—**Evelyne Sechaud**, *former president of the European Psychoanalytic Federation; former president, training and supervising analyst of the APF (French Psychoanalytic Association).*

"Psychoanalysts need to resort to as many luminaries in their field as they can, granted that no single author, no matter how great, can be credited with possessing the final truth. But then another problem arises: the multiple analytic idioms represent a challenge of their own. Levine brilliantly meets that challenge by displaying an exemplary capacity to navigate between many exponents of the British, French, North- and Latin-American analytic traditions and offering a personal synthesis rich with original ideas and clinical illustrations."
—**Dominique Scarfone**, *training and supervising analyst, Canadian Psychoanalytic Society Institute, Montreal French Branch.*

"Since Freud, psychoanalysis has acutely explored the architecture, dynamics and texture of psychic life: the logic and logistics of the soul. Howard Levine is at the forefront of thinkers who are currently examining these issues in a contemporary framework. He presents his reflections in crystal clear prose and with all the exciting commitment and enthusiasm of the best psychoanalytic thinkers at work today."
—**Elias M. da Rocha Barros**, *São Paulo Society and fellow of the British Psychoanalytical Society.*

# Affect, Representation and Language

This book presents and elaborates on the rationale and implications of the transformational dimension of psychoanalysis. In so doing, it attempts to extend psychoanalytic theory and practice beyond neurosis and beyond what were formerly thought to be the limits of analytic understanding. Its theoretical vision sits at the crossroads of the thinking of Freud, Bion, Winnicott, Green and the Paris Psycho-Somatic School. Other sources include the contributions of contemporary French psychoanalysts such as Laplanche, Donnet, L. Kahn, P. Miller and the Botellas, along with the work of Alvarez, Scarfone, Ferro, Ogden, and more.

In re-examining the very epistemological foundations of psychoanalysis and their implications for a theory of psychic functioning, it follows upon and extends the radical implications of Freud's 1937 Constructions paper, the thoughts of Bion on intuition and Winnicott's understanding of the working through of the consequences of early pre-verbal environmental failure. In so doing, it makes a case for psychoanalysis as a powerful treatment for borderline, primitive narcissistic, post-traumatic and other character disorders and conditions – including perversions, addictions, psychosomatic, autistic and panic disorders.

By presenting a revised metapsychology that is Freudian, contemporary and clinically near, *Affect, Representation and Language. Between the Silence and the Cry* offers practitioners at all levels of analytic experience a way of understanding and treating the expanding range of patients and disorders that present for treatment in our modern era.

**Howard B. Levine** is a member of APSA, PINE, the Contemporary Freudian Society, NYU Post-Doc's Contemporary Freudian Track and in private practice in Brookline, Massachusetts. He is the author of *Transformations de l'Irreprésentable*, editor-in-chief of the Routledge W.R. Bion Studies book series and a director and founding member of the Boston Group for Psychoanalytic Studies.

The International Psychoanalytical Association
Psychoanalytic Ideas and Applications Series
IPA Publications Committee
*Gabriela Legorreta (Montreal), Chair and Series Editor; Dominique Scarfone (Montreal); Catalina Bronstein (London); Lawrence Brown (Boston); Michele Ain (Montevideo); Carlos Moguillanski (Buenos Aires); Udo Hock (Berlin); Christine Kirchhoff (Berlin), Gennaro Saragnano (Rome) Consultant; Rhoda Bawdekar (London), Ex-officio as IPA Publishing Manager; Paul Crake (London), Ex-officio as IPA Executive Director*

**Permanent Disquiet**
Psychoanalysis and the Transitional Subject
*Michel de M'Uzan*

**Psychoanalytic Work with Families and Couples**
Clinical Perspectives on Suffering
*Susana Kuras Mauer, Sara Moscona, and Silvia Resnizky*

**Narcissistic Fantasies in Film and Fiction**
Masters of the Universe
*Ilany Kogan*

**Psychoanalytic Reflections on Writing, Cinema and the Arts**
Facing Beauty and Loss
*Paola Golinelli*

**Change Through Time in Psychoanalysis**
Transformations and Interventions, The Three Level Model
*Margaret Ann Fitzpatrick Hanly, Marina Altmann de Litvan, Ricardo Bernardi*

**The Infantile in Psychoanalytic Practice Today**
*Florence Guignard*

**Affect, Representation and Language**
Between the Silence and the Cry
*Howard B. Levine*

For more information about this series, please visit: https://www.routledge.com

# Affect, Representation and Language

## Between the Silence and the Cry

Howard B. Levine

LONDON AND NEW YORK

First published 2022
by Routledge
2 Park Square, Milton Park, Abingdon, Oxon OX14 4RN

and by Routledge
605 Third Avenue, New York, NY 10158

*Routledge is an imprint of the Taylor & Francis Group, an informa business*

© 2022 Howard B. Levine

The right of Howard B. Levine to be identified as author of this work has been asserted by him in accordance with sections 77 and 78 of the Copyright, Designs and Patents Act 1988.

All rights reserved. No part of this book may be reprinted or reproduced or utilised in any form or by any electronic, mechanical, or other means, now known or hereafter invented, including photocopying and recording, or in any information storage or retrieval system, without permission in writing from the publishers.

*Trademark notice*: Product or corporate names may be trademarks or registered trademarks, and are used only for identification and explanation without intent to infringe.

*British Library Cataloguing-in-Publication Data*
A catalogue record for this book is available from the British Library

*Library of Congress Cataloging-in-Publication Data*
Names: Levine, Howard B., author.
Title: Affect, representation and language : between the silence and the cry / Howard B. Levine.
Description: 1 Edition. | New York, NY : Routledge, 2022. | Series: IPA psychoanalytic ideas and applications series | Includes bibliographical references and index. | Summary: "This book extends psychoanalytic theory and practice beyond neurosis to what formerly were the limits of analytic understanding, presenting and elaborating on the rationale and implications of the transformational dimension of psychoanalytic practice. Offering readers a metapsychology that is both contemporary and clinically near, Affect, Representation and Language offering practitioners at all levels of analytic experience a way of understanding and treating contemporary patients"—Provided by publisher.
Identifiers: LCCN 2021022510 (print) | LCCN 2021022511 (ebook) | ISBN 9780367774356 (hardback) | ISBN 9780367774318 (paperback) | ISBN 9781003171331 (ebook)
Subjects: LCSH: Representation (Psychoanalysis) | Affect (Psychology) | Psychoanalysis.
Classification: LCC BF175.5.R43 V37 2022 (print) | LCC BF175.5.R43 (ebook) | DDC 150.19/5—dc23
LC record available at https://lccn.loc.gov/2021022510
LC ebook record available at https://lccn.loc.gov/2021022511

ISBN: 978-0-367-77435-6 (hbk)
ISBN: 978-0-367-77431-8 (pbk)
ISBN: 978-1-003-17133-1 (ebk)

DOI: 10.4324/9781003171331

Typeset in Palatino
by codeMantra

Language without affect is a dead language: and affect without language is uncommunicable. Language is situated between the cry and the silence.
Andre Green (1977, p. 205)

# Contents

| | |
|---|---|
| *Series editor's foreword* | xi |
| *Acknowledgements* | xiii |
| *Foreword - When something vital goes missing* | xvii |
| PATRICK MILLER | |

| | |
|---|---|
| Introduction: Freud's theory of psychic functioning and its relevance to the analytic process | 1 |
| 1 Psychoanalysis and subjectivity: a personal note | 6 |
| 2 Freud's theory of representation and the expansion of analytic technique | 19 |
| 3 Clinical implications of unrepresented states: effacement, discourse and construction | 36 |
| 4 The fundamental epistemological situation | 49 |
| 5 Psychoanalysis and the problem of truth | 63 |
| 6 The analyst's authority: suggestion, seduction, compliance and influence | 77 |
| 7 Trauma, process and representation | 91 |
| 8 Making the unthinkable thinkable: Autism, ASD and representation | 106 |

| | |
|---|---|
| 9 Word, body, thing: on the movement from soma to psyche | 122 |
| 10 Psychosomatics and unrepresented states | 132 |
| *References* | 143 |
| *Index* | 151 |

# Series editor's foreword

The Publications Committee of the International Psychoanalytical Association continues, with the present volume, the series "Psychoanalytic Ideas and Applications". The aim of this series is to focus on the scientific production of significant authors whose works are outstanding contributions to the development of the psychoanalytic field, and to set out relevant ideas and themes, generated during the history of psychoanalysis, that deserve to be known and discussed by present-day psychoanalysts.

The relationship between psychoanalytic ideas and their applications needs to be put forward from the perspective of theory, clinical practice and research, in order to maintain their validity for contemporary psychoanalysis. Our objective is to share these ideas with the psychoanalytic community and with professionals in other related disciplines, so as to expand their knowledge and generate a productive interchange between the text and the reader. The IPA Publications Committee is pleased to publish *Affect, Representation and Language. Between the Silence and the Cry* by Howard Levine as part of the Psychoanalytic Ideas and Applications Series.

This volume puts together many of the author's contributions which have been the subject of inquiry and elaboration over the past decade. The author skillfully weaves together his numerous contributions, to provide a holistic and coherent view of his theoretical and clinical stance on the themes of representation, transformation and construction in analytic work. It also elaborates on a number of related theoretical issues such as truth, psychosomatics, time and intersubjectivity.

Solidly grounded in Freudian metapsychology, the reader will get to appreciate the author's intellectual journey, which led him to integrate major ideas in post-Freudian psychoanalytic thought such as those of Bion, Winnicott, Baranger, Green, Laplanche and Tustin. This journey has resulted in Dr. Levine's innovative concept of "the fundamental epistemological situation." A chapter of the book is dedicated to this notion.

We are grateful to the author for having skillfully organized this book in ten chapters which underscore his original and rich contributions to the theoretical and clinical aspects of psychoanalysis. I have no doubt that this book will be of much interest to the psychoanalytic community and to health professionals interested in the notions of transformation, representation and construction in clinical work.

Gabriela Legorreta<br>
Series Editor<br>
Chair, IPA Publications Committee

# Acknowledgements

> Now that we are almost settled in our house
> I'll name the friends who cannot sup with us…
> William Butler Yeats (1919, pp. 130–133)

A book of this kind written in the late stages of one's professional career owes debts of gratitude to many more people than can possibly be mentioned by name: Family, friends, colleagues, teachers, patients and an untold number of contacts and connections that have been formative, have influenced and have made up one's life and experience. One of the most precious gifts of being able to have spent one's life as a psychoanalyst is that person and profession become intimately and inextricably entwined.

At this particular moment in time, the beginning of 2021, still in the midst of the ravages and uncertainty of the Covid pandemic, it is Yeats' memorial poem to those friends no longer with him, many of them comrades who perished in the Irish fight for independence and could not be present in the flesh at the joyous celebration of the housewarming at his new home, that has come to mind. In re-reading this manuscript for the final time before sending it off to the publishers, my thoughts have returned to a number of names and faces that I would like to mention, all but one of whom have passed on.

David Sidorsky, still living well into his late 80s or early '90s, was a young philosopher who taught my freshman class in Contemporary Civilization at Columbia. I was so impressed by him that although I was not a philosophy major, I took every class he offered in my undergraduate years. I learned many things, of course, but above all, I feel he taught me a discipline that I would call learning how to think, something that has stood me in good stead throughout my life.

Paul Myerson was chairman of the psychiatry department at Tufts Medical School when I arrived there in 1964. Paul was quiet, gentle, a man of deep intelligence, compassion and, along with some shyness and a bit of seeming social discomfort, grace. He was a teacher and supervisor and had confidence in me despite my rough edges. He helped arrange a special, extended rotation on the psychiatry service for me in my senior year, accepted me for residency and encouraged my application to the analytic institute. He was a role model that I quietly tried to emulate, not only as a psychoanalyst, author and teacher, but as an eminently sensible man.

Hal Boris, who was supervisor, teacher and then colleague and friend, holds a special place in my heart and mind, because it was Hal who first introduced me to Bion's writings. One of my assignments as a first-year resident was leading a five times per week, in-patient group on a very psychoanalytically oriented ten patient ward. Hal, who was the supervisor, had me read Bion's Experience In Groups and introduced me to Bion's group-as-a-whole manner of leading and interpreting the group. That was a brief three-month rotation at the time, but in my third year of residency, it was decided that it might go better if it became a full year's responsibility and if it was led by someone who had more experience. The department asked me to run the group and I agreed if Hal would be my supervisor. We met twice a week for a year and read Bion's *Attention and Interpretation* together, which had just come out. This immersion in Bion and Boris planted a seed that has grown into something enormously important in my intellectual development and has become a pillar of my professional self.

The final person that I will mention by name is Elvin Semrad, who was my training analyst. In those days, it was the custom for newly accepted candidates to the Boston Institute (BPSI) to visit a number of training analysts and decide with whom they would begin their analysis. Semrad, of course, was already a legend and after talking with him and a few others and consulting with teachers and friends I called him up and told him I would like to begin analysis with him. "Are you sure you want me to be your analyst?" he asked over the phone. I hesitated and answered: "I'll tell you when we're finished." (You can see why I needed Paul Myerson as a model!). If Sidorsky taught me to think, Semrad taught me to wait and to free associate and to feel. Although he was relatively 'atheoretical' in a sense, I always felt in my heart that Semrad, with his often silent, patient expectation of and focus on helping one know and bear and make sense of the griefs and disappointments of one's life was a Bionian fellow traveler, *malgré de lui*. One of the most important lessons he taught me was that "In analysis, you help a fellow to free associate and then you get out of his way." So much of this book and all of the work that I have done in the past 15–20 years on the unrepresented is about just that: what do you have to do to try to help someone to free associate, so that you can get out of their way and they can begin to lead a more coherent, meaningful and successful life for themselves.

Writing of those no longer with him, Yeats says:

> They were my close companions many a year,
> A portion of my mind and life

And in his final stanza:

> ... how bitter is that wind
> That shakes the shutter, to have brought to mind
> All those that manhood tried, or childhood loved
> Or boyish intellect approved...

Bitter, of course, at life's ending, but also sweet. For they are among those I have learned from and loved and upon whose shoulders the foundations of whatever better self I have managed to secure and the accomplishment embodied in this volume has rested. For all that I have received from them and innumerable others, I am grateful.

January 2, 2021<br>
Cambridge, MA

## Permissions

I would like to acknowledge and thank the following books and journals for permission to revise and reprint sections of previously published work.

Sections of chapter 2 previously appeared in Levine, H. B. (2014). Beyond Neurosis: Unrepresented states and the construction of mind. Revista di Psicoanalisi 60: 277–294.

Sections of chapter 4 previously appeared in Levine, Howard (2017): *Die grundlegende epistemische Situation. Die psychische Realität und die Grenzen der klassischen Theorie.* In: *Jahrbuch der Psychoanalyse.* 74 Stuttgart-Bad Cannstatt: Frommann-Holzboog, S. 203–229.

Sections of chapter 5 previously appeared in Levine, H.B. (2016). Psychoanalysis and the problem of truth. Psychoanalytic Quarterly 85:391–410.

Earlier versions of parts of chapter 7 appeared in Levine, H.B. (2021). Trauma, process and representation. IJPA 102: 794–809.

The case material in chapter 8 appeared in: Levine, H.B. (2020). Reflections on therapeutic action and the origins of psychic life. JAPA 68: 9–26.

Sections of chapter 10 previously appeared in Levine, H.B. (2012), Book Review: Psychosomatics Today: A Psychoanalytic Perspective. Edited by Marilia Aisenstein and Elsa Rappoport De Aisemberg. JAPA 60: 207–216.

Levine, H.B. (2017). *La psychosomatica y los estados no representados. Revista de Psicoanalisis* 79: 207–221 and Levine, H.B. (2017). Psychosomatics and unrepresented states. In: Not Knowing – Knowing – Not Knowing ed. by Mira Erlich-Ginor. New York: IPBooks, pp. 73–84.

Earlier versions of chapters 2,3,4,9 and 10 appeared in the French language volume, Levine, H.B. (2019). *Transformations de L'irreprésentable. Théories contemporaines de la cure*. Paris: Ithaque.

# Foreword - When something vital goes missing[1]

*Patrick Miller*

In *Learning From Experience,* Bion (1962b) asserted: "The problem presented by the psycho-analytic experience is the lack of any adequate terminology to describe it."

Becoming an analyst is a never ending quest, a permanent self-interrogation, a sustained dialogue and dispute with other thinkers, dead or alive, first and foremost with Freud, and a conversation with oneself.

This book invites us to follow the author in his theoretical endeavors and watch him grapple with clinical challenges that lead him to question some of the established ideas inherited from his training in the sixties and seventies within the psychoanalytic culture prevalent at the time in North America[2]

Howard Levine seems to have decided, early on, to travel far into the foreign lands of European and South-American psychoanalytic cultures. The book is, in part, the narrative of his journey, in that respect it reads like a Bildungsroman. It deals with his continuing transformation.

The home he starts from is a short autobiographical narrative, very much akin to Green's dead mother complex. His maternal grandmother dies, his mother retreats into depression, when he is 19 months old. Something vital is missing, not only the loss of an object but:

> (…) what I felt to be missing and what I have been continuously striving to recover and create, has also turned out to be some aspect of my *self.*
>
> (p. 13)

---

1 «We may discern a basic, recurring narrative theme (in the development of psychoanalysis), one that might almost be described as one of our 'foundation stories,' told and retold in various 'dialects' by the different iterations of theory and schools of psychoanalysis throughout the history of our field. A core element of this story is that psychopathology and symptomatic distress occur when something vital goes missing.» p. 20.
2 At that point in time, ego psychology and conflict theory were the dominant, almost exclusive theories in American psychoanalysis, and it was assumed for the most part that what the analyst could contribute to the treatment process followed from his or her capacity to be objective about the patient's external reality.

The wish to become an analyst is deeply rooted in such early experiences, the way in which they have been experienced, and then touched and untouched by personal analysis, permeates the theorizing stance and the way in which each analyst develops his own way of implementing theory and technique in the encounter with patients. Levine doesn't go into more autobiographical details, he only pinpoints this early dilemma: object loss/self loss, and how he had to grapple with it at every level of his clinical and theorizing struggles and interrogations throughout his analytic life.

The existential dilemma, beyond the fact that it permeates the analyst's theorizing activity, is part and parcel of his listening, not only as countertransference, but also, and maybe first and foremost, as a potential touchstone giving representational capacities for interpretation. Provided that it is allowed to come spontaneously to the analyst's mind and wording, and not used as a technical tool. Spontaneity is here a key dimension, rooted as it is in the living and life oriented processes taking place within the analyst's somatopsychic continuum.

> When you said that about the look on my face, I was thinking about something in reaction to what you had been telling me. I'm not sure if it will be of interest or use to you, but I thought I would mention it in case it would prove helpful. My thought was about how painful and irrevocable life's losses can sometimes feel and be.
>
> (p. 67)

In this case the analyst's intervention is not a self-disclosure. Actually I think it is quite the opposite. It relies on what the patient thinks she has perceived on the analyst's face. Instead of denying the analysand's perception, the implicit theoretical stance is: something actually showed on my face, the reflection of a complex set of internal psychical events. I'm not going to tell you: « You have imagined this. It's all in your fantasmatic life ». But the analyst doesn't share with the patient the specifics of his personal history. The important point is not to deny the patient's perception, and then bring the rest to a more universal standpoint, sharing something that is common to human beings emotional life: « My thought was about how painful and irrevocable life's losses can sometimes feel and be. » An acknowledgment that something of an interaffective and interpersonal experience has taken place in the hic and nunc of the session, something that goes against the repetition of early traumatic events in the patient's psychic life, something that may suspend the usual defence mechanisms and open up a possibility for a new beginning.[3]

---

3  The notion of new object, instead of only transferential object, and new beginning, comes from Ferenczi's and Balint's tradition.

Truthfulness and spontaneity are tantamount to questions of vitality, as highlighted by André Green:

> Sometimes, paradoxically, it will be less damaging to the process to allow a lively countertransference reaction to be expressed, even if negative, in order to gain access to the internal movements animating the analyst. These are all evidence of ... spontaneity ... having more value for the patient than a conventional pseudo-tolerant discourse which will be experienced by the patient as artificial and governed by technical manuals.[4]

At the heart of Levine's «free-floating theorization» (Aulagnier) during the sessions and in the background of his theoretical and clinical thinking, lies an implicit theory of trauma. Which becomes quite explicit and complex as the book's writing unfolds.

Levine refuses easy and seemingly obvious oppositions, derived from a simplified reading of Freud's thinking:

> (...)the seeming dichotomy between what we might call 'drive/phantasy/wish related pathology' and 'trauma related pathology' appears to be a false one.
>
> (p. 162)

By suggesting that a « trauma of some kind lies at the heart of *every* process that we view as pathogenic » (p. 168) he recalls that Freud suggested that a kernel of actual neurosis might lie at the heart of every neurotic conflict and he brings us back to Freud's « On the psycho-analysis of war neuroses » (1919): « We have a perfect right to describe repression, which lies at the basis of every neurosis, as a *reaction to trauma* – as an *elementary traumatic neurosis.* » (p.210, italics added).

The notion that repression might be a reaction to trauma, an elementary traumatic neurosis, may help us reconsider the drive theory in its relationship to what Green was calling for: a general theory of representation. The issue of « unrepresented states », central to this book, can be worked through and better understood from that perspective.

Freud's conception of the drive, as an elementary form of psychic expression resulting from a demand made upon psyche due to its relation to the body (soma) seems to indicate that the traumatic force lies in the endosomatic excitation. That excitation is both the source of the work resulting

---

4   Green, A. (2005). *Key Ideas for a Contemporary Psychoanalysis. Misrecognition and Recognition of the Unconscious.* Trans. A. Weller, London and New York: Routledge. Cited by Levine, p. 130.

in the drive expression, as a first degree of psychic expression, object seeking and aiming at satisfaction, just as it is what constantly threatens psyche of its deconstruction. In that perspective the origin of trauma is essentially internal. The elaborative trajectory of the drive, from endosomatic excitation to the representational facet of the drive, cannot happen without the qualifying action of the maternal object. Even Freud conceded that psychic development cannot happen without the action of a helpful other. The drive transformation implies an overlapping of internal and external.

We could say that the demand for psychic elaboration stems out of the necessity to « make sense » of the trauma. Meaning happens in the encounter between the infant's drive force and the maternal interpretation that enables the passage from quantity to quality. Major difficulties arise when the object cannot play its qualifying, metabolizing role. The absence of a qualifying function acts as a negative trauma with dire consequences on the infant's representational capacities.

This is what draws the line between neurotic and non-neurotic states and calls for what Levine names « a two-track theory of therapeutic action », one that is archeological and the other generative (Roussillon) and transformative. The latter is not primarily centered on uncovering the repressed, because repression failed in its conservative task, but to help develop the patient's internal capacities that are needed to engage in this specific form of psychic work called psychoanalysis, and actually create a condition (i.e a here and now environment within the dynamics of the session and of the analytic process as it becomes progressively internalized) that will allow for a capacity for repression. Levine uses this very telling image of a long pregnancy:

> The analytic process must often begin and be maintained for long periods of time within the person of the analyst.
>
> (p. 148)

Levine eventually comes to what he calls « a radical conclusion »: what is at stake in the analyses of non-neurotic patients is « the very creation of the psyche itself ». I am not sure that I can follow him in this demiurgic representation of the analyst's action and of the analytic process.

Let's not forget Freud's citation of Ambroise Paré, a « surgeon of ancient times »: « *Je le pansay, Dieu le guérict* », quite consistent with Freud's representation of the analytic process as a pregnancy, where the analyst gives the impetus (the desire and the seed) but the baby is not created by him, it grows in the mother's womb, according to the laws of Nature. Even though we can assume that the mother's somatopsychic state has a « say » in the way the laws of Nature make the fœtus grow and how it interacts with its development.

Nobody can create a mind, but the analyst can try and free the mind from hindrances that prevent it from growing and developing. In one of his novellas, Enfantines, French writer Valery Larbaud wrote: « Let me go back to where I was. » Through what we call regression, and especially formal regression, the analyst's frame of mind and state of consciousness, modified by the demands of the analytic setting and stance, can facilitate for the patient to go back where he or she was. To re-experience some of those early moments of choice and put into question the massivity of some defence mechanisms, which were, at the time, the only manner to survive, both somatically and psychically.

The analyst can accompany the patient back to where he or she was and enable new potential by creating a safer environment, allow some defence mechanisms to become obsolete, help to let them go by maintaining a sufficient homeostasis within the emotional events during the session. In so doing the analyst helps suspend the repetition compulsion and facilitates for the patient to find new possibilities of transformational metabolization and new capacities to translate and interpret different levels of psychic organization. This comes close, although it is expressed in a different metapsychological language, to what Levine pleads for: intersubjective assistance:

> (...) compulsive repetition may signal the active presence of a blind – and « thoughtless » - repetitive action driven by *unrepresented* forces. In addition to defensive and aggressive ends, this repetitive action may contain a desperate plea for ***intersubjective assistance*** in dealing with and helping to relieve primitive agonies.
>
> (p. 174)

Rather than the creation of a mind it allows for the liberation of the potentialities needed to develop a mind. Once those potentialities are internalized in the patient's own capacities, it becomes the patient's task to develop his/her own mind.

Aulagnier wrote that we are « condemned to cathect ». Her metapsychological teaching was an attempt to demonstrate that the human psyche, throughout life, must constantly effectuate a work of translation and interpretation between three dimensions of the psyche that are formally heterogeneous to each other, and stemming out of the « ground » of the soma: the primal or the original (locus of pictographic activity), the primary and the secondary. The original is the first degree of psychic transformation from the somatic, and Aulagnier defined the pictogram as both the representation of the affect and the affect of the representation.

The issue of unrepresented states, central in Levine's book, is a complex one.

Are those states unrepresented because they are lacking representation and hence need to become represented, or do they belong to a dimension of representation that is alien in terms of the logics of primary processes and phantasies or in terms of secondary logics and connection of word presentation with thing presentations? What seems certain is that they do not belong to the repressed unconscious, but rather to the unrepressed.

> Is there experience, perhaps deriving from the soma, the preverbal period of infancy or from traumatic states, that is inscribed – somewhere, somehow – but not yet *psychically* represented? (…) Or do we believe that some registrations are pre- or proto- psychic, not yet organized, and a theory of frontier crossing, perhaps from soma to psyche, is necessary?
>
> (p. 40)

Is there any such thing as a frontier crossing? Here we are in somaland and now in psycheland? This notion of a frontier implicitly refers to a duality of body and soul, with a line drawing a separation. Freud has invited us to do away with the philosophical tradition of duality, but language, and its implicit categories informing thought, tends to bring us back to that duality. Freud's theorizing of the « becoming psychic » is always in terms of gradual process and transformation, be it the drive theory or the conception of the Id.

Can we say that there is no representation or knowledge in the somatic dimension? Or rather that they exist in a form that is unknown to us, and maybe not knowable as such, but from which our representational capacities are derived?

Levine often refers to Bion, and especially to the question asked by Bion himself: « Whether the 'beta-element' or 'bizarre object' are to be classified as *thought* or not is a matter of scientific convenience. »

The alpha function, as metabolizing capacity, could not transform beta-elements if it didn't have a « knowledge » of what they are made of, that knowledge deriving from a previous 'intimacy' with beta-elements state of being.

Beta-elements in themselves are not the issue, but rather that in some instances they remain split off from an alpha function that can enable their transformation (given that it is a constant process and that beta-elements are food for psychic life, if there is, in Bionian terms, a capacity for digestion).

Does the analyst's alpha-function (or the drive related transformational process in Freudian terms) transform the beta-elements (unrepresented states) *for* the patient because the patient *lacks* that capacity?

Levine mentions Green's expression: 'tears in the fabric of the psyche' that are a consequence of « traumatic disruptions of psychic organization (that) can produce areas of psychic voids, de-cathexis, disintegration or other discontinuities in psychic organization and functioning ».

As far as early, sometimes massive, traumas are concerned, the issue is not a rupture of a pre-existing organization or integration but rather the great difficulty to reach a possibility for organization or integration. To pursue the textile metaphor, it is of no help to mend or patch over the tears in the fabric if the loom is dysfunctional and keeps reproducing the tears indefinitely. In terms of therapeutic aim it is more efficient to help mend the loom and render it functional rather than constantly patch over the tears. Only when the loom functions well enough does the patient become independant from the analyst's mending abilities. The aim is not to repair or change the content but to help modify and install new capacities for producing content, for weaving.

> Before one can support, foster or guard a psychoanalytic process, one must often help the patient develop the internal capacities needed to engage in this form of psychic work.
>
> (p. 153)

Each psychoanalytic encounter re-enacts some aspects of the primordial encounter between the somatic dimension and the psychic maternal dimension, in particular the issue of a capacity to cathect a representational activity.

What is needed to effectuate that cathexis, according to Piera Aulagnier, is a quantum of pleasure, and even the shared experience of a pleasure associated with forming a representation.

In the analytic encounter that experience of pleasure in forming a representation and investing representational capacities, coming from the analyst, plays a great role in developing more elaborate representational capacities for non-neurotic patients. The « bonus » of pleasure experienced by the analyst in passing a threshhold of representational level, in the face of a, sometimes, extreme tendency to annihilate and erase coming from the patient, goes back to his/her own early cathexis of the pleasure to represent shared by the maternal environment, and possibly retrieved in his/her own analysis. The nature of that pleasure that is both bodily and sublimated, lies at the very heart of psychic life.

# Introduction
## Freud's theory of psychic functioning and its relevance to the analytic process

> The unconscious is the true psychic reality; in its innermost nature it is as much unknown to us as the reality of the external world, and it is as incompletely presented by the data of consciousness as is the external world by the communications by our sense organs.
>
> Freud (1900, p. 613)

Freud's first topography, the topographic theory, was described by Andre Green (2005a) as a theory of *representations (Vorstellung)*, whose model was the nighttime dream. Condensation, displacement and symbolization produced a resonance of symbolic meanings between conscious and unconscious *thoughts* analogous to that which existed between manifest and latent dream thoughts. Freud's second topography, the structural theory, was a theory centered on the vicissitudes of the unbound force of the *drive*, manifested as affect (e.g., panic attacks, affect storms) and action (*agieren*).

Taken together and viewed as a dialectical pair, representation and drive reflect and encompass the oscillating dynamism between formed and unformed, saturated and unsaturated, conscious and unconscious elements and potential elements of the psyche. Representation reflects the end product of processes of the binding of raw, untamed psychic energies that, to the degree to which they are successful, will infuse a life with vitality and meaning, eventuate in the organization and structuring of the psychic apparatus and allow for the emergence and functioning of the processes that govern psychic regulation and homeostasis.

Based on clinical experience, we could hypothesize an evolutionary determinant of our need to perform these transformational and binding processes, the aim of which is to regulate and harness the potentially unruly and assaultive impulses and feelings of raw existence. Bion spoke of the psychic apparatus as a late evolutionary adaptation, the purpose of which was to try to reduce and regulate the inevitable overwhelming tensions of existence. (Think here also of Freud's Nirvana Principle.) I have referred to the force of this regulatory need as "the representational imperative" (Levine, 2012).

> *psychic activity is governed by an inherent pressure to form representations and link them into meaningful, affect laden, coherent narratives.* This pressure, which I shall call *the representational imperative*,[1] originates in internal (e.g., drives) or external (e.g., perceptions) sources, exerts a 'demand upon the mind' for psychic work and ranges from catalytic to traumatic. If kept within optimal bounds, it has the potential to activate capacities for representation, which serve a vital protective role as they create, structure and organize the mind. It is the creation and linking of representations that will in part determine whether or not any given pressure can be contained within the bounds of what is 'optimal' or will exceed those bounds to become 'traumatic.'
>
> (p. 609)

Bion's description (1962b, 1970) of alpha function and container/contained is especially relevant, because it indicates the role of attachment and object seeking in the search for intersubjective help in these processes of psychic regulation.

It is the search for regulatory assistance that is an important unconscious determinant of the patient's discourse, feelings and actions in the analysis. To the extent that this intersubjective help, when successful, results in some form of useful response, that response is marked by the production of representations – in both self and object. Consequently, a significant part of psychic development and the analytic process could be encompassed and described under the heading "Representations and Its Vicissitudes."

If we assume that representation is not a given – for example, not a "hardwired," inborn cognitive or neurological capacity – but is a developmental achievement through which previously unbound or inchoate forces become bound and contained in the psyche, then we must also assume the existence of processes that achieve this transformation. How then might we describe the means by which we get from one state or condition to the other? What is the original condition that is worked on by transformations and what are the products of that process?

For Freud, the starting point or "raw material" was the psychic force or energy that he called drive (*treib*). It originated in the soma and made a demand on the mind (the psychic apparatus) for work. The "work" demanded was a kind of binding, containment and transformation of that primal force or energy and the end product of that work was expected

---

1 Jean-Claude Rolland (1998) speaks of a "compulsion to represent" (*compulsion de représentation*).

to take the form of representations. The latter are the building blocks of thoughts and ideas.

> It was Freud's genius to have understood that in order to create an inner world, a *psychic* reality that points, reflects and stands in for concrete internal (somatic) and external (perceptual) reality, the mind uses 'manifestations' and signifiers, which are connected to and reflective of past experiences, especially object relations, invested with emotional quality and significance.
>
> Levine (2012, p. 610)

Following Freud's use of the term, I will assume that "representations" are organized, structured psychic entities that are potentially verbalizable as thoughts, ideas or images. Representations can be invested with emotions, linked together into narratives and, if put into a suitable form [the unification of word presentations and thing presentations (Freud, 1915a)], they may be eligible to pass censorship and enter consciousness.

While the representational process is ongoing throughout life – that is, there is a continual gradient of motion that goes from untamed, inchoate forces of the id via transformational processes in the psychic apparatus that eventuate in representations that are the foundation for emotionally invested thoughts, ideas and fantasies – attention to its functioning and dysfunctioning is especially important in the treatment of patients whose difficulties lie 'beyond neurosis' [e.g., borderline and other "limit cases" (Green, 2005a)]. In these patients, difficulties and deficits in representational capacity manifest as or are associated with psychic regulatory disturbances that leave patients subject to affect storms, perverse and impulsive actions, somatic discharge and significant ego splits and distortions. One often discovers that the very means by which these patients have forestalled the real or imagined threats of catastrophic abandonment, annihilation anxiety and nameless dread – that is, the defensive organizations that allow a part of their psyches to achieve some degree of organization, regulation and development – are responsible for the distress that brings them to treatment.

I have found that with these patients a good deal of the analytic process and the work of the cure revolves around the analyst's role not only in uncovering and helping them to discover organized, unacceptable but hidden aspects of themselves (unconscious or split-off wishes, fantasies, fears, defenses) but in strengthening and developing their capacities for representation. The latter results in a greater capacity for psychic regulation and, while it cannot change the reality of the traumatic and pathogenic influence of failed environmental provision in the past, it can offer remediation by working *après coup* within a new object relationship to help initiate or reinforce the psychic structures that are essential to autonomous homeostatic processes.

It has not always been recognized that Freud assumed that this representational, transformational process of binding could never fully represent the essential nature of the world as it exists and could never be fully complete. In this sense, Freud's epistemology followed that of Kant, whose "Copernican revolution" consisted in the idea that "human cognition is a matter of how our peculiar capacities as epistemic subjects actively 'form', and in that sense constitute, the world we seek to gain knowledge about" (Stanicke et al., 2020, p. 289).

This means that "[w]e can only *approach* truth about reality; we can never fully reach it" (ibid., p. 283, italics added). Some parts of the raw material, drive force or energy, will always remain beyond the power and limits of psychic transformation and therefore representation – beyond the binding power and nomination of the spoken word.[2] Thus, Freud's (1900) assertion that each dream possessed an umbilicus that would always defy interpretation or his intuition in his Screen Memories paper that in regard to emotionally important events, historically complete memories *of* childhood may not exist (Freud, 1899) (see Chapter 2).

An important implication of the persistence of an untranslated, unarticulatable, unbound "residue" of drive or force is the recognition that in addition to a *dynamic unconscious*, there is an *unstructured unconscious*. In the former, wishes, fears, fantasies and other potentially verbalizable psychic ideational elements are saturated in regard to meaning, but banished from consciousness because they are potentially too anxiety provoking and unacceptable to one's superego. In the latter, a partial degree of containment, structure and potentially verbalizable meaning may become possible in the context of an intersubjective relationship. The meaning that may result will be emergent, and possess the potential to be captured in many different ideational forms.

Freud (1915a, 1923) implied the existence of these two levels of organization of unconscious psychic elements, when he described a category of psychic elements that were structured like the elements of the system

---

2 Kahn (2018) writes that the "event," the thing-in-itself "defies the familiar grasp of the mind" and resists "totalisation of meaning" (p. 58). Infancy,

> is therefore not a stage of life but an incapacity to represent and bind something that is not even repressed as it has not been perceived, an unmanageable stasis dwelling as presence without any representation or scene. And passibility is not the opposite of activity. It is a form of enduring, an ability to host whatever thought [one] is not prepared to think, which is exactly what can rightly be called thinking. For the mind must nonetheless bear witness to and contain such immemorial that silently persists and is signaled by turmoil. Delusion or anxiety; it must analyse it, historicise it, in short, it must give form to this amorphous mass by endowing it with a place in space and a moment in time.
>
> (pp. 62–63)

Cs.-Pcs., but, nevertheless, remained unconscious. That is, they possessed the structural organization that ordinarily lets representations pass the censorship barrier, but their content was so anxiety provoking or unacceptable that they had to be hidden away from awareness.

A further confirmation of Freud's recognition of the unstructured unconscious can be inferred from his 1937 Constructions in Analysis paper. There he acknowledged that for some patients, the alleged traumatic pathogenic events of infancy and childhood remained forever outside the realm of being captured in words and could never be recalled to memory. Presumably, they either took place in the early pre-verbal period or were the occasion of such a traumatic disruption of psychic memory capacity that they were somehow, somewhere "registered," but in a nonverbalizable, unretrievable form. These events, Freud said, would have to yield to construction – a plausible conjecture on the part of the analyst that did not necessarily conform to or attempt to describe an actual happening, but that produced a feeling of conviction in the patient and acted dynamically in the cure in the same way as the recovery of an actual traumatic memory of childhood.

It is these four concepts – Freud's theory of representation; the existence of unrepresented states; the conceptualization of both a dynamic and unstructured unconscious; the central role of transformation, construction and *après coup,* along with Bion's idea of the communicative dimension of projective identification taken to its logical conclusion – and their implications for understanding and treatment of non-neurotic patients that lie at the conceptual heart of this volume. Together, they attempt to cast light on the unique epistemology of Freud's psychoanalytic thinking endorsing its relevance for our own and extend the limits of our theory to an ever-widening scope that will encompass and include the understanding and treatment of a broader range of non-neurotic patients.

# Chapter 1

# Psychoanalysis and subjectivity

## A personal note

> There is a crack in everything.
> That's how the light gets in.
>
> Leonard Cohen (1970)

## I

Psychoanalysts gravitate toward the theoretical positions that they favor, not only because those theories possess some clinical usefulness, explanatory value and perceived correspondence with "truth" as they believe that they have experienced it but because those favored theories also fit in some fashion with analysts' personal needs and past history, with how they construe and wish to construe the world and its ways. It is no accident, then, that I have become interested in the dialectics of separation and union, self and other and the emotional interpenetration of the analytic couple; in the places where words may go missing and fail to represent and convey the thoughts and experience of the speaker; in the unrecognized and unacknowledged performative use of words as concrete actions and memories-in-feeling; in the impossibility of the analyst's ever achieving a state of pristine and absolute objectivity; in the implications of the analyst's subjectivity; in the ways in which that subjectivity flows, in part, from the patient's inner world and helps shape and create the phenomena of the patient's experience of the analytic process; in the analyst's struggle to recognize inevitable moments of countertransference feeling and enactment as being of potential value; and in the unending struggle to transcend and transform the unrepresented and weakly represented inscriptions associated with trauma and the pre-verbal period of infancy and to bring order to, make sense of and contain and control some small part of the inchoate, vast and formless void within us.

These preoccupations spring not only from my clinical struggles and experience but from deeply personal roots, as well. I believe, however, that the observations and insights to which they have led go beyond the solipsism of my own wishes and needs and may be of value to others. It is in this spirit that I offer the ideas and experiences that follow, fully aware that this book, as perhaps all books written by and about one's experience as a psychoanalyst, will reflect a deeply personal journey, one that has taken place at the intersection of psychoanalysis as it has evolved as a field, as it is or was understood – or misunderstood – by me, and the inevitable changes that I have experienced as the result of immersing myself in the lifelong task of and commitment to the study of the mind, my own as well as that of my patients.

I was drawn to psychoanalysis, in part, because of a significant early emotional loss, one that left me feeling restless, incomplete and in search of something. My maternal grandmother, to whom my mother was extremely close, died in the seventh month of my second year. Although never corroborated by family lore and certainly not remembered by me as an ideational "event," I have developed a strong conviction that this loss precipitated a significant depressive withdrawal on my mother's part that had profound effects on my emotional development. After much reflection, analysis and life experience, I have come to believe that although in terms of *historical reality*, the early emotional loss was that of an *object*, in an important sense of *psychic reality*, what I felt to be missing and what I have been continuously striving to recover and create has also turned out to be some aspect of my *self*.

In trying to formulate and speak analytically about what I believe that I have lost and what I have been seeking, I am confronted with a seeming dilemma. What do I view as bedrock: self or object, object or self?

How a given analyst or theory answers this question can have far-reaching consequences for any description of the psyche and conceptualization of its development, for analytic clinical theory and technique. Historically, in our profession, different choices have led to different theoretical emphases and different analytic schools of thought – ego psychology, object relations theory, self psychology, relational psychoanalysis, and so on. What I shall emphasize is that *particularly at the level of emerging psychic structure, self and object, object and drive develop from a common matrix and form indissoluble pairs*. Each helps constitute and is revealed by the other (Green, 2005a). While complex and intimately connected to the fate and functioning of the drives, the relationship of self and object, particularly at the origins of their psychic representation and as they emerge from some unintegrated, unstructured infantile state or become structured in the analytic interaction, is reciprocal, dialectical and kaleidoscopic.

The complexity and interconnection of self and object has not always been clearly appreciated in psychoanalytic theory. Perhaps the origins of this inattention began with an emphasis on Freud's (1911a) initial contention that in relation to drive satisfaction, the object was relatively interchangeable and therefore by implication the least important element in the sequence "drive-frustration-desire-satisfaction."

From our current perspective, we can now see that this description fit within a certain view of Freud's topographic theory, with its emphasis on what was psychically represented. It applied best to neurotic patients, whose psyches were conflicted, but well organized and structured. These patients possessed more or less well-functioning emotional regulatory capacities and demonstrated robust linkages between word presentations and thing presentations, and between primary and secondary processes.

For better or for worse, however, contemporary clinical experience has repeatedly taught us that this degree of psychic organization and the functional capacity that it supports cannot always be assumed to be present. More often, we are faced with patients and those parts of our patients' minds (and sometimes our own!) in which the connections between words and things, primary and secondary process and the constitution, continuity and separation of self and object are not the starting points for analytic treatment, but instead its goals. To the extent that the treatment process goes well, these attributes will appear as *emerging phenomena that are highly dependent on the specificity and the actual nature of the external object (e.g., the analyst): its receptivity and responses and the interactions that these determine.*

Freud, himself, was aware that not every patient was "neurotic" and thereby suitable for the treatment method he was discovering. Thus, early on, he distinguished "transference neuroses" from "actual neuroses" and "narcissistic neuroses" and at times he seemed to believe that only the truly neurotic were suited for his therapeutic method. It was not until the revolutionary reformulations of 1920 and after, as Freud began to lay the groundwork for our appreciation of the radical discontinuity that exists between represented (neurotic) and unrepresented (non-neurotic) mental states, that analysis could begin to more fully develop in new directions, ones that were already indicated and implied in many of Freud's own early writings. As it did so, analysts began to more closely consider the formulations, interventions and clinical stances needed for the successful treatment of non-neurotic patients and sectors of the mind.

These matters have been taken up at length by many authors, foremost among them for me, Bion (1962b, 1970), Winnicott (1962, 1971) and, especially, Andre Green (1975, 1980, 2005a, 2005b). Following Green's close reading of Freud – and in line with my own experience (e.g., Levine, 2012) – I have come to accept that there is a radical discontinuity between the drive dominated, unstructured sections of the id and unconscious ego and the word-embedded, structured sectors of the conscious and preconscious mind. This discontinuity determines markedly different challenges to clinical theory and technique that are presented by neurotic and non-neurotic (borderline) patients and states of mind. It is reflected in two different, often-interlaced modes of discourse and communication.

To put it simply, the neurotic is able to semantically describe and recognize descriptions of their inner states and feelings, because they can more or less put their feelings into words. In contrast, the non-neurotic patient unconsciously relies on speech as action in order to transmit and induce emotions in their objects. This non-verbal (para-verbal) form of communication poses considerable challenges for analysts and our "talking cure."

Despite these challenges, however, and in contrast to Freud's initial impression, my clinical experience has convinced me that psychoanalysis is an appropriate treatment for both sets of conditions, neurotic and non-neurotic – which, parenthetically, should be expected to occur together in any given patient to various degrees. What has not always been recognized, however, is that the work of psychoanalysis may be quite different for the two groups of patients and/or mental states. What is crucial may depend on whether or to what extent the issues at hand concern what is already represented and can be expressed in words, saturated in regard to ideational meaning, and involve the uncovering of what is hidden, disguised or forgotten versus the very difficult problems of how to foster and participate in a relationship that will help make a portion of previously silent, inchoate forces verbalizable; how to organize and help bind previously unnameable terrors; and how to help catalyze and create the emergence of psychic structure and a true sense of self.

If our theories are to aid us in our struggles to engage with, understand and help all of our patients, the non-neurotic as well as the neurotico-normal, they must clearly alert us to both sides of this discontinuity and divide. They must not be restricted to formulations and descriptions that apply only to neurotic patients, nor must they valorize one side of the seeming dichotomies that we face – one person versus two person psychology; intrapsychic versus relational; self versus object; drive versus object; and so on – at the expense of the other. Instead, our theories must recognize and take into account that, in addition to being opposites at some points of development, at others, these seemingly dichotomous terms form dialectical pairs that at some level are inseparable.

In retrospect, much of my clinical work has been conducted at or beyond the limits of neurosis. This has involved attempts to address these complex issues and to discover with each patient a unique therapeutic course that could address the difficulties that arise in relation to both neurotic and non-neurotic states of mind. I think that I can now see the extent to which my early experiences of loss and its consequences, in conjunction with my clinical experiences, have drawn my attention to these problems of *infans*, allowed me to try to forge a particular language in which to think about and express their vicissitudes for my self as well as for my patients and have informed a number of the important themes that have engaged my professional interest. It is these problems and themes to which I have turned in the writing of this book. I have been supported in this task by the observation that many others, analysts as well as patients, have had analogous personal experiences and have been encouraged and assisted by my attempts to write and speak about them. Ultimately, these experiences have come to form the kernel of something that, having been lived through myself and recognized in others, I have come to value as important life events.

These are not, by any means, the only terms in which emotional experience and growth can be formulated or achieved, nor are they meant to supplant the more usual iterations of psychoanalytic clinical and developmental theory, although they may prove to comprise an important component of them. Rather, I offer the thoughts that follow as a complementary perspective, a point of entrée from which to approach other theories and an additional lens through which to view the clinical encounter (see also Levine, 2010a, where I propose a two-track theory of psychoanalysis, *transformational* as well as *archeological*).

## II

If we stop a moment and think about the development of psychoanalysis from the perspective of missing self and/or missing other, we may discern a basic, recurring narrative theme, one that might almost be described as one of our "foundation stories," told and retold in various "dialects" by the different iterations of theory and schools of psychoanalysis throughout the history of our field. A core element of this story is that psychopathology and symptomatic distress occur when something vital goes missing – from one's awareness, from one's self, from one's facilitating environment, from one's ability to use one's mind, and so on – and that relief may follow when that absence is discovered, acknowledged, spoken of, compensated for, restored or corrected.

In one seminal version of this narrative, it is *the contents of the unconscious* that is "the missing other" and that need to be uncovered or discovered. Indeed, in many places, Freud himself often referred to the unconscious as the *Nebbenmensch*, the stranger within. Though these contents have been characterized in different terms at different points in the development of psychoanalytic theory – the unacceptable facts of reality that conflict with one's "dominant mass of ideas"; the forgotten memory of a childhood fantasy or trauma; the unknown or unacknowledged derivative of a forbidden infantile wish; and so on – the outlines of the story have remained the same. Whether embedded in the seduction theory, the topographic theory ("making the unconscious conscious") or the structural theory ("where id was there ego shall be"), the implication was always this: what you don't know *can* – and usually does – hurt you,

No matter that urgent security needs – for example, the attempt to stabilize and preserve one's sense of being or self or one's foundational primary object in the face of some form of annihilation anxiety and/or to avoid an unbearable agony – led to your not knowing in the first place. As much as hysterics – and by extension, all neurotics - suffer from reminiscences – that is, what we cannot recall and stand to let ourselves know – we might say that non-neurotics suffer even more from that which was never clearly experienced as part of an integrated self and articulated to begin with (see, e.g., Winnicott, 1974). It is the latter that is associated with what I have called unrepresented or weakly represented mental states that are too often the results of pre-verbal, cumulative and/or massive psychic trauma.

The knowledge (neurotic) or not-yet-knowledge (non-neurotic), whatever it may be, internal and/or external, that is fought against, forgotten, disguised, ejected, foreclosed or otherwise disavowed, disowned and/or dissociated is intimately related to who we are, how we see ourselves and what we might become. In this sense, then, the struggle to grow emotionally often involves the search for – at times the creation of – a "missing self/missing other/missing capacity for containment and/or psychic processing" and the recognition, acceptance and redress of its absence.

At times, the distinction between object and self is indistinct and only emerges in the course of a work of construction, creation or discovery. Perhaps there is an analogy here to modern physics, where light can be described as both wave and particle, depending on the circumstances in which it is measured. Words and language are central to these matters, and yet, especially when we are dealing with non-neurotic structures, speech is often found to be an inconstant ally in our attempts to think about and understand this process, our patients and our selves.

As Bion (1970) said, words can reveal and words can conceal and what may appear to be "words" spoken in an attempt to lexically communicate something is often better understood as unconscious acts meant not only to defend, control and attack but also – perhaps always – to signal a desperate need for psychic regulatory assistance. That the means of trying to do so takes the form of what appears to be attacks on and attempts to control the object or through the evacuation or other concrete manipulation of bizarre or empty fragments or bits of sensation and feeling often obscures the potential *communicative* value of these gestures.

What I have come to believe and what I hope will be conveyed in the chapters of this book is that whatever else these "words-as-acts" may semantically convey or concretely attempt to do, there is a perspective from which they may be viewed as a potential distress signal whose very form and unconscious purpose contains a plea for specific address of some psychic regulatory need. That is, like Freud's (1911a) description of the drive, the quasi-concrete use and action component of the words that are determined by the unrepresented and unstructured parts of the patient's unconscious make a demand on the mind of the object for regulatory work. This work can be conceptualized as assistance in helping to bind and transform the previously *unspeakable unspoken*, allowing some part of it to emerge in a contained and verbalizable (represented) form.

## III

The interpenetration and interconnectedness of self and object that is so central to my thesis is often obscured in the English language and by the positivist, empirical philosophical tradition that underlies modern medical and psychological thought (see Kahn, 2018). However, behind and embedded in the more usual ways of parsing the world into subjects and objects, separate but in relation to one another, lies another perspective, equally relevant, equally valid, in which subject and subject may be intimately and inextricably related and interconnected, interpenetrating and held together in a subtle, ever-shifting blending of boundaries. It is this mutuality of deep involvement that is at the heart of the way that I view *intersubjectivity*, a subject that I will address at length and is an important cornerstone of this book.[1] And, of course, the recognition of intersubjectivity in psychoanalysis inevitably moves the subjectivity and person of the analyst to a central position in the analytic process.

This matter of how each analyst's unique subjectivity contributes to the creation of the analytic process has been a topic of increasing psychoanalytic study and interest across my psychoanalytic lifetime (1971– the present). Looking back over developments in that time, we might say that, in one sense, psychoanalysis, in its various iterations, has taught us to help our patients search for the "missing other": the affects accompanying unacceptable ideas; the repressed memories of infantile trauma or sexual fantasy; the disavowed mental processes and functions and parts of the self; the absent, lost or otherwise unprovided "good enough" objects and selfobjects needed to facilitate homeostasis and development; the container needed for emotional growth; the enlivening object needed to counteract the stasis of the death instinct; and so on.

At the same time, psychoanalytic theory itself has also, in a sense, been in search of a "missing other." This "other" has often proven to involve the actuality of the emotional state and participation of the external object: in analysis, the subjectivity, interaffectivity and unconscious contributions of the analyst to the psychoanalytic process. As these factors were increasingly taken into consideration, our theories have evolved from one-person to two-person psychologies, escaping the pulls of external (consensually validated social) reality, embedding their vision ever more deeply in the highly subjective and fantastical world of psychic reality, requiring our theories to try to account for the subjectivity of both analyst and patient in their inevitable interactions, interconnections and interpenetrations.

## IV

Without my realizing it or appreciating the extent to which its elaboration would take up so much of my thought and that of so many colleagues in

---

1 See also Levine and Friedman (2000).

my professional lifetime, I first encountered this problem in 1972, when, as a third-year psychiatric resident, I attended a course in psychoanalytic metapsychology taught by Dr. Leon Shapiro. At that point in time, ego psychology and conflict theory were the dominant, almost exclusive theories in American psychoanalysis, and it was assumed for the most part that what the analyst could contribute to the treatment process followed from his or her capacity to be objective about the patient's external reality.

Despite this then prevailing view, the seminar began with Shapiro (1972) making the following observation:

> One problem with psychoanalytic theory is that it is like watching an American football game on television, but only being able to see one of the two teams. Players line up, run around, inexplicably fall down, line up and do it over and over again.

While this description may have been exaggerated for emphasis, the point was well made. Psychoanalysis, at least as practiced and understood in the United States, for the most part, had developed a refined and sophisticated way of looking at one-person, *intrapsychic* phenomena, such as conflict and defense, but was much less successful when it came to conceptualizing the *interactive*, the *interaffective* and the *intersubjective*. And except for the occasional descriptions of mysticism (Freud, 1930) or the creative process (Kris, 1952), the realm of the *interpenetrating* was mostly relegated to severe psychopathology and primitive functioning (e.g., symbiosis and other failures of self-object differentiation).

In my formation, as in the formation of so many of my American contemporaries, to the extent that the analyst's subjectivity was considered as part of the analytic process and relationship, it was almost always synonymous with the analyst's countertransference. And unlike contemporary formulations, in which the latter is conceptualized as a possible source of information about the patient and the analytic relationship, countertransference was viewed almost exclusively as a potential interference that required elimination or suppression.

"Proper" technique was thought to be objective, something that, once the prospective analyst had been sufficiently analyzed, could be taught, learned and applied. For the well-analyzed, well-functioning, "good enough" analyst, one's own specific psychology was assumed to be moot and irrelevant to the analytic process, unless and until the analyst became enmeshed in some countertransference difficulty. Then, the analyst's task was to resort to self-analysis, supervisory consultation and/or assisted analysis to remove the impediment, at which point it was assumed that the analytic process would then continue per force.

While a great deal of what has been written and taught about countertransference in the narrow, classical sense remains true and of value, in retrospect, the state of affairs that I encountered is puzzling, even ironic. Early in his career, Freud recognized the universality of the unconscious and of transference and described transference phenomena as quintessentially interactive: the intrapsychic lived out in the realm of the interpersonal. Freud also took careful note of interactive phenomena, such as unconscious communication, and was aware of its importance in the analytic process. In 1913, for example, he wrote,

> everyone possesses in his own unconscious an instrument with which he can interpret the utterances of the unconscious of other people.
> Freud (1913, p. 320)

Two years later, he observed,

> it is remarkable how the Ucs. of one human being can react upon that of another, without passing through the Cs.
> Freud (1915a, p. 194)

And when he formulated the structural theory (Freud, 1923), he placed the development of the psyche squarely in a two-person, object relational context, by declaring that the ego was the precipitate of abandoned object relationships.

As clinicians, even the ego psychologists had recognized, at least to some extent, that the analytic *relationship* was central to the process of therapeutic change and struggled in their theory to try to acknowledge that recognition. (Think, for example, about all that was written about the therapeutic and working alliance, the real relationship and the unobjectionable positive transference.) But the American mainstream had barely begun to take into theoretical account the implications for the psychoanalytic situation of the role played by the psychology of the analyst and the shift from a one-person to a two-person psychology. We remained, for the most part, wedded to a view of the traditional classical model, which portrayed an objective analyst engaged in treatment with a subjective patient or – taking into account the ego psychological concept of the "therapeutic split" (Sterba, 1934) of the ego into experiencing and observing parts – an objective analyst engaged in treatment with a subjective part of the patient. Here, objectivity was equated with a clear vision of what was "real" and subjectivity with a neurotic distortion of reality.

## V

There were two other problems of my early training that should be taken note of, as they would prove quite relevant to my development as an analyst and to the work that would follow. The first was the seeming contradiction between what I was being taught in my introductory seminars on "analyzability" and what I was hearing in the clinical presentations of fellow candidates. In the former, I was taught that certain initial diagnoses – for example, hysterical, phobic and obsessional neuroses – would have a strong correlation with positive analytic outcomes. In regard to my colleagues' cases, however, I noticed that some patients who had dire prognoses based on their initial diagnosis could do very well in analysis, while others, whose diagnoses were presumptively optimistic, could turn out poorly. Later on, I discovered that the research literature on analyzability corroborated my initial impression that there were only weak correlations, at best, between initial diagnosis and analytic outcome. Apparently, who the analyst was and how he or she understood and responded to the patient were far more important in determining outcome than was the initial diagnosis. Eventually, this contradiction between received wisdom and clinical experience led me to attempt to examine the analyst's participation in the analytic process (Levine, 1994) and intersubjective role in the *creation* rather than the assessment of prospective analytic patients (Levine, 2010a).

The second problem followed from the tacit assumption on behalf of supervisors and seminar leaders that patients in analysis would be capable of psychic representation and that the words they used would have symbolic value. As a result, it was assumed that if the analyst remained abstinent and neutral and sufficiently analyzed the patient's defenses, then whatever was relevant to the analysis would appear in the patient's verbal discourse. While this assumption may have held true for the seldom-encountered, so-called good (neurotic) analytic patient, in relation to most of the patients I was seeing or hearing about from colleagues, it proved to be the exception rather than the rule.

My clinical experience involved the treatment of patients with significant non-neurotic difficulties: borderline, perverse and narcissistic patients, adults who were sexually abused as children, patients with eating disorders and psychosomatic disturbances and other patients in the so-called widening scope, for whom words were often concrete actions and in whom actions often spoke louder than words. For these patients, I often found that the "relevant data" would never appear in the dreams or associations of the patient, no matter how long the analysis, how patiently I waited or how effectively I tried to analyze their resistances. Instead, a broader theoretical net was required than the one with which I had emerged from training: another channel of information was needed besides that of the patient's verbal discourse and the search for historical truth would need to be joined by the centrality of construction (see Freud, 1937; Levine, 2011a).

It was my work with anorexic patients and adults who had been sexually abused as children (Levine, 1990) that convinced me of the extent to which the relevant material, missing in the patient's discourse, could appear in *the analyst's* thoughts, feelings and impulses to action. From here, it was a short step to the work of Paula Heimann (1950), who extended the definition of countertransference to include "all the feelings which the analyst experiences towards his patient" (p. 74) and argued that the analyst's emotional response to the patient in the analytic situation "is not only part and parcel of the analytic relationship, but it is the patient's creation, it is a part of the patient's personality" (p. 74).

Following a logical progression, I moved from Heimann to Klein and the contemporary Kleinians of London and then to Bion and container/contained. What I encountered in the writings of Bion, Segal, Joseph, Britton, Steiner, Feldman et al. helped broaden my thinking and sharpen my observational capacity. In particular, my deepened appreciation and understanding of projective identification as a theoretical concept and clinical phenomenon allowed me to form the impression that like transference, it was ubiquitous and universal and should therefore apply to both parties in the analytic situation.

Ultimately, I came to two conclusions about its centrality and relevance to the analytic process. The first was that it was *the mutuality of projective identification between patient and analyst, exercised in the service of seeking help with psychic regulatory processes, that helped define the analytic situation as inherently and inevitably intersubjective* (see Levine, 1994; Levine and Friedman, 2000).

Having reached this point, I felt that I could now better appreciate the work of analysts such as Heinrich Racker (1968), who described the psychological symmetry that existed between analyst and patient in the following terms:

> The first distortion of truth in the "myth of the analytic situation" is that it is an interaction between a sick person and a healthy one. The truth is that it is an interaction between two personalities in both of which the ego is under pressure from the id, the superego, and the external world; each personality has its internal and external dependencies, anxieties and pathological defenses; each is also a child with his internal parents; and each of the whole personalities – that of the analysand and that of the analyst – responds to every event of the analytic situation.
>
> (p. 132)

And Bion (1962b, 1970), who gave further credence to this view when he emphasized that the analyst's mind and the way that it functioned – the quality and specificity of its receptivity, attunement, creativity, and so forth – were significant variables in the creation and the development of the patient's analytic situation. Through study of Bion's later writings, I have come to appreciate how much he saw the intersubjective in the analytic situation. In the words of the contemporary Italian analyst Antonino Ferro (2005), whose work uses the field theory of Baranger et al. (1983) as well as Bion as important points of departure,

> the analyst's mode of functioning in the session, characterized by greater or lesser receptivity, greater or lesser reverie and greater or lesser narrative competence, partly determines the form assumed by the session itself.
>
> (p. 10)

Thus, "the psychoanalytic situation is determined jointly by the patient-analyst couple" (Ferro, 2005, p. 60).

The second realization that later followed concerned the implication of Bion's description of the communicative dimension of projective identification. In addition to what Freud, Klein and so many others have taught us about the search for relief from erotic and destructive *wishes*, Bion – and Winnicott – have alerted us to the extent to which the patient's *needs* for psychic regulatory assistance are signaled and embedded in the ways in which they communicate by unconsciously inducing feelings in the mind and body of the analyst. Despite the seemingly peremptory, aggressive, controlling or psychotic quality of their behavior, non-neurotic patients are often – perhaps always – unconsciously trying to signal and draw attention to their regulatory needs, often by presenting – that is, embodying and enacting – the analyst with the consequences of the object's failure to recognize, receive, transform and help attenuate situations of emotional crisis and urgency.

This book, then, follows the broad sweep of psychoanalytic clinical theory as it has evolved in the course of my lifetime as an analyst. It reflects the movement within psychoanalysis from a one-person to a two-person psychology and presses toward the recognition and working out of the implications of a truly intersubjective perspective on our understanding and description of the psychoanalytic process. It moves as well from the exclusion of unrepresented mental states or their relegation in technique to the "art of psychoanalysis," to their inclusion in a robust attempt to conceptualize these states along with the processes of transformation needed to inscribe them in the psyche and make them usable for psychological processes. Although we have been aware for some time of many of the preliminary observations needed for the completion of this task, psychoanalysts have been reluctant to take the final step and follow through to their logical conclusion the implications of Freud's introduction of the structural theory and our subsequent recognition of the "irreducible subjectivity" (Renik, 1993) of the analyst and patient.

While there are good reasons for this reluctance, I believe that the ubiquity, universality and ineradicability of the unconscious, of transference and of primitive areas of the mind where words remain as actions and projective identification of unmetabolized proto-thoughts and proto-feelings persists leave us no other option. Our clinical theory must recognize and take account of the fact that for the psychoanalytic relationship, as with any significant, intimate and affectively charged relationship, self and other are, to some extent, mutually constituted, as each is subjected to a continual stream of inchoate external sensations, drive impulses and blind tendencies toward action, as well as unconscious wishes, needs and desires emanating from the other. Consequently, the resulting analytic relationship and process are not determined by the patient's spoken discourse or internal factors alone; rather, they are brought about by unconscious forces that recruit and reject intersubjective participation by the other. These forces are active in *both* participants. It is my hope that this book will contribute to the ongoing effort to demonstrate this perspective and elucidate its implications for psychoanalytic listening and technique.

# Chapter 2

# Freud's theory of representation and the expansion of analytic technique

## I

The central epistemological questions are these.

Is there experience, perhaps deriving from the soma, from the preverbal period of infancy or from traumatic states, that is inscribed – somewhere, somehow – but not yet *psychically* represented? If so, how do we understand such inscriptions and speak about their impact? What kinds of theories are available to us to do so? Do we hold a theory that assumes that all registrations of drive derivatives and perceptions, internal and external, are psychic in some sense and so there is no "frontier" in need of crossing? Or do we believe that some registrations are pre- or proto-psychic, not yet organized, and a theory of frontier crossing, perhaps from soma to psyche, is necessary?

In retrospect, the ego psychology and conflict theory that I grew up with seemed to make the tacit assumption that all experience, internal and external, was psychically represented, even if unrecoverable or too deeply defended against to ever become conscious. Similarly, one reading of Kleinian theory implies that all internal experience is organized and stored as "unconscious fantasy" ("I or a part of me wants to do this to you or a part of you") somewhere in the mind and so by definition is both psychic and represented.

In contrast – elaborating on a very different set of assumptions that can be found, but not yet fully developed in the work of Freud – the theories of Winnicott, Bion, Andre Green and the Paris psychosomatic school allow that traumatic disruptions of psychic organization can produce areas of psychic voids, de-cathexis, disintegration or other discontinuities in psychic organization and functioning: what Green (2005a) called "tears in the fabric of the psyche." These, in turn, can lead to or are associated with weakness, loss or failures of representation that clinically manifest themselves as "overload phenomena," such as impulsive discharges, affect storms, somatic illnesses, structural failures of the capacity for thought and symptoms associated with massive economic imbalances and breakdowns.

Each psychoanalytic theory leads to a somewhat different hierarchy of therapeutic goals and aims. Classically, the therapeutic task of analysis has been seen in relation to neurosis,[1] as described in Freud's *archeological* model, as the recovery of repressed memories, the healing of splits and/ or the uncovering and reworking of the unconscious dimensions of a patient's conflicts, pathological defenses and compromise formations. More and more analysts today,[2] however, see their task, in addition to the traditional *archeological* analysis of neurotic parts of the mind, as including the need to work *transformationally*, together with or even *for* the patient – to create, or strengthen psychic structure that was previously weak, functionally inoperative, or missing (Levine, 2010a, 2012). This work has been described, for example, by Bion (1962b, 1970) as "alpha function" and container/contained, by Botella and Botella (2005) as the "work of *figurabilité*" and by Green (2005a) as "working as a similar other," and in Ferro's (2002) field theory as the work of narrative co-construction.

No matter how they are spoken of, these iterations of analytic theory have begun to shift from the conception of a universe of presences, forgotten, hidden or disguised, but there for the finding, to *a negative universe*, one of absences or voids, where *creation* rather than discovery of missing content and structure becomes of necessity part of the cure.

Concomitantly, the aim of the cure has also shifted, away from an exclusive or predominant focus on the healing of splits, the recovery of repressed childhood memories and the reworking of pathological compromise formations to the strengthening, creation and development of psychic capacities. What is needed is a "metapsychology of process rather than a metapsychology of content" (Roussillon, 2014), one that helps us and our patients "work not so much on insight, …. as on the development of the instruments for thinking" (Ferro, 2015).

The development of "psychic capacities" or the "instruments for thinking" is intimately connected with and dependent on *the capacity for representation (Vorstellung)*, a term with roots in Freud's metapsychology that we confuse with similar terms from neuroscience or child development at our conceptual peril. Representation in the Freudian, psychoanalytic sense is the culmination of a process through which drive (often manifest in the conscious mind as an aspect of affect), object, ideational content and unconscious or disguised fantasies must all be linked. It is also the prerequisite for the creation of symbols, the linkage of associational chains and the production of nighttime and waking dreams.

It is important to emphasize that references to representational "weakness" or absence do not necessarily imply a complete lack of

---

1  As I shall use the term "neurosis," it implies organization, psychic representation, symbolization, conflict, compromise formation and defense (Levine, 2012).
2  Aisenstein (2017), Bergstein (2019), Botella and Botella (2005), Eekhoff (2019), Ferro (2002), and Press (2016), to name a few.

"registration" or "inscription" in the psyche or soma, but instead different levels or gradients of registration or inscription, with representation being among the most highly organized and advanced.[3] Such references, however, present epistemological problems, as they shift the ground on which psychoanalytic technique must stand from that of the discovery or recovery of veridical and objective historical truth toward the phenomenological ambiguity of the *creation* of psychic reality, the necessity of co-construction and beyond, toward the *actual* and the truly ineffable.[4]

## II

One of the cornerstones of analytic technique has always been Freud's 1914 paper Remembering, Repeating and Working-Through, which asserted that what cannot be remembered in words, because it was unacceptable, too threatening or anxiety provoking and therefore had to be repressed, would be expressed and repeated in action. Think of Dora fingering her reticule, and thereby signaling her masturbatory activities. This image reflects the genius and enormous clinical power of Freud's first topography (topographic theory). In the face of repression, in the absence of the capacity to consciously recall, action and repetition will serve as a defense against, but also as a way station toward, the recollection of what cannot yet be remembered.

Behind this clinical observation lies the assumption that what is repressed and unconscious has a structure that is symbolic, psychically organized and integrated into and linked up with other, similar ideas and affects that are connected via chains of association. It is these links that make classical technique based on free association possible. Freud (1915a) delineated this portion of the unconscious, when he noted that some unconscious instinctual impulses are "highly organized, free from self-contradiction" (p. 190), relatively indistinguishable in structure from those which are conscious or pre-conscious and yet "they are unconscious and incapable of becoming conscious." (pp. 190–191). He continued, *"qualitatively* they belong to the system *Pcs.* but *factually* to the *Ucs.*" (p. 191, original italics).[5]

---

3 The presumed "location" of non-representational registrations or inscriptions will depend on the particular theory one holds.
4 I believe that this was, in part, what Bion (1970) had in mind when he said that psychoanalytic inquiry is dependent on the recognition and exploration of a kind of experience that is not of the senses: "the realizations with which a psycho-analyst deals cannot be seen or touched; anxiety has no shape or colour, smell or sound" (p. 7).
5 He maintained this distinction when he introduced the structural theory (Freud, 1923, p. 24).

This description links representation and neurosis and when we are operating therapeutically in this psychically organized domain, what is most important and necessary is to wait and follow the patient's associations, perhaps clearing resistances out of the way by interpreting and exploring their presence and function. Sooner or later, the content of the underlying "message" will reveal itself and either the patient will discover it for him or her self or the analyst will interpret it to the patient. That is, what is repressed, signals and "points" to its presence the way an otherwise invisible atomic particle indicates its presence and path by leaving a trail through a cloud chamber.

But as Freud (e.g., 1920, 1923) later came to realize, the repressed unconscious was only a small part of the totality of that which is unconscious. The *actual*, which includes not yet processed, raw existential experience, the less structured – I would say unrepresented and weakly represented – strata of the id and the areas of the psyche that relate to preverbal experience and/or that have been disorganized and de-structured by the "too-muchness" of the kind of Experience[6] that we would call "traumatic," these are better conceptualized as *force without ideational content*, something that is closer to affect than ideation.[7] (Think of *pulsion*, the French translation of the word, drive, with its implication of "pulse"). This is the realm of non-neurotic psychic organizations; of patients, who suffer from ego deformations, psychic disruption and discontinuity and of the less structured parts of the mind, which functions "beyond the pleasure principle."

These considerations force us to raise the awkward question: is there something akin to "memories" that cannot be "*re*-membered" because they have never been *membered* in the first place? Things that first need to be constructed ("membered") before they can be forgotten and then re-membered?

At the end of his Screen Memories paper, Freud (1899) suggested that we may not have memories *from* childhood, only memories *about* childhood, implying that childhood memories are not retrieved fully formed

---

6 "Capital E" Experience is "actual." It is what happens to us in the world, independent of whether or not we are able to know or articulate it. "Small e" experience is that part of "capital E" Experience that we are able to notice and/or articulate. The difference between the two is the difference between what Bion called **O** and **K**, and is directly related to how we think about the unconscious.

7 This assertion is based on the assumption that affect is something that is not fully psychic, but is rooted in the soma and extends into the psyche. That at its somatic end it is force without ideational content, linkage or containment and that only at its psychic end it is linked to mental content and "about" something, rather than being relatively ideationally unbound, a more purely economic entity (see also Chapter 9).

from hiding, but are shaped and assembled moment-to-moment to serve a particular dynamic purpose. From this perspective, "remembering" is not just about recall and retrieval or, in the case of neurosis and the analytic process, about the lifting of repression or the healing of splits. It is an essential component of ongoing processes of *creation of meaning and enriching meaningfulness* in one's personal world.

These processes are central to the formation and consolidation of a personal identity, which, in the sense of Bion's "waking dream thoughts," is continually being *dreamt into being*. Their hallmarks include *subjectivization* and the *instantiation of temporal order*, both of which reflect and further foster movements toward psychic organization and structuralization that define and affirm one's sense of self. What I wish to emphasize is the difference between *memory as structure* versus *remembering as process*; the difference between recovery or retrieval of memory versus *the experience of remembering*. (It is, for example, the difference between the scene recounted versus the emotional world evoked by the taste of Proust's madeleine.)

In this sense, "remembering" is a component act of the work of creation of a personal narrative that takes place at the crossroads of – and probably also knits together – past and present into a coherent, although not necessarily seamless, and subjectively felt state of "selfness." (This is an awkward neologism, but I hope that it conveys the sense of *this* memory belonging to me and therefore being *mine* and what makes me *me*.) Thus, while historical truth and veridical reality matter, especially and often painfully so in the case of trauma, in an analytic therapy, one can never categorically choose between historical truth and psychic reality, but it is always a matter of both being intertwined and relevant to whatever is being communicated.

While almost all that I have said holds true for neurotic organizations and states of mind, where representation holds sway and is robust, it is particularly applicable to non-neurotic organizations and states, where unrepresented and weakly represented proto- or pre-psychic emotional turbulences make a constant demand on the mind for "membering" – that is, for emotional relief via *figurabilité* and representational transformation, much as a grain of sand "catalyzes" an oyster to produce a pearl.[8]

---

[8] Bion has written eloquently about this demand and the processes associated with it in his descriptions of the communicative function of projective identification, reverie, negative capability, alpha function and container/contained. In my own writing, I have suggested that this demand is at the heart of an essential psychic regulatory mechanism that I have called "the representational imperative" (Levine, 2012; See also Chapter 4, this volume).

## III

The two different categories of psychic organization that I am trying to delineate have different implications for analytic technique. While classical psychoanalysis has taught us to rely on *observation* and *inference* as we search for or await the emergence of something organized but *hidden* in the minds of our patients, this alternative formulation reminds us that since it is the very capacity to think that is at issue in these patients, what we are after may not yet have achieved a level of specificity and organization so as to be discernible and hidden; may not yet be embedded in a network of associated meanings; may not yet have achieved a specific form and so may only "exist" as a spectrum of possibilities that have yet to come into being. And, if these not-yet-emerged elements are to achieve any form at all (become fixed in meaning and associatively connected to other psychic elements – memories, thoughts, feelings, fantasies, desires), that form will only be shaped as a result of the analyst's unconscious, spontaneous participation in an active, intersubjective process in which we support, catalyze and co-construct affectively imbued, symbolically meaningful, plausible thoughts and constructions with and sometimes even for our patients.

For those patients in whom – or in the sectors of mind in which – this analytic action is required, mental contents are not – or are only weakly – organized, fixed in meaning, structured by language or firmly linked to other representations and chains of associations; self and object may feel fragmented, inconstant and poorly differentiated. Emotional states may be overwhelming and peremptory or vague, amorphous and poorly defined. Speech may be more evacuative, fragmented and empty of feeling and meaning than symbolic, expressive and suffused with unconscious signification. It may reflect the pressures that arise from inchoate feeling states that are not yet structured, bound or specified by attachment to words.

Bion (1962b, 1970) described this level of communication when he spoke of the communicative dimension of projective identification. No matter how defensive, aggressive or unruly and disorganized this form of communication might appear, *it may also be understood as a covert distress signal and an unconscious plea for assistance in psychic regulatory function*. This form or dimension of discourse depends more on the unconscious induction of emotion in the object than it does on the semantic meaning of the words used. Consequently, at this level, the patient's speech, rather than reflecting the use of words as symbols and signifiers with which to communicate meaning, may utilize words more as "things" that tend even more than is usually the case toward action, evacuation and discharge or paradoxically, may be and feel empty, stripped of affect and meaning.

To illustrate the difference, think of the psyche as metaphorically possessing an inner theatre, akin to Joyce McDougall's (1985) metaphor of the "theatre of the mind," a stage on which various characters (internal objects) appear, speak their lines and live out their parts.[9] Neurosis and the repressed unconscious might be thought of as a play in which some actors exert influence while remaining out of sight. For example, we might know H.G. Wells's "invisible man" is on stage, although we can't see him, because objects inexplicably seem to levitate or move about, other characters' paths are suddenly blocked by something present but unseen, and so on. In contrast, what Green and Winnicott might have us think of is that the stage or theatre itself has been wrecked or dismantled or there are black holes and other powerful, invisible voids in the very air of the stage setting that suck things into them unexpectedly. Without seeming reason, things explode or implode, fragment and disappear.

Still another possibility is that the void itself becomes a kind of character that is clung to and cherished (Green, 1980). It is more difficult to illustrate this kind of negative presence, but one might think here of Lewis Carrol's Cheshire Cat, whose smile remains after he is long gone. We might say the actor while on stage in the cat suit "represents" the Cheshire Cat, but the smile that is left behind continues as *presence* rather than becoming a memory. The smile is a "registration" of some sort, but not a "memory" and not what Freud or Green or others would call a "representation" in the psychoanalytic sense of the term.[10]

The challenge that faces us then is how to articulate a conceptual stance toward these phenomena and begin to spell out the clinical implications and possible changes in listening stance and technique that this stance may require.

At times of emotional crisis, the discourse of patients who are at the mercy of the unrepresented may demonstrate a failure of meaning at a fundamental level (Green, 2005a). It is for this reason that carefully following these patients' associations and then interpreting fantasies or defenses may prove insufficient for the analytic task at hand. Instead, or in addition, *the analyst may have to act* (spontaneously and often unconsciously) so as to help the patient create words with which to form associations, imbue those words with consistent symbolic meaning and link those associations to other narrative fragments. The process that I am trying to

---

9 Green (1980) spoke of this internal, psychic "space" as a "framing structure."
10 Bion (1970) might categorize the smile of the cat as a "beta-element" or "bizarre object." "Whether the beta-element or bizarre object are to be classified as *thought* or not is a matter of scientific convenience" (p. 10, italics added). This was a matter that he left unsettled, although in my reading, he seemed to lean toward the assumption that beta-elements and bizarre objects did not qualify as "thoughts."

describe, which should be recognizable to practicing analysts, is analogous to that of weaving a patch to repair the unity of a torn fabric or, sometimes more aptly, first operating the tool and die press so as to create the tools that are necessary for the repair!

In my work (Levine, 2010a, 2011a, 2012; Levine et al., 2013), I have emphasized the importance of "myth making" (i.e., helping to build presumptive thoughts and along with that, strengthening the capacity to think them) and the analyst's construction of plausible sequences of cause-and-effect narratives of emotional interaction and reality in the here-and-now of the analytic relationship.[11] In doing so, I have argued for a kind of analytic action that may appear to an outside observer as intuitive rather than deductive, anticipatory rather than reactive; and inspired rather than fully grounded in the patient's manifest associations. By "action," I mean not only physical acts, but also – and more often – acts of spontaneous, intuitive, internal emotional resonance and/or expression (feeling or imagining what the patient may not yet clearly feel or know) that effect and reflect psychic figurability (*figurabilité*; Botella and Botella, 2005) (forming an image that structures or conveys something implicit or imminent but not yet represented in the patient's or analyst's psyche).

While these "internal acts" may be preferable to motor acts, sometimes the latter are inevitable and necessary to actualize or call attention to some aspect of a newly emerging Experience. Often, these "actions" (often classified as enactments) are the external markers of an act of figurability through which the unrepresented acquires specific ideational form. Cassorla (2013) has described how the unwinding of a temporary stalemate may begin with and even require an unconscious, jointly created enactment, which not only gives form to something nascent, not yet or only weakly represented, but also calls attention to its emergent existence.

In retrospect, the kind of action that I am trying to describe may be seen as a reflection of and response to unconscious communication from the patient. While to an outside observer it may seem prosaic, supportive or cognitive, it is, in fact, intersubjective and transformational, as the analyst's actions contribute as catalyst, co-constructor or alter ego to the patient's ongoing strengthening of representations and formation of psychic structure. Conceptually speaking, it is an open question as to whether the dividing line between this kind of transformative action and more traditional descriptions of countertransference are very difficult to discern or do not in fact exist!

What I am proposing is that the analyst must not only use his or her subjectivity as a source of data about the patient and the analytic situation, but must expect that in addition to helping patients discover and explore

---

11 See also Chapter 3.

their dynamic unconscious – that is, helping them search for something that is hidden, but discernible by the effects it has on what *is* available to consciousness – the analyst may also be faced with the challenge of helping patients *create* that dynamic unconscious. The latter occurs as the analyst initiates or catalyzes processes that strengthen and/or integrate patients' abilities to think by helping give form to something that was previously weakly or un-represented. Thus, analysts must expect to find themselves unconsciously participating in dialogical and interactive processes, which have the effect of offering patients – or helping them to create or approximate – something that may not yet have achieved sufficient "presence" in a figured form. It is only after figuration has taken place that there may be anything that can then be repressed and subsequently "uncovered" or "de-coded."

Prior to being strengthened or created, this "something" may make its presence known via vague or eruptive states of emotional turbulence, impulsive action or difficulties in thinking and psychic regulatory processes, but it may be "invisible" or only weakly discernible *as content*, unless or until its trace is strengthened or transformed into being (achieves representation) by an intersubjective process of construction or co-construction. The potential plasticity of the forms it may assume once it is transformed implies that its eventual figuration may be highly influenced by the unique subjectivities of each member of the dyad and the unique, moment-to-moment conditions of their relationship.

In practice, it may be almost impossible to answer the question, "Whose construction is it?" The questions of to whom the final content of the representation "belongs" or how to distinguish a truly intersubjective act of figurability from the imposition of an analyst's countertransference need or the expression of a patient's transference compliance remain complex, enigmatic and perhaps can never be resolved. And in the case of severely traumatized patients and/or those with primitive personality disorders, the unintended imposition of an "analytic false self" that, nevertheless, offers structure and facilitates the patient's capacity to think, defer action and regulate affects may be the best or only – outcome possible (Donnet, 2010).

If we assume that there is not a hidden meaning waiting to be uncovered or discovered behind every action, but rather sometimes the action is or contains an element of pure discharge connected with a pre- or proto-psychic "registration" or "inscription" that is connected with a psychic failure to represent related to immaturity (preverbal period; failure to develop sufficient capacity for verbalization; etc.) or trauma (overwhelming of the capacity to represent and think and symbolize and verbalize), then the "outbreak" may *acquire meaning from the context in which it occurs.*

Once it has done so, the memory of the interaction around which that meaning was generated and acquired may serve as the "patch" that can "cover" the consequences of the earlier disruption and function dynamically as a plausible construction (Freud, 1937). The memory of some aspect of the current interaction will then stand in dynamically for a past experience, which can never be "*recovered*," not because it is repressed or defended against, but because it is unstructured, unformed or not yet sufficiently psychic. However, unlike the prototypical construction that Freud offered – for example, "when you were 4 years old you must have noticed X and only later when you came to understand sexuality you realized that your parents …." – the constructions that we make in regard to unrepresented states are often made out of the factual and emotional details of here-and-now interactions in the analytic relationship that the patient is continually "effacing" (Green, 1998).[12] Without these details, the cause-and-effect comprehension of emotional life becomes distorted or even impossible. Once they are re-presented and then represented, meaning, coherence and continuity can be restored or achieved for the first time.

The unrepresented probably never appears clinically isolated in pure form. It is most inferable when its presence is marked by some kind of eruption, but it is also probably always present at the heart of every representation, which "wraps around" and "covers over" an enigmatic core. Freud implied as much when he wrote that an actual neurosis lies at the heart of every psychoneurosis and that each dream contains an "umbilicus" that is inherently unknowable. Laplanche's argument for infantile sexuality as an unconscious, enigmatic, untranslatable implantation from the Other rests on similar ground. The implication of this view is that transformational work is probably going on silently in even the most seemingly structured processes and highly organized moments of mental functioning.

Let us now turn to a clinical case.

## IV

Ellen[13]

I began work with Ellen when she was depressed, angry, hopeless and dangerously suicidal. The first period of treatment, face-to-face at three to four times per week, lasted 12 years and helped her to weather numerous hospitalizations and suicidal crises, finish university and begin to stabilize her life.

Ellen's mother was a severe alcoholic: depressed, unreliable and emotionally unavailable. During Ellen's latency years, mother was repeatedly

---

12 See also Chapter 3.
13 Portions of this case material have appeared previously in Levine, H.B. (2012). The colourless canvas: Representation, therapeutic action and the creation of mind. *Int. J. Psycho-Anal.* 93: 607–629.

hospitalized and out of even telephone contact for prolonged periods of time. When mother was home, Ellen lived on the verge of continual panic, emptying mother's hidden whiskey bottles, hiding the car keys to prevent mother from driving while drunk and sneaking into the bedroom where mother was passed out to see if she was still breathing and alive.

Ellen's father was a terrifyingly angry man, whom Ellen viewed as despotic and intrusive. His mood would shift without warning and he would erupt in dangerous rages. Her siblings were described as envious and cruel.

In the early years, once treatment began to take hold, Ellen soothed herself by holding and counting a hidden supply of sleeping pills, reminding herself they were her escape from an unbearably painful, incomprehensible reality. In sessions, her thinking became blocked or disorganized, her mind went blank and her discourse was often empty and flat. I barely made sense of what she was saying or what was going on between us. It is likely that my state was both a response to her fractured discourse and an identification with her disorganized self.

I attempted to clarify and explore what Ellen was feeling or thinking or describe what was happening between us. While this activity reflected standard technique, in helping her to name her feelings and make plausible sense out of what seemed to be going on within her mind and between us, I was also working as an alter ego or "double," supporting her – or lending her my – ability to create, link and strengthen representations, thereby reinforcing her capacity to think.

Gradually, we developed a picture of her mind that named and described her terror of abandonment, murderous and suicidal rage and desperate need for aid and comfort. Some elements of these reactions were presumably based on representations of early objects, fantasies and relationships. For example, one could surmise that her fears of closeness were determined, in part, by her need to defend against her oral rage and hunger or avoid a traumatic repetition of internalized memories of abandonment by her mother. One could postulate a defensive, aggressive identification with her raging, paranoid father or view her suicidal preoccupations as murderous revenge against abandoning and sadistic parents and sibs. At the same time, however, in addition to these presumed manifestations of more organized, represented mental states, the vagueness and incomprehension of her discourse, the paralysis of her thinking, the intensity and eruptive quality of her affects and the confused and impulsive action that permeated her life all spoke to a presumptive weakness or failure of representation.

For most of our early years together, interpreting these presumed dynamics or addressing these phenomena as possible ego defenses – for example, "perhaps your mind stops working so you don't have to feel or know how angry you are; or how much you feel that you need me to be here;" – or the surface markers of unconscious fantasies – for example, "you seem afraid that your needs and anger will destroy me" – or memories – for example, "when I go away you feel abandoned by me as you did by mother when she left for the hospital without explanation or opportunity to visit" – did not make sense to her or lead to a more usual process of working through. These phenomena, which were associated with intense states of confusion and a disorganization of her ability to think that left Ellen unable to make coherent sense of her emotional life, were linked to a disorganized and disorganizing discontinuity of experience and a loss of meaning and meaningfulness, which I believe reflected a failure or weakness of representation. In this context, I wish to emphasize the *role of my clarifications as coherence-building constructions* that provided and sustained the building blocks of thought within a significant object relationship, rather than uncovering or decoding interpretations of defenses or organized but hidden content.

As I clarified and tried to help Ellen make sense of affect storms, feelings of abandonment, sudden emotional withdrawals and suicidal crises and interpretively put the here-and-now interactions of our relationship into some plausible and comprehensible explanatory, cause-and-effect narrative sequence, our separations – around vacations and absences, between appointments and so on – assumed increasing importance. Instead of fingering and counting her pills when distressed, Ellen began to call my answering machine to hear my voice or drive by my office to visualize and be close to my surroundings.

Much later, when she became able to speak of these experiences, she could only repeat that she was trying to hold on to the sense that I was "real." Attempts to explore and help specify what "being real" meant or how it worked for her emotionally yielded little success. We never uncovered a pre-existing, specific defensive meaning or unconscious fantasy related to these actions. Like Winnicott's (1971, p. 115) infant struggling against the disorganizing impact of de-cathexis, Ellen seemed to be in the realm of the concrete rather than the symbolic: I was either there or not there; she was either organized in and by my presence and able to think or disorganized and unable to think when abandoned and alone.[14]

The shift in Ellen's attachment, from thoughts of suicide to thoughts of me, seemed to mark the beginning of her achieving a representation of me that assumed an increasingly important, stabilizing role within her psychic economy. She seemed to be intuitively attempting to counter the destabilizing consequences of de-cathexis by acting in ways that reinforced her sense of my presence. Concrete "reminders" of my existence or contact

---

14 My best guess is that "being real" was connected to my willingness to think about and remember her and hold a place for her in my mind.

with things that reinforced her sense of my "being real" seemed to modulate her affects, "refuel" (Mahler et al., 1975) her capacity to think and help maintain the cohesion and coherence of her self.

Eventually, her sense of my "being real" became more stable and, except under greatest duress, she managed increasingly longer separations without becoming suicidal or showing indications of disorganization or loss of vitality, stability and coherence. Subsequently, the concrete need to call to hear my voice during separations was replaced by her preemptively asking me to tell her where I was going. Once I understood the stabilizing role that that information could play, I willingly shared it with her. She used it to locate me in space and reaffirm my existence, imagining where I was, what my surroundings might look like, and so on. Ellen seemed to be developing a representational means to hold on to a sense of my presence in my physical absence. This helped her to stabilize my image and presence within her mind, thereby keeping me with her, preventing a disorganizing fragmentation and allowing her to "think" of me and maintain self-cohesion and psychic stability in my absence.

Years later, as the fruits of this work ripened further, she announced that she now understood that there were *two* people in the room. While it is possible that this announcement marked or was associated with relinquishing a defensive denial or *discovering* an organized but deeply hidden fantasy, I believe that it reflected the achievement of her capacity to hold on to a sense of my continuity and separateness as a sustaining object despite my absence and to observe, think about and put into words an aspect of her Experience that was previously unnamable.

During the 15 or so years that followed the end of our first period of treatment, Ellen kept in touch intermittently by mail or occasional phone contact. Was this an unconscious titration of her need to maintain a concrete, "refueling" (Mahler et al., 1975) relationship needed to support her psychic functioning by preserving a representation of my existence within her mind? While we have never answered this question decisively, it did seem to be her way of holding on to the "reality" of my existence.

She returned to treatment, face-to-face, three times per week, after her father died. Despite becoming a mature woman with grown children and a successful marriage and career, her sensitivity to separation and possible loss was still acute and verged on the catastrophic. One important reason for her return seemed to be her vague intimation that the small inheritance she received on her father's death could make it possible to try to address the fact that her well-being and sense of adequate functioning remained tied to her sense of my physical existence and connection to me.

During this second phase, Ellen's strengthened capacities for self-observation and affect tolerance allowed her to observe and discuss her experience of our separations with a new competence. Eventually, she reported that what was so destabilizing in my absence was not just fantasies, fears or wishes that I would die or wish not to return – these were associated with primitive transferences built on representations of her violent father or abandoning mother – *but her terror that the me who returned would not be the same as the me who left*. While this terror may have been based on a fantasy connected with unconscious fears from childhood in regard to mother's emotional absence and/or hospitalizations, the *loss of continuity in her sense of the object*, the fragmentation of self and Ellen's dependence on my presence in order to effectively think and address these problems offer presumptive evidence of de-cathexis and weakness of representations.

In the ensuing years, despite having strengthened her capacities for thought and representation, Ellen still showed a propensity – although one that she now more rapidly recovered from – to revert to mind-numbing states of disorganization, confusion and frozen silence, to lose her ability to regulate her feelings, observe herself or meaningfully associate in the face of impending or actual separations or loss of my emotional attunement. My role in what now became the work of *her* increasing ability to manage her own acts of figurability became much less evident, but was discernible, nonetheless.

In the midst of a discussion of still powerful reactions to a recent break in the continuity of our sessions, Ellen impulsively asked if my eyes were blue. My spontaneous, intuitive reply was neither inquiry nor interpretation, but a statement of "fact" in the form of a personal story. I replied that I thought my eyes were brown, but that when I was a little boy, my mother would tell me they were hazel. As I spoke, I did not know why I chose to respond in this way or why I added this personal detail at that time, but I was aware that for me, it reflected a deeply meaningful, warm and loving memory. It is uncharacteristic of me to speak of my personal history with patients and the detail emerged spontaneously without my thinking about it.

In retrospect, it introduced "the mother" as an "affective hologram" (Ferro, 2002) into the field. In so doing, I was not only "being real" (Renik, 1998) or "self-disclosing" to Ellen but was assisting her in a spontaneous, intersubjective act of the creation of meaning. In introducing "the character of the mother," I was discharging a tension of my own – perhaps seeking solace and comfort from a loving, maternal introject in the face of a hostile or barren relationship with my patient – but also doing something akin to "adding a (verbal) prop" to the "playset" with which a child analyst engages a youngster: an iconic mother, who could lovingly see her child and imagine something wonderful and distinctive ("hazel eyes") in him – a mother who was more like the facilitating, consistent, caring and engaged analyst-mother in the positive transference.

In response to my comment, Ellen settled down and realized that *in her mind's eye*, she was transposing onto my face – that is, she imagined seeing – *the blue eyes of her mother*, that quintessential figure of abandonment. Her "hallucination" of a blue-eyed analyst was a "visual slip" reflecting the presence and use of an internalized representation and actualizing a transference reaction. At the same time, my introduction of a mother who sees and idealizes her child challenged her "transference distortion" and silently reminded her of how vitally different our relationship was from that of her childhood with her parents. The latter helped to patch a "micro-tear" in her psyche, restoring her equilibrium and allowing her to differentiate the change of separation from the catastrophe of absence, loss and psychic annihilation.

Still later in the treatment, faced with several cancellations necessitated by her work, Ellen was once again talking about how panicky and disorganized she could become when threatened with being out of contact with me. She continued with descriptions of chaos (at work) and her need to be hyper-vigilant and in total control as she faced intrusive feelings of panic. I commented that there seemed to be two panics pulling her in opposite directions: one she could feel at being out of contact with me. This sometimes damaged her sense of my being friendly and real, and then disorganized her sense of herself. It led her to desperately seek contact with me and try to reschedule any appointments that we might have to miss. The second panic was at the thought of her knowing or my seeing how dependent on me and needy she felt. This made her feel vulnerable and led to her wanting to appear indifferent to the cancellations. As a result, she was being pulled apart in opposite directions. "Welcome to my world," was her response, as she smiled (in relief?) and exhaled deeply.

A phrase she used as she described the work conflict that necessitated her missing her sessions triggered my memories of a past, lost love object and as I continued to listen to her, I began to fall into a deep and painfully mournful mood marked by hopelessness, desperation and daydreams of suicide. Dividing my attention between Ellen and myself, I reflected on and silently articulated something about my own state of mind. I recognized I was reworking a painful personal memory of irrevocable loss and with that thought as an object of reflection and with the question of whether it might somehow be tied to Ellen and the session, I returned my attention more fully to her discourse.

Her associations had led back to her own painfully traumatic childhood:

> It's a wonder that I ever got interested in learning, because no one ever read to me as a child. I remember a babysitter once told me a story about Peter Pan using the pictures in a book. My mother came home and became very angry. I thought we must have been doing something wrong.

She then talked further about her panic at our separations, her terrible dependency and need, but suddenly interrupted herself and angrily said,

"Don't look at me like that." Startled, I asked about my look, and what she had been thinking and feeling just before she noticed it. In the short run, this was "helpful." She quickly put her reaction aside by announcing that she had been "projecting" (her words) and seemed to recover a positive, helpful sense of my presence. However, it felt to me that she had used my intervention as more of a "reality check" than an opportunity for true thought, reflection and exploration. I therefore decided to use my reverie as the basis for an intervention and said,

> When you said that about the look on my face, I was thinking about something in reaction to what you had been telling me. I'm not sure if it will be of interest or use to you, but I thought I would mention it in case it would prove helpful. My thought was about how painful and irrevocable life's losses can sometimes feel and be.

Her response was that as a child, she had never lost anyone "irrevocably." I replied I wasn't thinking so much of a person, but of her childhood itself, of the opportunity to have been raised and to have lived in a secure and helpful family. She saddened and agreed. As she did so, a picture of her barren childhood emerged in my mind against the backdrop of her current incipient panic attacks and her attempts to stabilize herself on her own so that she could keep them hidden from me and avoid the panic of my seeing how needy she felt. I commented on this and she replied there was a third panic: that she would use me up or destroy me out of her neediness.

At that point, my thoughts shifted to Li'l Abner, a comic strip from my childhood, in which the characters lived in great poverty, but were nourished by a mythical set of friendly animals called "schmoos," who willingly turned themselves into hams and lovingly allowed themselves to be eaten by hungry humans. Beneath this memory was a series of half-formed images of breastfeeding, being breast-fed, the warmth of my first analyst and his extraordinary capacity to help patients acknowledge, bear and put into perspective the disappointments and heartbreaks of their lives.

I asked Ellen if she had ever read Li'l Abner and did she know about the schmoos? She had, but didn't remember them, so I told her about their role as loving food source and suggested that since her feeling while growing up in her own family was that nobody felt loving or giving in that way and because her needs must have felt so ravenous and great, she could not really believe that I might *want* to help her and not feel or be used up or destroyed in the process. She sadly agreed and added, "That's why people have children; so that they can find and give the love they never got themselves."

This triggered in me the image of a good friend reading the comics to my then 4-year-old son. Based on this flash memory and aware that the session was at its end, I said,

> You know what I think just happened? You'd said that no one ever read to you as a child and in telling you about Li'l Abner, I think I was also reading you the Sunday comics!

She smiled as she left the office and I warmly imagined her thinking, *The things analysts say!*

What I wish to call attention to in this last sequence is the way in which an area of representational weakness or absence (produced by the traumatic absence of the mother particularized as absent loving, seeing, comic reading presence) may appear embedded in a more usually represented conflict (the panic, shame and wish to hide her hunger or the extent of her dependency). I would suggest that coupled with her defensive negation (Freud, 1925) that she had "never" experienced an irrevocable loss were hints that we were approaching an area of representational absence or weakness (*my* unexpectedly becoming filled with mournful feelings and suicidal thoughts, followed by her sudden paranoid response to my "look"). Alongside her "neurotic" defensive denial was a disavowal or "ejection from the psyche" (McDougal, 1978) of an unbearable pain, which I unconsciously absorbed, resonated to and transiently identified with, returned to representation for both of us via an unconscious act of "figurability" and re-presented to her in the form of the words, "irrevocable loss" and in the memory of Li'l Abner and the schmoos. The latter condensed for me a series of warm memories of love and loss: my mother reading to me, my friend reading to my son, me reading to my son, warm and loving moments from my own analysis, me analyzing this patient, and so on. And like my introduction of the mother who sees special hazel in the everyday brown of her son's eyes – the analyst who sees the possibility that this suicidal teenage girl could grow up to be a successful mother and professional – the Li'l Abner story represented and re-presented an important structural support to Ellen's damaged psyche.

I believe that processes of unconscious communication were taking place between us. What is at question is the extent to which these processes involved the communication of more or less fully formed and organized unconscious fantasies and memories or of something more inchoate and far less saturated that was being projected into, taking root in and being transformed by the mind of the analyst so that it could then be re-presented to Ellen in a more structured form and then internalized by her to help solidify and form the representational basis of her own psychic functioning.

# Chapter 3

# Clinical implications of unrepresented states

## Effacement, discourse and construction

**I**

Western philosophy has long debated the true nature of "reality": Can we know it directly? To what extent does "reality" correspond to what we think we know and experience as "real"? Do our sense-based perceptions of what we assume to be real *create* our sense of reality or do they reflect and therefore confirm a pre-existing "something" that is independent of our perceptual capacities that we thereby discern? And what do we make of what we call psychic reality?

> [Freud] inherited from Kant the view that experience is not a raw given and that our understanding constructs … [experience] by arranging the material of sensation …. From this perspective, the world's objects are never accessible as such but only as phenomena, i.e., within limits of *possible* experience.
> 
> Kahn (2018, p. 25, original italics)

That is, the *sources* of experience (*noumena*) and the *forms* of experience as we sense them (*phenomena*) are not necessarily the same. Their relationship is analogous to that of the objects that are the source and the shadows that the objects cast on the walls of Plato's cave. From observations and experience of the one, we can make inferences and conjectures about the essential nature of the other.

In order to negotiate everyday life, we assume that the things of material reality have concrete existence in time and space and can be known empirically through our senses. However, quantum mechanics tells us that the true nature (i.e., the *reality*) of the atomic particles that make up the physical universe is impossible to know. We cannot measure or know atomic "reality," but only what that reality appears to look like as it is transformed in the act of our observing and measuring it.

The argument becomes even more complicated in regard to psychic reality – that is, the realm of the dynamic and the unstructured

DOI: 10.4324/9781003171331-4

unconscious – and the objects of psychoanalytic investigation. We lack direct access to knowledge of the unconscious:

> just as reality is not as it appears to us, the "internal foreign territory" … the unconscious … can only be accessed indirectly (Freud 1900: 668; 1915a: 170; 1933: 57).
>
> Kahn (2018, p. 25)

Whatever access we do have will always inevitably be partial and incomplete.[1]

Bion (1970) made the same point when he distinguished between **O** – raw existential experience – and **K** – that part of **O** that can come to be known.[2] He noted that the experience of psychic states and emotions is different from the experience of material facts. Psychic states and emotions can be known only indirectly by *intuition* and conjecture and not empirically via our senses:

> … the physician is dependent on realization of sensuous experience in contrast with the psycho-analyst whose dependence is on experience that is not sensuous. The physician can see and touch and smell. The realizations with which a psycho-analyst deals cannot be seen or touched; anxiety has no shape or colour, smell or sound.
>
> Bion (1970, p. 7)

The "instrument" by which we assess both material and psychic reality is of our mind.[3] But we have no way of stepping outside the mind to directly gauge and calibrate that instrument. To the extent that we believe that material or psychic reality is discoverable, we cannot know whether or not that purported discovery is necessarily accurate, partial or complete. In regard to what we believe we *can* know, we must remain uncertain if what we deem to be "real" is truly so or if it is to some extent *discovered, shaped* or *created* by our senses in the act of perception and the accompanying processes of neural organization.

Psychoanalysis teaches us that perceptions, memory and intuition are all subject to conscious and unconscious forces. The ideational forms in which they appear are not necessarily veridical (historically "true"), but may be shaped by our conscious and unconscious wishes, fears and needs.[4]

---

1 See Chapter 4.
2 See Levine (2016b).
3 Freud (1900) said that consciousness was "a sensory organ for the perception of psychic qualities" (p. 488).
4 See, for example, Freud's (1899) discussion of screen memories. Also Reed and Levine (2015) and Chapter 2.

Additional problems in accurate knowing arise from the anxieties produced by our experience of our ignorance:

> ... when we are at a loss we invent something to fill the gap of our ignorance – this vast area of ignorance, of non-knowledge, in which we have to move. The more frightening the gap, the more terrifying it is to realize how utterly ignorant we are ... the more we are pressed from outside and inside to fill the gap ....
>
> ... in a situation where you feel completely lost; you are thankful to clutch hold of any system, anything whatever that is available on which to build a kind of structure. So from this point of view ... we could argue that the whole of psychoanalysis fills a long-felt want by being a vast Dionysiac system; since we don't know what is there, we invent these theories and build this glorious structure that has no foundation in fact – or the only fact in which it has any foundation is our complete ignorance, our lack of capacity.
>
> However, we hope that it isn't completely unrelated to fact, that psychoanalytic theories would remind you of real life at some point in the same way as a good novel or a good play would remind you how human beings behave.
>
> Bion (2005, p. 2)

To complicate matters even further, there is general agreement that observation, which we rely on to furnish us with the raw material from which our theories might be derived, is never theory-free.[5] Observation is inevitably structured and directed, both made possible and limited, by pre-existing theories, implicit and explicit, conscious and unconscious. The philosopher Auguste Comte (1974) summarized this problem when he wrote,

> If it is true that every theory must be based upon observed facts, it is equally true that facts cannot be observed without the guidance of some theories. Without such guidance, our facts would be desultory and fruitless; we could not retain them: for the most part we could not even perceive them.
>
> (p. 27)

These are the epistemological problems surrounding psychic reality, the unconscious and ideas, thought and perception. Additional limitations and problems accrue once we attempt to put what we think we can know of experience (**K**) into words. Language and thought always fall short of

---

5 Parsons (1992): "we cannot regard theory as derived purely from observation alone, because the observations that we make are already dependent on the theory we use in making and describing them" (p. 111).

fully rendering or translating the "event," the thing-in-itself. The latter, "defies the familiar grasp of the mind" and resists "totalisation of meaning" (Kahn, 2018, p. 58).

Green (2005a) offered a similar perspective in discussing Freud's shift from the topographic to the structural theory:

> What Freud is trying to tell us … is that the unconscious can only be constituted *by a psyche which eludes the structuring of language.*
>
> (p. 99, original italics)

In his formulations of the communicative dimension of projective identification and his theory of container/contained, Bion (1962b, 1970) shifted the emphasis of his thinking from the study and discovery of elements of the dynamic unconscious – that is, what was organized, but hidden because it was anxiety producing and unacceptable to the superego – to the study and creation of the capacity to *have* an unconscious – that is, the ability to map the infinite space of the unstructured unconscious onto the three dimensional and temporal "geography" of psychic space.[6]

An important clinical implication of Bion's (1962b) formulation of the beta screen and the psychotic part of the mind implies that in addition to what can be represented (as alpha elements) and therefore communicated via the lexical meanings of words, analytic discourse may also reflect a second level of communication that attempts "to produce an emotional involvement" (Bion, 1962b, p. 24) with an object by unconsciously inducing feelings and impulses toward action in the listener.

Green (1975) re-affirms Bion's findings when he notes that

> More and more frequently we see analysts questioning their own reactions to what their patients communicate, using these in their interpretations along with (or in preference to) the analysis of the content of what is communicated, because *the patient's aim is [unconsciously] directed to the effect of his communication rather than to the transmission of its content.*
>
> (p. 3, italics added)

---

6 Bion's understanding of the unstructured unconscious and the autonomous and intersubjective transformations through which it might be contained and metabolized came out of his work with psychotic patients. He later extended this to the pre-verbal infant and the infant–mother relationship and realized that these were universal phenomena of normal life. He designated the unstructured unconscious as "the psychotic part of the mind." This I believe was an unfortunate choice of terminology, because as De Masi (2020) has argued, while both psychosis and infantile psychic functioning involve the vicissitudes of the unstructured unconscious, psychosis is a particular psychic organization and structure that is very different from that of the normal psyche of the pre-verbal period.

We should expect, then, that in the analytic situation each participant will potentially be communicating to the other on two simultaneous, often contradictory channels: one lexical and manifest, the other affective, unconscious and inductive. This second channel reflects the unconscious communicative capacity of projective identification.[7]

To summarize, when it comes to matters of what can be known of the world and our experience, materially and emotionally, consciously and unconsciously, empirically gathered evidence is never "immaculate." Veridical "truth" of memory, perception and psychic reality must always to some extent remain ambiguous and suspect. We are always in danger of "shaping" and "filling in" what we perceive, recall or believe that we know according to our wishes, fears and needs.[8] And in treatment, a conjectural shaping in the form of constructions may be required, especially in the treatment of non-neurotic patients. Rather than certainties and hard facts, we are more often – perhaps always – left to some extent with beliefs, hypotheses and speculations; plausible theories rather than empirically verifiable facts. That is, rather than uncovering and naming repressed, hard factual truths that correspond to historical reality, our interpretations are often constructions.

## II

At the heart of Freud's (1937) Constructions in Analysis paper is his acknowledgement that *constructions may function dynamically in the analytic process and the cure in the same way that the recovery of a once repressed traumatic childhood memory did*. Under certain conditions, a good enough conjecture could stand in for and perform the same work as a recovered, previously repressed memory. This realization gave further credence to Freud's earlier assertions that psychic reality and material reality were distinct, but functionally equivalent modes of thought. It also exposed the deep epistemological divide concerning the nature of evidence in psychoanalysis, the truth-value of interpretations and any expectations of exact

---

7 "In psychoanalysis, two regimes of language operate side by side and blend: one refers to the semiological plane of lost meanings, the other to the performativity of uttered statements .... [This duality of discourse, via words as semantic conveyers of meaning and words as inducers of emotion] means that words will be heard for what they mean, including in the form of divided signifiers. They will be listened to for what they do not want to say and, most importantly, for what they cannot say: i.e., the part that only makes itself known via the acts which the utterance of speech performs in analysis" (Kahn, 2018, p. 93).
8 See Chapters 4 and 5 for further discussion.

correspondence between psychopathological etiological factors and the findings of external reality.[9]

The key terms in Freud's reformulation are "construction" and "conviction." As nouns, they refer respectively to ideas (constructions) and feelings (convictions) that appear as end products of psychic processes that seem to arise spontaneously and appear unbidden. These are processes not of *deduction*, but of *induction*. Their arrival in consciousness without awareness of the intermediate steps involved is usually surprising and unexpected.

Freud (1937) defined construction as a presumptive formulation or understanding, an "imaginative conjecture,"[10] that comes to the analyst's mind unbidden in the midst of the analyst's reverie. This definition conforms closely to Bergstein's (2019) description of *intuition*:

> an unmediated knowledge or understanding of truth, not supported by any information derived from a familiar sensual source ... [one whose basis] cannot be communicated to another and cannot be corroborated by a rational method of scientific knowledge.
>
> (p. 30)[11]

In this sense, constructions are the end products of transformations of inchoate forces and sensations originating in the unrepresented, unstructured unconscious that result in representations (ideational forms). This process is experienced as *intuition* and the emotional state or feeling associated with the sense of rightness, relief and fit that a useful construction may produce is experienced as *conviction*.

Constructions are not intended to be statements of historical fact – the latter are what Freud (1937) termed "reconstructions" – and so should not be evaluated in regard to the factuality of their content. They are, instead, something broader and more open-ended: statements of beliefs or possibilities offered as possible instruments for mental growth (Bianchedi, 1991).

> [Their] merit lies in their *capacity* for *generating psychic movement*, transforming psychic barriers into caesuras, affording a multidimensional

---

9 In Chapter 4, we will speak further about the epistemology of the seduction theory – the idea that the etiology of psychopathological states always will be found to relate to actual historical events – and question whether, to some extent, it has continued subliminally in the minds of analysts who hold the expectation that an actual set of causal traumatic events will always be discovered for every psychopathological outcome.
10 "We do not pretend that an individual construction is anything more than a conjecture which awaits examination, confirmation, or rejection" (Freud, 1937, p. 265).
11 See also Bianchedi (1991).

view, and enabling the patient to move from a preoccupation with [concrete and actual aspects of] external reality to an observation of his internal reality.

Bergstein (2019, p. 178, original italics)

Like any intuition, constructions can serve as containers for what otherwise may be "experience [that] remains non-mental, as an overwhelming frenzy of stimuli inside the mind and body" (Bergstein, 2019, p. 13). In the clinical situation, this "non-mental experience" can reflect pre-verbal, perhaps even pre-natal events and sensations, the consequence of trauma and the surging, unbounded and not yet represented drive derivatives and excitations of the id. In addition to providing containers for that which is unrepresented, constructions can help produce a space for emergence of the not yet knowable and stimulate a reorganization of already represented and known elements that can modulate excitation by naming it and making it an object of thought, producing openings to new possible meanings or understandings through metaphor, polysemy and implication.

As is any intuition, a construction is an extension in the domain of myth, something that Bion (1963, p. 12) deemed a "necessary dimension" of the analyst's interpretation.[12] It's necessity follows, in part, from the fact that a *major task of the human psyche is representation of the previously unrepresentable* (Levine, 2012).[13] This is a lifelong, homeostatic task in which the inherently traumatic sensations of being alive and suffering Existence[14] are contained, ameliorated and made somewhat more tolerable.

## III

In a previous paper (Levine, 2011a), I traced the evolution of earlier assumptions about the clinical use and role of construction in analysis, noting that constructions were:

1   Originally seen as a means of bringing previously repressed memories to light – "building a bridge towards the repressed" (Chianese, 2007).
2   Then seen as filling in by conjecture the missing pieces of a patient's actual history – along the lines of how one might sketch in the picture

---

12  See Levine (2016a).
13  See Chapter 4.
14  I use the "capital E" Experience to refer to raw existential experience in the domain of O. That part of Experience which can be known (that can enter the domain of K) is what we commonly refer to as "experience" in everyday speech and is written here with a small letter e. See Chapter 4 for further explication.

of a real but once shattered vase or urn from the incomplete set of fragments found at an archeological site.
3   And finally, with Freud (1937), as standing in dynamically for – that is, serving the same functional role as – an actual memory of childhood memory that had been repressed and continued to remain inaccessible.

I then considered the work of Green (1975) in an attempt to describe the value and role of construction in regard to remediating the effects of psychic voids and other "tears in the fabric of the psyche" (Green, 1975) produced by negative hallucination, de-cathexis and effacement in the treatment of borderline and other non-neurotic patients.

At the 1974 London IPA Congress, Green (1975) differentiated repression (*Verdrangung*) from what has variously been called "abolition," "foreclosure" or *effacement* (*Verwerfung*). In retrospect, we can see that in Green's formulation the former referred to a neurotic form of organization in which an unacceptable, anxiety arousing mental content – thought, feeling, perception or fantasy – remains intact, even as it is banished from conscious awareness at the behest of the superego.[15] In contrast, in effacement, "the processes of symbolization are impaired" (Green, 1998, p. 652) as *negative hallucination is directed against the perception of thought and representations* (p. 658), *including representations of reality* (p. 655). (In his 1924 paper "The Loss of Reality in Neurosis and Psychosis," Freud described "representations of reality" as "ideas and judgments which have been previously derived from reality and by which reality was represented in the mind" [p. 185].)

To return to Green (1998),

> Repression keeps the representation as far as possible from consciousness. It [the representation] is conserved in the mind though out of reach, impossible to awaken to memory, but still there. In the case of negative hallucination, the thoughts, some capital thoughts, are lost, because they have been erased. There is no trace of their ever having existed or of their 'underground' performance.
>
> (pp. 658–659)

To put the matter in terms of our spatial metaphor, this means that the result of that erasure (*effacement*) is that the ideational representation is

---

15  Recall Freud's (1915a) comments that a certain layer of the system Ucs. referred to elements that were structured like elements of the system Pcs./Cs., but were, nevertheless, inaccessible to consciousness because of their content and meaning. We would now say that these were elements of the dynamic unconscious.

replaced in the unconscious by some unstructured force that then lacks specific ideational meaning. The force will signal its relatively asymbolic presence by impulsive action, an overflow of affect, somatic discharge or the profound turning away from reality that Green (2000a) described as the central phobic position. In contrast, in the case of elements banished to the dynamic unconscious, a representation with full ideational saturation persists.

What this means clinically and practically is that in the presence of negative hallucination, de-cathexis and effacement, we cannot trust or rely on the patient's ability to notice or continually know their thoughts or feelings. What is said or reported as felt in one moment cannot be expected to be retained and used in an emotional sense in the next. Links between mental elements are easily lost or severed. Whether or the extent to which, in any given instance, this de-linkage is due to attacks on linking (Bion, 1959) or a structural deficit of the psyche remains an open question. In either case, representations of reality in the patient, especially emotional reality, cannot be securely relied on to be present.

As a result, the mind of the borderline patient operates as if it was a computer with an inconstant "save memory" function. The RAM is quickly overwhelmed and what is or may be expected to be "known" one moment is lost sight of the next. When added to the defensive distortions and denials that are commonly produced by the more intact, neurotic portion of the mind, we can see how the analyst may easily be confronted with a patient who cannot make sense of their being-in-the-world. Too much relevant information goes missing to have a comprehensible picture of their internal, emotional life, because it has been effaced. As a result, the patient has only very partial information with which to piece together a plausible and coherent cause-and-effect picture of their self-states or psychic functioning. Life feels disjointed and chaotic or else achieves a maladaptive stabilization by means of rigid, reductive pseudo-explanations.

Abensour (2013), talking of the absence in the psychotic – and borderline – patient of a stable and coherent "foundation for the personality" and emotionally operational sense of their "individual and family history" describes a similar situation:

> It is like a book from which some chapters or pages have been removed, so that reading it leads either to confusion or incomprehension.
>
> (p. 8)

Consequently, if a coherent, flexible and meaningful discourse or self-understanding is to emerge, the analyst must help name, preserve and remind the patient of what has just been said, felt or has just occurred; must help the patient to hold this in mind and help fill in the many missing pieces in order to create the possibility of forming a plausible, cause and effect, sequential picture (representation) of their emotional reality. This has far more to do with naming and describing actual and/or plausible feeling states of the patient and cause and effect emotional sequences in the here-and-now interactions of the session and less to do with interpreting extra-analytic dynamics or transferences or making genetic interpretations of the kind more suited to the neurotic patient or portions of the mind.

The means through which the kind of work that I am trying to describe will be achieved include *sustained inquiry* on the part of the analyst designed to raise questions and reinforce possible links between cause-and-effect happenings, *clarification* (e.g., underlining and reminding the patient of what has just happened or what they have just felt or said, "putting the feelings into words") and *construction*. To the outside observer, the resulting dialogue may look prosaic, "cognitive" or like a form of supportive psychotherapy, but it is in fact *an intersubjective process with a powerful analytic rationale that is required in order to support and help repair an otherwise fragmented, torn and continually disrupted psyche.*

As Green (1998) reminds us, there is "all the difference between a hole in the mind and an evanescent dream as something embarrassing to tell that can easily be forgotten" (p. 656). He further cautions that "Contemporary psychoanalysis is in great need of structural differentiations in order not to mix up the material coming from different types of patients in a one and only matrix." (p. 661).

The metapsychological basis for this work goes back to Freud's (1911b) formulation of psychotic delusions as an attempt to repair an internal state of radical withdrawal (de-cathexis) from a sense of external reality. Chervet (2013), in his introduction to Absenour (2013) describes this situation as follows:

> ... in a psychotic situation, the task given to words is that of repairing the lack of drive-related thing presentations, in order to self-cure, as it were, that lack.
>
> (p. xvii)

Treatment is therefore based on the "hope that thing-presentations able to fulfill their role as representatives of the drives [i.e., drive derivatives]" will arise from various word-based or word-mediated interactions in the patient's *current* life situation.

> The treatment of psychotic patients requires the creation of reality traces to make good the lack of memory traces; that is what is required if the patient is to become able to deal with the reality of the *missing link*, that drive-based reality that remains divorced from any possibility of being represented.
>
> Chervet (2013, p. xxi)

In Green's (1998, 2005a, 2005b) terms, effacement, negative hallucination, de-cathexis and the *work of the negative* are the bases for a lack of representation and memory. They are the reasons that the links fail, disappear or go missing in the first place.

Over the past 70 years, the very nature of what is constructed in analysis and the underlying reasons for doing so have shifted considerably. While some treatments today may include the kind of constructions of past historical events that Freud was concerned with – for example, his construction of the early observation of a primal scene in response to the dream of the Wolfman – *what is more commonly constructed now are aspects of the patient's affective experience of the here-and-now interaction in the analytic relationship*. These constructions concern themselves with actual, inferred and emergent plausible, emotional mind states of the patient and narrative cause-and-effect sequences in the present.

Bion (1970) considered these, the events of the analytic session, as the true north of psychoanalytic inquiry and regarded anything else as *hearsay evidence*. The aim of these constructions is less that of helping patients remember what was once known but then forgotten, and more to counteract effacement, negative hallucination and de-cathexis, thereby initiating or facilitating a transformative process that will help patients achieve a more stable and comprehensible psychic representation of reality; to make thinkable previously inchoate proto-emotions (Bion, 1970). That is, to help patients recognize previously ineffable and unarticulatable feelings and put them into words.

The latter process is especially important in the treatment of non-neurotic patients, whose difficulties are intimately connected to unrepresented or weakly represented mental states (Botella and Botella, 2005; Green, 2005a, 2005b; Levine, 2010a; Reed, 2009). In these analyses, the literal, historical truth-value of an interpretation may sometimes be less important to the therapeutic process than the potentially transformative and/or catalytic movements that may – and often *must* – emerge from the interaction and relationship between analyst and patient. Hence, Hartke (2013) has noted the important shift in the goals of contemporary analysis, which he suggests aims "primarily at the expansion of the mental container, instead of the predominant work on unconscious contents" (p. 132) and Green (2005a) has argued that it is sometimes better for the analyst to express his or her countertransference in action than inhibit it in favor of a lifeless or artificial discourse. What these assertions point to is the fact that our formulation of the constructive "work" that the analyst must perform has, in the case of unrepresented and weakly represented mental states, expanded to include transformative mental processes and even interpersonal actions (containment, reverie, alpha function, unconscious actualization, affirmation, etc.).[16]

---

16 See also Botella and Botella (2005) for a discussion of *figurability*, and Levine et al. (2013) for a discussion of unrepresented and weakly represented mental states and some of their technical implications.

## IV

If we return to Freud's (1937) Constructions in Analysis paper from the perspective outlined above, we will come to the radical conclusion that what is at stake in the analyses of non-neurotic patients is the very creation of the psyche itself. How then are we to re-interpret the meaning of his brilliant insight that what has once occurred is never lost, but remains inscribed somewhere (p. 260)? Does Freud mean that these events remain encoded in the psyche? In the body? And at what level of organization? Verbal? Sensorial/somatic?

Here is Marucco's (2007) formulation of the problem:

> What is the archaic that repeats itself? Is it something that emerges in the act from the regressive push toward a state almost prior to the encounter with the other? Or is it the product of the intrusive force of an object that imprinted the destructive trace of the unbinding where the path toward the potential for representation should have been opened? We are 'far away' from the repressed unconscious and, at the same time, very close to the cauldron of the id.
>
> (p. 315)

Note the similarity to Green's (1998) formulation (following Winnicott, 1971) of the consequences for psychic structure of the *de-cathexis*, which can follow an insurmountably traumatic loss or absence of a primary object. Rather than stimulating the psychic work needed to produce mental representations, in such circumstances the loss or absence will provoke,

> a wound in the mind; producing a hemorrhage of representation, a pain with no image of the wound but just a blank state … or a hole … The total picture of the situation is either blotted out, or leaves remains of fragmented pieces (which will later become bizarre objects) with no bonds to unite them.
>
> (p. 658)

Patients with a deficient capacity to represent and/or mentalize cannot "(1) represent feeling states meaningfully in symbols and words, (2) experience affects as [their] own, (3) relate to [themselves] as an agent" (Killingmo, 2006). Their discourse is apt to be fragmented or empty of meaning. The anxiety that these patients feel is not associated with unconscious forbidden wishes, but is apt to be tied instead to nameless dread: loss of the self and disorganization of the psyche; fusional fears of engulfment and abandonment; rage at the terror of coming in contact with or confronting the emptiness or void; or fragmentation of self in an explosion of infinite expansion into limitless space. At this level, we are no longer talking about punishment for the gratification of dangerous or forbidden desires (e.g., castration or loss of the object's love), but annihilation and the sense of one's very *existence*. At stake is the formation, cohesion and maintenance of the experience of a sense of identity and self.

In these circumstances, the patient is dependent on the analyst in order to regain, maintain or perhaps develop for the first time the capacity to think. What is required of the analyst is to lend his or her transformative capacities to the patient in the process not of recall, but of the *creation* of thought and/or memory, its symbolic linkage with other psychic elements and its insertion into a coherent narrative story and time line. This work takes place as part of an intersubjective, dialogic process that is inexorably tied to the analyst's individuality, intuition and creativity. When it is successful, a "memory" of a here-and-now present day interaction in the analysis may work to dynamically "patch over" a "hole" or "psychic void" left in the wake of previous pre-verbal or massive psychic trauma. This is the functional meaning of the working through, *après coup* in the analytic process.

# Chapter 4

# The fundamental epistemological situation

> It ain't no good, it ain't no good
> I gotta use words when I talk to you.
>
> T.S. Eliot, *Sweeney Agonistes*

## An epistemological[1] challenge

Reflecting on what he felt was a fragmentation of analytic thought into opposing theories, Andre Green (1997) suggested that psychoanalysis needed to be placed within a contemporary epistemological framework, so as to "overcome that which, in Freud's work, was hampered by the [the limitations of the] thinking of his time" (p. 11). Green's aim was not that of creating still another post-Freudian school or discourse, but rather providing "the foundations of a new contemporary paradigm: a new *Freudian* matrix, pluralistic, extended, and complex" (Urribarri, 2017, p. 134, italics added).

This matrix, which involved a shift from an almost exclusive concern with the removal of defenses, healing of splits, resolving of conflicts and the uncovering and de-coding of hidden psychic *contents* to attempts to facilitate the development of the patient's creative capacities to think, feel and dream, has encouraged analysts to extend their psychoanalytic understanding and technique beyond the previous limits of analyzability. Thus, Ogden (2004) writes of the need to help analysands find the capacity to "dream undreamt dreams" and Botella (2014) insists that the true goal of psychoanalytic treatment is not the "remembering" of facts, but the supporting of processes that lie behind, generate and form what we call our memories and make them capable of reorganizing psychic life.

While a formal essay devoted to psychoanalytic epistemology never appeared in English,[2] Green's descriptions of the work of the negative,

---

1 Epistemology is defined as *the study of the theory of knowledge, especially with regard to its methods, validity and scope, and the distinction between justified belief and opinion.*
2 For readers of French, see Green, A. (1995). *La Causalité Psychique: Entre Nature et Culture*. Paris: O. Jacob.

DOI: 10.4324/9781003171331-5

de-cathexis, effacement and psychic voids (e.g., Green, 1975, 1997, 1998, 2005a) seemed central to the task. His was "an innovative program of investigation centred on patients at the limits of analyzability, studying their representational function (and dysfunction) in the analytic setting" (Urribarri, 2018, p. 66).

In addition to the classical goals of helping neurotics discover already formed, pre-existing truths about their wishes, fantasies and fears that they could not allow into consciousness, Green emphasized the importance of helping limit-case patients develop the capacities to *create* the personal truths of their being. This often required the provision of a setting and a relationship capable of "Supply[ing] … content to what … [was previously] experienced only in unrepresentable form" (Green, 1997, p. 211).

He argued that borderline and other non-neurotic,

> patients, who are dependent on affective communication, seem to need *a sharing of their experience*, which does not mean collusion with it, in a non-intrusive exchange which *gives them a feeling of existence*, in which sufficient space can be formed, albeit manufactured space, for their silent self, and where the defensive meaning of their state can be acquired without there being a compression of their inner world.
> Green (1997, pp. 200–201, italics added)

Green's emphasis on the "sharing of experience" rather than interpreting the hidden content, on the need to feel that one's true self can exist, that psychic space is being *manufactured* and meaning *created* ("acquired") rather than *found* ("uncovered") builds not only on the work of Freud, especially his Constructions paper (Freud, 1937), but that of Winnicott (1965, 1974) and Bion (1962b, 1970). The latter each described the essential role of intersubjective, affective communication in infant development and the analytic process, especially in the treatment of non-neurotic patients. And each noted that the analytic situation offered and/or helped create conditions for the emergence, recognition and expression of potentially disruptive and/or traumatic events that reflected and were based on unrepresented registrations of infantile and childhood events.

These events – environmental failures of provision in Winnicott's theory; failures of maternal reverie and examples of reverse projective identification in Bion's theory; the Dead Mother dynamics in Green's (1980) theory – had occurred, but had not yet been "experienced" by an organized sense of self. The internal situation thereby produced is ever present and yet always remains outside of conscious awareness. It is not consigned to the "ordinary" dynamic unconscious, but is frozen in the temporal dimension that Scarfone (2015) calls "the unpast," because the actual experience in question occurred in the pre-verbal period in the presence of an ego that was "too immature to gather all the phenomena into the area of personal omnipotence" (Winnicott, 1974, p. 104).

Thus, Winnicott (1965) concluded,

> There are very roughly speaking, two kinds of human beings, those who do not carry around with them a significant experience of mental breakdown in earliest infancy and those who do carry around with them such an experience and who must therefore flee from it, flirt with it, fear it, and to some extent be always preoccupied with the threat of it.
>
> (p. 122)

## Truth, sense, psychic reality and experience

Bion (1965, 1970) believed that the mind needed truth in order to grow the way the body needs physical nourishment.[3] In analysis, he said,

> There can be no genuine outcome that is based on falsity. Therefore the outcome depends on the closeness with which the interpretive appraisal approximates to truth.
>
> Bion (1970, p. 28)

However, as we shall see in Chapter 5, the questions of what truth is, how one arrives at it and recognizes that one has arrived and whether one can ever, in their descriptions, do more than "closely approximate" to psychic truth remain very complex matters indeed.

In Chapters 2 and 3, we have noted that the *objects of psychoanalysis* – emotions, states of mind, the unconscious – are psychic qualities. As such, *they are ineffable, unavailable to perception via the modality of the senses* (Bion, 1970, p. 28). Attempts to fully capture them in words will always, to some extent, prove insufficient to the task of conveying their full meaning. Consequently, in analysis, we "are faced with communicating about an experience which by definition is impossible to [fully] translate into words" (Green, 1997, p. 204).

Thus, Kahn (2018) writes that infancy – literally, *in fans*, meaning without words,

> is therefore not a stage of life but an incapacity to represent and bind something that is not even repressed as it has not been perceived, an unmanageable stasis dwelling as presence without any representation or scene. And passibility is not the opposite of activity. It is a form of

---

3   In a memoir, Francesca Bion (1995) said of her husband: "First and foremost he placed respect for the truth without which effective analysis becomes impossible. It is the central aim and as essential for emotional growth as food is for the body; without it the mind dies of starvation" (p. 106).

enduring, an ability to host whatever thought [one] is not prepared to think, which is exactly what can rightly be called thinking. For the mind must nonetheless bear witness to and contain such immemorial that silently persists and is signaled by turmoil. Delusion or anxiety; it must analyse it, historicise it, in short, it must give form to this amorphous mass by endowing it with a place in space and a moment in time.

(pp. 62–63)

This "giving form" to the "amorphous mass" of the not yet represented, that can never be fully represented, is the result of a demand made on the psyche – of the self or of the intersubjective other – for a work of binding and containment. That is, it requires and elicits the creative act of construction.[4] *Thus, there is always a gap that requires binding and that offers the possibility of being filled in with something new.*

One implication of this inevitable shortfall is that it is impossible to ever *fully* know one's own mind or that of another.[5] Another implication is that there is often a huge difference between theoretically valorizing "the truth" in psychoanalysis and finding the actual words needed to approximate it when we attempt to state it to ourselves or describe it to another.

Much of Bion's later work centered on the structural problem of how the truth of psychic qualities can be discerned and to what extent that truth can come to be known. In the previous chapters, we have described how he argued that psychoanalytic inquiry is dependent on the recognition and exploration of a kind of experience that is not "of the senses." Inferring the presence of a psychic quality or state is not the same as directly observing it. Thus, there is a limitation in knowing or speaking about psychic qualities and psychic reality that implies that *there is always an enigmatic space that exists and that can be filled with a variety of suitable, but always approximate, ideational forms.*

In Chapter 3, we noted that Bion (1970) proposed that in place of the senses and empirically deduced evidence, psychoanalysts must rely on "intuition" (p. 28). The latter implies unconsciously spontaneously grasping (intuiting) "the psychic reality (the truth) of the session by becoming one with it" (Ogden, 2015, p. 287).

But this formulation creates more problems than it solves. As a psychic quality, intuition will have its own enigmatic, ineffable dimension and

---

4 See Chapter 3.
5 This implies that one can never fully overcome one's countertransference. "One of the essential points about counter-transference is that it is *unconscious*. People talk about 'making use of' their counter-transference; they cannot make any use of it because they don't know what it is" (Bion, 1980, p. 16).

will also be subject to all of the vicissitudes of unconscious influence and distortion. How then to be sure of the correctness or "truth" of one's intuition when one is intuiting the psychic state or psychic reality of another? Although not *of* the senses, not a subjective state in the way that ordinary, concrete reality is assumed to be, psychic reality is felt to be a kind of *experience*. But of what kind? And how – and to what extent – is it to be known? Therein lies the problem.

## The fundamental epistemological position

Up to this point, I have spoken, quite colloquially, of "experience," but this term requires further explication. Following Bion's (1962b, 1970) distinction between **O** (raw existential Experience) and **K** (that part of Experience that one can come to know and specify in words) and accepting his view, following Plato and Kant, that Experience (**O**) itself is never fully knowable, I (Levine, 2010b) have suggested using the convention of distinguishing between "capital E" Experience (**O**) and "small e" experience (**K**), that part of Experience that can become known. Only parts of "capital E" Experience may come into the domain of that which can be known (**K**) and thereby become part of our "small e" experience.

This means that *transformations from* **O** *to* **K** *(T(**O**)->**K**) are not necessarily fixed, one-to-one correspondences and never move from a fully saturated element in one domain to a fully saturated element in another. Whether we are speaking of perception, memory, somatic sensation, drive movement, affect or other psychic qualities, there is always a gap or potential space, some enigmatic, ambiguous, not-yet-completed ideational form that is potentially emergent and context-specific. In analysis, the context is the emotional link – or its absence – between the pair within the setting.*

The unfinished, unsaturated, context-dependent, pair-dependent or group-dependent quality or component that needs to be added to complete and determine the moment-to-moment nature and meaning of small e experience is the very open space and potential for emergence in which analytic therapeutic action and *après coup* operate. It reflects a basic quality of human psychic functioning that I propose that we call *the fundamental epistemological situation*. Here is a fuller description of that situation:

*The nature of lived Experience is such that the human organism initially registers bits of that Experience, internal and external, drive and perception, as vague somatic sensations that must be transformed – ("dreamed" in Bion's (1962b, 1970, 1992) terms) – given meaning and made personally meaningful: "subjectivized," "personalized" and instantiated into a fixed temporal sequence. This transformation and the final (saturated) form that any given sensation will ultimately acquire are dependent, in part, on forces generated by the conscious and unconscious, internal and external, context – relational or self-generated – in which they occur. This means that meanings (final ideational content) will often, perhaps always, be contingent on and carry the imprint of the specific context and dynamics of their construction.*

Another way of describing this is to say that each stimulus – internal or external, drive, somatic sensation or perception – is a *turbulence, presence* or *thing*, which has the potential of being or producing an excitation or sensorial disturbance that then needs to be bound within a suitable container and transformed. This process of containment and transformation inevitably implies construction.[6] When this occurs, the specific finalized form of the product of that transformation will not be fully pre-determined, but will be one of several possibilities that while fitting and unique are also context dependent.

As part of a general theory of psychic representation, Freud (1915b) described the drive as a "frontier concept" that originated in the soma, where it produced a pressure, turbulence or vague sensorial disturbance that, when it reached the psyche, "made a demand upon the mind for work." This work allowed it to acquire psychic representation in the system Ucs. as a "thing-presentation." He further suggested that it was only when united with a "word-presentation" that the ideational content of that drive derivative became knowable or verbalizable, as it crossed the censorship barrier and entered the system, Pcs.-Cs. (Freud, 1915a).

Although Freud de-emphasized representations and their vicissitudes in his second topography, he maintained the enigmatic, not-yet-ideational, status of drive elements in his conception of the Id. For example, in Lecture 32 of the New Introductory Lectures, Freud (1933) speculated that "nothing corresponding to an idea or content exists in the id. Nothing but instinctual impulses seeking discharge" (quoted by Green, 1997, p. 186). This implies that rather than being a "seething cauldron" of ideationally saturated wishes and desires, *Id impulses are force without fully saturated ideational content.*

Thus, Freud left open the question of whether or not the ultimate form of the ideational content of the drive derivative was singular, fixed and fully pre-determined by its origins or whether there was some potential flexibility in the determination of its ultimate form; and whether the word-presentation that bound and transformed the thing presentation was always self-generated or could also come from the Other (the object or group – e.g., culture). Was there a tentative recognition here of an undifferentiated space in which the final form taken by mental contents (ideas) could be shaped to fit the dynamic exigencies of the moment; of the gap between Experience and what is describable in language?

We earlier saw (Chapter 2) that similar considerations were raised in regard to memory in Freud's (1899) Screen Memories paper. There, he suggested that memories were not pristine and stored fully formed, but

---

6 For a more extensive discussion of construction, see also Levine (2011a, 2015a).

remained partly unsaturated until recollected; that their ultimate specific ideational form and content were dependent on the context in which and aims for which they were retrieved.

> It may indeed be questioned whether we have any memories at all *from* our childhood: memories *relating to* our childhood may be all that we possess. Our childhood memories show us our earliest years not as they were but as they appeared at the later periods when the memories were aroused. In these periods of arousal, the childhood memories did not, as people are accustomed to say, *emerge*; they were *formed* at that time. And a number of motives, with no concern for historical accuracy, had a part in forming them, as well as in the selection of the memories themselves.
> 
> Freud (1899, p. 322)

Thus, Freud implied the existence of an unformed, unsaturated space in which memories could emerge and reach final saturated ideational form, *completed in the present at the moment of recall and assembled with a specific unconscious purpose in mind.*

Avzaradel (2015) offers a contemporary elaboration of this argument, noting the distinction that must be made between the mnemic trace, an initial somatic registration that is not yet psychic, and memory, which is a form of psychic ideation that is the product of a process of transformation and elaboration that moves via alpha function (Bion 1962b, 1970) – *regredience* and *figurabilité* (Botella and Botella, 2005) – from mnemic traces to the level and status of thoughts.

Roussillon (2011) found neuro-scientific confirmation of this description in the work of Gerald Edelman (1989), who suggested that the contents of memory systems are always approximate rather than complete and fully formed. Roussillon (2011) also noted that the process through which the final end product of memory is constructed often reflects some elements of the intersubjective role of the object (as "other/subject"). He further extended this co-constructive dimension to psychic development in general:

> Development and gradual integration are not automatic or dependent solely on the self's internal processes; they become structured only when they are accompanied by an appropriate response from … [one's primary] objects.
> 
> Roussillon (2011, p. 180)

The self and the ideational, verbalizable description of that self that emerges is then *"constructed in accordance with the nature and type of adjustment and mirroring that the primary object proposes"* (p. 139, italics added). This dependence on the other for discovery of the self is what Roussillon calls,

> *the paradox of primary narcissism*: cathexis of the object is superposed on that of the self, with no antagonism as long as the cathexis of the object reflects back to the self its own states of feeling, not necessarily in the same mode.
>
> (pp. 139–140, italics added)

Thus, for Roussillon, the primary object is inevitably a "symbolizing object," one that "subjectifies the self or enables the self to take on board the feeling of being a subject" (p. 171). But as it does so, there is an object specific and context specific flavor that is given to the ideational result. The shadow of the object, as Freud (1917) said in Mourning and Melancholia, inevitably falls on the ideational and/or affective shape of how the "small e" experience is organized, felt and described or remembered. It is this dimension of psychic development that is repeated in the analytic process and determines an important element of its therapeutic action:

> The treatment setting … becomes the arena of an intersubjective relationship in which the interplay between the transference and countertransference becomes a decisive factor. *The shadow of the psychoanalyst falls on the analytic process and treatment*, as it were, *and, with it, the shadow of all the objects that have contributed historically to constructing the self's mental apparatus.*
>
> Roussillon (2011, p. 52, italics added)

It is for this reason that construction, the analyst's subjectivity and attention to the here-and-now of the total transference situation assume such importance in the cure:

> The here-and-now of the psychoanalytic dialogue is the focus of the analyst's attention and lies at the very heart of how the transference is seen; the analysand's actual past has, thus, only a secondary role to play – since meaning is not already there, it has to be constructed in the here-and-now of the analytical process.
>
> Roussillon (2011, p. 54)

And the "flavor" of that construction will vary with the subjectivity, temperament, personal history, etc. of each individual analyst.

Consequently, in regard to drive derivatives, memory, formation of the self, indeed in regard to all "small e" experience, whether internal or external, drive, memory or perception – that is, that which is or has or can become knowable:

- Knowable experience is the end product of a process through which somatic sensorial turbulence and inscription becomes psychic and achieves specific (saturated) ideational form.

- The processes through which this happens are initially intersubjective (e.g., mother/infant, container/contained) and later autonomous (self-generated alpha function).
- The resultant end product may be expressed in a variety of potential forms that, in part, will reflect the context and purpose for which they were formed and/or the subjectivity and specificity of the co-participating object.

## Archeological analysis and transformational analysis

### Clinical implications

Let me begin with Freud's archeological metaphor. If the principle aim of archeological analysis is the discovery of the dynamic unconscious – what is and remains already formed and is disguised, buried or hidden behind a screen – then the principle aim of transformational analysis is the construction of something that may *then* be hidden behind the screen, and sometimes even *the creation of the capacity to have a screen and the space behind it in which the something that is created can be hidden*. In regard to the (already formed but repressed) dynamic unconscious, Freud (1915a) argued that adding a word presentation to a thing presentation was needed in order to pass from the Ucs. to the Pcs.-Cs. I have tried to show that in regard to the not yet represented, it is in the nature of "capital E" Experience that, *in their raw, essential state, drive, affect, impulse, action, somatic sensation, and memory all involve a degree of incompleteness, a potential that is not yet fully formed and that awaits completion, and that when this transformational act of construction and completion occurs, it can assume many different possible ideational forms.*

In regard to an interpretation that he had offered, but which his analysands did not recognize as "correct," Bion sometimes said, "You do not now agree with what I have said. Perhaps some time in the future you will agree with what I have suggested to you" (Brito, 2015). Parsing this intervention, one can see several possible meanings of Bion's remark. At its most direct level, it is possible that he felt that the patient had not yet arrived at the point at which they could understand and accept an existing "truth" about themselves that he was pointing out.

At a more ambiguous level, Bion may have been planting a seed or laying down a direction in which the patient's thinking *might* evolve. But at its most ineffable and complex, he was perhaps saying to them something like what Pablo Picasso said when Gertrude Stein complained that his portrait did not look like her: "Some day it will" (Stein, 1990, p. 12). What I believe Picasso was saying was not that he saw something already there that others did not, but rather that he had an intuition about what Stein would become, and the truth of that intuition might emerge over time. For

## 58  Epistemological situation

purposes of my argument, I am proposing that both Bion and Picasso had an *imaginative conjecture* about something that was potential and emergent, but that did not yet exist, and that perhaps in the future, this conjecture would achieve realization through further evolution of the subject.

Formulation of the two track model (Levine, 2010a) makes clear that the challenge for the patient is not simply to overcome repression and tolerate knowing what is unacceptable, terrifying, or painful, but that the patient must appropriate and assimilate the sources of that terror or pain to their sense of self in the service of psychic growth. Roussillon (2011) described this eloquently, when he said,

> The work of analysis has to take into account the conditions and preconditions under which meaning can be brought forth and become conscious … Meaning, therefore, is no longer always there, hidden somewhere in some corner of the analysand's unconscious. It will *gradually be produced* within the psychoanalytic process itself and with the—often active—help of the analyst. *Meaning, therefore, is more produced than revealed; by the same token, it is inevitably more relative than a truth that has been placed somewhere awaiting revelation; it is more polysemous.* Interpretation and hermeneutics make way for the work of construction or of reconstruction of meaning and of psychic impulses; *associative or symbol-making generative capacity replaces the quest for truth.*
>
> (p. 53, italics added)

### A clinical vignette

With this in mind, and as an illustration of the combination of "found," uncovered and constructed/created meanings that evolve and emerge in a psychoanalysis, let us consider a vignette from the long analysis (4 times/week) of Prof. M, a successful, but deeply isolated and retreated single man in his 50s. At the time of these sessions, M had begun to make certain moves for the first time – buying and taking pleasure in decorating an apartment as his first permanent, "real" home; accepting social invitations instead of staying withdrawn and isolated; risking dating a woman he might care about, instead of maintaining a part-time and limited sexual relationship with someone persecutory and "unacceptable"; and so on. As he has done so, the issue and images of his "deadness" have assumed more prominence in the sessions, allowing his female analyst to interpret M's struggles between his wish to become more alive and his fears and anger that leave him deeply attached to a sense of deadness and locked into a schizoid withdrawal and retreat.

Contributing to his difficulties is a long history of maternal absence and depression that lasted throughout M's childhood and centered in his mind around the death of an infant sister 10 months before he was born. To the extent that his birth and existence failed to restore his mother to a more vital and affectively alive emotional state, M has felt like an inadequate, unsuccessful replacement child. To add to his sense of deadness, at the time of these sessions, his mother, with whom he has been deeply and depressively identified, was quite elderly, partly demented and in failing health. His father, whom the patient felt could never compensate for mother's emotional unavailability, had died a few years before.

In recent sessions, M has bemoaned the fact that neither parent provided him with a sense of vitality and life, but allowed that there may be a spark of that life in the analysis. A slip of the tongue, in which he says in reference to his mother and her failing health, "I am my mother's daughter …," indicates his identification with his dead sister and perhaps a feeling of having to remain locked in a universe of the dead in order to search for or be close to his mother, whom he feels has never really been free of her preoccupation with the dead child and so has emotionally lived in a world of the dead. (The slip indicates a *formed unconscious fantasy* [neurotic organization], while the metaphoric image of mother "living" mostly/only in the world of the dead is a new creation, a *construction* in the mind of the analyst that puts words to a certain depressive emotional cast and dilemma that the patient seems to continue to struggle and live with, but has never before assumed a fully saturated ideational form.)

These affects and feelings are complicated by the Christmas holidays and the patient's travel schedule, which make for interruptions in the flow of sessions and threaten M with a devitalizing separation from a vitality supporting contact with the analyst. In sessions, M reports feeling useless, old, tired, and that his life is without meaning. He feels alone, but too vulnerable to put aside the "iron shield" that keeps others out. While the shield protects him, it also keeps him isolated and empty.

His analyst's recognition of and comment on his distress brings an angry insistence that he does not want to be contacted – "Fuck off!" – followed by memories of a girl he liked in grade school (age 9), but never tried to get to know and of a kindly nurse, who gently touched his arm when he was injured. (Free association implying representation, symbolization, linkage and psychic organization.)

"Perhaps you want something like that from me, here," his analyst says. "If you did that, I would leave immediately. The iron shield would go up at once," he declared. As the session ends, his analyst is left with the thought that perhaps the "nothing" and depressive deadness is not only a feeling state but *signifies* the depressed maternal object and/or the dead sister. (This intuition is a way of spontaneously putting something that was not yet formed into words; a construction.)

The next session begins with his description of a flare up of genital herpes and disgust with his physical body and the sexual act. M next introduces a metaphor (*his* construction), as he complains about the endlessness and length of the analysis – "We have been circling Jericho for over 15 years" – and says that to imagine that a woman would find him acceptable "is unthinkable." His analyst responds with a familiar comment about how M may be once again making himself inaccessible. M acknowledges his mistrust and tendency to push others away, but then recalls a teacher, who came to visit him at home at the age of 7 when he was ill. He still cannot believe she did so out of concern for him. Although he liked her, he refused to leave his room to greet her. (The transference implication here – representation, symbolization, displacement – is quite obvious, as is the saturation and organization of the psychic structure.)

In the next session, M begins by asking to reschedule some upcoming appointments so that they won't be missed. He reports dreams of great threat and danger – sharks, crocodiles – and acknowledges that he is holding back from sex with a potential new girlfriend – and contact with others in his life. He says he feels like the little Dutch boy in the fable with his finger in the dyke. (The metaphor is his spontaneous construction that gives specific narrative form to a set of emotions.)

The analyst comments on M's fears of being flooded by closeness and the enormity of his needs, with her and elsewhere, and the dangers of letting anyone be close; of inviting anyone in. (The metaphor and image of flooding belong to the patient, and although M may have some specific ideational contents in mind [saturation], consciously or unconsciously, the potential possible extent of the meaning of "the flood" leaves room for further creative elaboration. For example, it might include his hunger for contact, anger at being frustrated, rejected or emotionally abandoned; erotized versions of these feelings; fears of being without boundaries and so absorbed or swallowed up by his objects; and more. There is space here for creative, interpretive elaboration, the exact form of which will depend, in part, on how the analyst intuits it, frames it to herself and responds to the patient.)

In a subsequent session, again filled with themes of deadness and despair, the associated "memory"/image of a frog fetus in a school biology lab prompts the analyst's interpretation that a part of M has been "trying unsuccessfully to live on formaldehyde, instead of the fresh air of human contact." In contrast, there is also evidence of something in him that feels or is trying to feel alive, as reflected in his asking to reschedule potentially missed sessions and reporting the sense of vitality he derives from aspects of his work. (The formaldehyde comment, appropriate in the context of the moment in the session, is a construction and transformation of the "iron shield" metaphor into something that moves the link to the dead sister/frog fetus closer to the narrative description of the self-imposed causes of the patient's schizoid isolation.)

## Epistemological situation  61

Two sessions later, after announcing a cancellation required by his work that cannot be rescheduled, M reports feeling an overwhelming urge to leave the session and acknowledges,

> You were right. I stubbornly refuse to live. As a child, I was never good enough for my mother. Now, I feel disgusted by her illness and what it has done to her body. I also feel disgusted by my own body and feel it is dirty and rotting inside.

The next week, in a more positive mood, he announces his determination to resume a book project, the writing of which has made him feel more vital and alive. (That this connection has in the past been pointed out to him by the analyst is no doubt an additional meaning, as it is connected to life and to their relationship.) Despite this determination, however, he continues to feels lost and alone. "I've always been an outsider. I don't know what life really is." He feels lost and rattles around in his life "the way a foot feels in a shoe that is oversized and too wide." It is also what he feels in the sexual act, lost and alone when he enters and is inside a woman. That is why he has often preferred to remain celibate.

"So it's not just avoiding sex, it's avoiding contact," his analyst says. M responds by returning to the Jericho image and then suddenly thinks of the gusher that explodes when one strikes oil. His analyst says, "That's how it often is in life. Unexpectedly, things suddenly happen." M references Jericho once more in his reply, but this time, he describes himself as looking down on the scene from the outside, as if from a great height. (In writing this, it occurs to me that this could be a reflection of his trying to withdraw from the scene defensively or his placing himself in the image of God looking down at the scene from the heavens. Neither possibility seemed to occur to the analyst, as you will see from her comment, but this is exactly the point I am trying to make about the continual shaping of things within the dyad by the way in which the enigmatic and indeterminate, incomplete pictures are generated, interpreted, constructed and shaped as the process evolves.)

What the analyst does say is, "Jericho. And who holds the trumpet?" to which M replies, "When the walls came down a great massacre followed." The analyst's retort was, "That doesn't sound very attractive!"

Perhaps influenced by a wish or need to be pleasing or relieved by the analyst's acceptance of his violent aggressive response (the massacre), M then begins talking about a very beautiful ("attractive") medieval painting of Jericho: the bright blue of the sky, the intense yellow of the sun. The analyst notices that his tone has shifted and comments on the change: "You seem to be talking so lively now. The way you described yourself sometimes talking with your father. It is as if we had just struck oil and hit a vein of vitality and life." (His "gusher" image is here woven into the narrative as a positive force. The analyst has made an implicit link between Jericho, M's destructive wishes [the trumpet] and his need to fight for life. In the Hebrew Bible, the Israelites must conquer Jericho in order to fulfill their destiny in the Promised Land. Perhaps – and this is *my* construction – this man needs to destroy the hold that death has on him and his mother or destroy the bond between his mother and his dead sibling, if he is to free himself from the iron shield of "living on formaldehyde" and have a true life of his own.)

With continued vigor in his voice, M says to his analyst, "You should be a writer. Have you ever written anything? I've never googled you to see." He imagines that if he did, he would find hundreds of hits. (He has reacted to the fertile imagination reflected in the analyst's construction, perhaps picturing her as a fecund mother, able to give birth to live baby writings unlike his own mother, whom he feels has only been entranced with the dead.)

In the next session, M mentions another medieval image, one that he imagines he might use on the cover of his not yet completed book, because he likes its bright colors. (From fertile life-giving analyst to fertile, life-giving self?) This moves into associations of sexual desire and sexual conflict, but these are the vicissitudes of, for this moment, being alive and in contact with objects and feelings.

## Conclusion

In this brief example, I have tried to illustrate some of the narratological consequences of the continual creation, presentation and elaboration of the "open space" that is an essential part of what I have described as "the fundamental epistemological situation." This "space" is the metaphoric place in which a continual possibility of a construction of meaning, intersubjective or autonomous, takes place. It is the locus of the verbal Squiggle Game (Winnicott) that is an inherent part, call and response, of every analytic process. To be sure, this ongoing co-creative construction occurs side by side with more traditional archeological work of uncovering and interpreting more fully formed but repressed, split-off or otherwise hidden or disguised mental elements. The two processes go on intertwined in a continual evolution and creation of mind. They are at the heart of psychic development and the clinical therapeutic process.

# Chapter 5

# Psychoanalysis and the problem of truth

> Psycho-analytic procedure pre-supposes that the welfare of the patient demands a constant supply of truth as inevitably as his physical survival demands food.
>
> Bion (1992, p. 99)

## Does truth matter in psychoanalysis?

In the background of Freud's thinking, there is an epistemological thread that runs from Plato through Kant and assumes that we can never fully know the thing-in-itself (noumena), but only its derivative phenomena as they become manifest empirically to our senses or intuitively to our minds. In previous chapters, we have seen that Freud "inherited from Kant the view that experience is not a raw given and that our understanding constructs ... [our understanding of experience] by arranging the material of sensation" (Kahn, 2018, p. 25). This applies to all of lived experience, but especially to "whatever it has been impossible ... to incorporate fully into a meaningful context" (Laplanche and Pontalis, 1973, p. 112).

It is the inability to place experience into a singular meaningful context that opens up the opportunity for deferred revision (*nachtraglichkeit*) and aligns with the conclusion that while it is possible to know and put into words *some* of our existential Experience, it is impossible to ever *fully* know and specify its contents. The difference or gap between what we presume *is* (i.e., Exists) and what we can know of Existence, especially in regard to psychic reality, defines and determines what I have called the Fundamental Epistemological Situation.[1]

In the debates about the incidence and reality of childhood sexual abuse and incest that raged in the United States throughout the 1980s and 1990s, the epistemological basis of Freud's thinking[2] was often overlooked.

---

1 See Chapter 4.
2 That "the world's objects are never accessible as such but only as phenomena, i.e. within the limits of *possible* experience" (Kahn, 2018, p. 25, original italics).

DOI: 10.4324/9781003171331-6

What seemed of vital importance to many clinicians, some of whom were sharply critical of psychoanalysis, was that analysts recognize the truth of reported incidents of sexual abuse and incest. While some analysts may have previously overemphasized fantasy at the expense of destructive external reality, the proposed corrective, coupled with the discrediting of metapsychology and the abandonment of the concept of drives, re-instituted in certain quarters a turn to historical reality and a search for "the perpetrator," who was expected to be discovered in every case.

The expectation that one would discover some actual happening that produced the psychopathology repeated the "one size fits all" assumptions of the seduction hypothesis. It also helped foster the furor of charges and counter-charges about false memory syndrome vs. repressed childhood abuse that attracted so much attention. In doing so, it once again brought forward questions of suggestion and compliance and tended to reify the idea that psychic pathology was always based on *actual* occurrences that were presumed to operate in a linear, determined cause-and-effect sequence. This, of course, was not what Freud (1897) had in mind when he renounced his "neurotica" in his famous letter of September 21, 1897 to Fliess.

There, Freud was proclaiming the potential pathogenic importance of *psychical reality* – "everything in the psyche that takes on the force of reality for the subject" (Laplanche and Pontalis, 1973, p. 363). That is, that psychical reality could play the same role in the etiology of psychopathology, as did forgotten memories of trauma tied to actual historical events. Freud never discounted "the existence, prevalence and pathogenic force of scenes of seduction [that were] actually experienced by children" (Laplanche and Pontalis, 1973, p. 406). He did maintain, however, that it was the later revision of the meaning of past events (*nachtraglich*) that "invests them with significance and ... pathogenic force" (Laplanche and Pontalis, 1973, p. 406).[3] Thus, he broadened the field of etiological factors, adding the role of "psychical reality" to that of external reality as a potential source of neurosis.

In regard to the matter of knowing "the truth," however, this complicates things even further. The more that meanings and facts may be subject to subsequent revision, the more truth is recognized as potentially emergent and never fully defined, then the more apparent it becomes why *the whole of one's truth can never be known*. As the Italian playwright Luigi Pirandello (1998) said, *Truth is a blur in motion*. And if, as we have seen in previous

---

3 Another feature of Freudian thinking that is often overlooked is that he held a two-stage theory of the formation of trauma. A first scene or event is experienced, but its traumatogenic nature is not unleashed or recognized until a later time, when a second scene clarifies or assigns it new meanings.

chapters, the words to describe the truth originate in the intuition and construction of the analyst, then what roles might suggestion and compliance play?[4] How then are we to understand and what are we to make of the role of interpretation in psychoanalysis? Of Bion's assertion that truth is to the mind as nutrition is to the body? Or of the many assertions, implicit and explicit, that the search for truth is at the heart of the psychoanalytic process?

Throughout a good deal of his career, Freud analyzed patients with the explicit goal of unearthing the forgotten, unacceptable, anxiety-producing "true" facts – repressed traumatic memories – and the forbidden fantasies, wishes, and desires of early childhood. Hence the therapeutic power inherent of his archeological metaphor, a certain understanding of neurotic symptoms, the structure and dynamics of dreams, the psychopathology of everyday life and the analytic technique to which all these gave rise.

In the accounts of Freud's actual clinical practice that have survived, either in our literature or by word of mouth, we have the archetypal scene of Freud deducing or intuiting a crucial childhood wish or experience that had been repressed, interpreting it to a patient and thereby setting off a dramatic chain of events. Two well-known examples are (1) his interpretation that the Wolf Man (Freud, 1918) had witnessed and then repressed all conscious memory of the *actual experience* of the primal scene and that the memory was forgotten until it later returned, disguised, in the wolf dream; and (2) his reconstruction given to Princess Marie Bonaparte that presumably sent her rushing back to Paris to confront her governess and receive third-party confirmation of Freud's conjecture. More recently, a newly discovered diary of an account of an analysis with Freud in 1921 reaffirms the kind of fact-based, reconstructed "truths" that were so central to many of Freud's interpretive interventions.[5]

Subsequent clinical experience has reaffirmed the value of revealing and helping *neurotic* patients acknowledge, reclaim, and reintegrate the organized but hidden "truth" of the split-off, conflictual, often hostile, sometimes depressive, envious, omnipotent, libidinal, aggressive, destructive wishing parts of themselves. This enables mourning processes to occur that prove essential for further psychic development. But what of those parts of the mind and especially those patients whose diagnoses lay beyond neurosis?

---

4 Previously (Levine, 2011a), I had suggested that Freud (1937) was too quick to dismiss the role that suggestion and compliance might play in the work of construction. See also Chapter 6.
5 The account, described in Maetzener (2015), is, *"We Bennimt Sich Der Prof. Freud Eigentlich?" Ein Neu Entdecktes Tagebuch von 1921 Historish und Analytisch Kommentiery* ["How Does Professor Freud Actually Behave?": A Newly Discovered Diary from 1921 with Historical and Analytic Commentary], ed. A. Kollreuter. Giessen, Germany: Psychosozial-Verlag, 2010.

As indicated in previous chapters, Bion believed that "truth is essential for mental growth. Without truth the psychic apparatus does not develop and dies of starvation" (Grinberg et al., 1977, p. 108).[6] This statement is especially crucial in regard to those "truths" that are achieving containment and expression and emerging from the unstructured unconscious into representational, ideational form for the first time. For Bion (1970), the vital subject matter of analysis – psychic qualities, the unconscious, and indeed any experience viewed from the *psychoanalytic vertex* – was a matter of intuition and not available to perception via the modality of the senses.

> The ... psychic qualities, with which the psycho-analyst deals, are not perceived by the senses but as Freud says, some mental counterpart of the sense organs, a function that he attributed to consciousness.
> 
> Bion (1970, p. 28)

In *Transformations*, in addition to the many levels of defensive reasons for not wishing to know one's psychic truth, Bion (1965) discussed the structural, epistemological limits to what can be known about the psyche. He felt that the crucial task of the analyst was discerning the difference between those situations in which the obscurity of the patient's communication is due to a wish or need to conceal – for example, defense, attack or avoidance – and those situations in which obscurity reflects the inevitable limitations of language when faced with the essentially ineffable nature of what the patient is attempting to communicate. That is, the "obscurity due to the difficulty of the matter of the problem for which [the patient] seeks help" (p. 22). As indicated earlier, if we take Bion's formulation of the normal, communicative function of projective identification to its logical extreme, we would expect to discover a potentially valuable "cry for help" even in the most destructive seeming defensive operations and "attacks on linking" (Bion, 1959).

Given all that we know about the way that unconscious forces impact on the mind, a "mental counterpart of the sense organs" that is an "attribute of consciousness" seems a rather shaky foundation on which to build a search for truth. This is especially so in those situations in which the recognition of some truth is apt to be painful, because it may:

- Force us to recognize our ignorance and lack of omniscience;
- Require that we tolerate frustration;
- Be linked to the disturbing concomitants of psychic growth that Bion called *catastrophic change*.

---

6 See also Francesca Bion (1995, p. 106).

Thus, Grinberg et al. (1977) repeat Bion's warning:

> The human being's capacity to tolerate truths about himself is fragile; truth is a permanent source of pain and the wish for knowledge can never be satisfied or completed; therefore the tendency to evasive action is great and the mind is always prepared to create lies to oppose this pain.
>
> (p. 110)

Clearly, the problem of truth is not a simple one.

## Definitions of truth

Traditionally, "truth" has been defined as "that which is in accordance with fact or reality; conformity to fact or reality; exact accordance with that which is, or has been; or shall be" (*Merriam-Webster Dictionary* __1913__). At the heart of this definition is a *correspondence theory* – that which is "true" is a statement or proposition that asserts something that *corresponds* to something else that exists or is real. We might hesitate at the thought of truth conforming to what is "not yet but shall be," because how do we know what shall be when it has not yet happened? But for the most part, this definition seems to make good sense in terms of everyday parlance and experience.

But does this definition serve as well for psychoanalysis? If Bion is correct and psychic qualities cannot be directly perceived by the senses, does this definition hold up when examined in the light of psychic reality, intersubjective narrative co-construction, and other transformations of unrepresented and weakly represented states? How does it fare in regard to conceptualizations of the *unformulated* or *emergent unconscious* and the investigation of psychoanalytic objects? Is there some inherent difficulty in the concept of truth in psychoanalysis that produces an inevitable slippage or even confusion in usage as we try to define and apply it? Will psychoanalytic truth inevitably lie in a transitional area that resists categorical assertions and absolute closure?

Consider, for example, Ogden's (2015), paper "Intuiting the Truth of What's Happening: On Bion's 'Notes on Memory and Desire.'" I feel very much aligned with the main thrust and conclusions of this paper, which affirm Bion's assertion that analytic interpretations of the unconscious rely more on the analyst's *intuition* and *at-one-ment* than they do on objective, empirical observations.[7]

---

7 It was Bion's distrust of empirical evidence in relation to the *psychoanalytic object* that led to his admonition to attempt to encounter the patient at each moment without memory or desire (see, e.g., Bion, 1970, 2005).

## 68  Psychoanalysis and truth

Among the many cogent and useful points that Ogden (2015) makes are the following:

- "Bion supplants 'awareness' from its central role in the analytic process and, in its place, instates the analyst's (largely unconscious) work of intuiting the psychic reality (the truth) of the session by becoming one with it" (p. 287).
- *"Genuine thinking, which is predominantly unconscious, seeks out the truth (reality)"* (p. 290, italics in original).
- "Without the truth (O), or at least openness to it, thinking is not only impossible; the very idea of thinking becomes meaningless" (p. 290).
- "The realm of the unconscious, Bion vehemently insists, is the realm of the psychoanalyst …. The unconscious is the realm of thinking and feeling that together form the psychic reality (psychoanalytic truth) of an individual at any given moment" (p. 292).
- "If the psychoanalyst is to be genuinely analytic in the way he observes, he must be able to abjure conscious, sensory-based modes of perceiving, which draw the analyst's mind to conscious experience and to modes of thinking (for example, memory and desire) that are fearful/evasive of the perception of the unconscious psychic reality (the truth) of what is occurring in the session" (p. 293).

What I would like to call attention to in this selection of excerpts are the different but related assertions or equations concerning *truth* and *psychoanalytic truth* that they contain. Truth is equated with "reality" (p. 290), "psychic reality" (p. 287), "unconscious psychic reality" (p. 293), and O (p. 290), and there is a reference to something called "psychoanalytic truth" (p. 292) that may or may not be equivalent to any of these or to the more common and socially validatable meanings of the word *truth*.

If we look closer and assume that these cognates are not all equivalent and interchangeable, we must then ask: what *is* "truth" in psychoanalysis, and is there a "psychoanalytic truth" that is different from what we mean by *truth* in its ordinary social sense? This parsing of the truth and truths inevitably leads us back to some of the foundational questions that have bedeviled psychoanalysis from its inception and are perhaps insoluble in any definitive form: What do we think we know and how do we think that we come to know it? What is our data and what is our evidence in regard to our observations, assumptions, and beliefs? How are each of these categories verified or proven false, and do they affect and influence each other?

Later in his article, Ogden (2015) refers to "multiple coexisting, discordant realities, all of which are true" (p. 300). If there are "multiple coexisting, discordant realities," are there also multiple coexisting, discordant truths? In the everyday world of external reality, truth tends to *feel* singular and never discordant: a shirt is blue or not blue. It might be blue and white, but its white stripes do not nullify the fact that it is also partly blue; its blueness is not in question.

As described by Ogden (2015), his patient Ms. C (pp. 297–300) both loved and didn't love her baby. One could characterize this condition and try to solve the problems that it might entail by saying that she was ambivalent or that she possessed both feelings, alternately or even simultaneously. But I would suggest that to do so might miss something of what Ogden was describing: that perhaps an oscillating or ambivalent "love/no love" relationship with the baby did not feel "true" to something of this patient's feeling state or Ogden's belief about it, and that "all love and only love" *and* "all no love and only no love" felt more to Ogden to be the "truth" of the patient's **O** – what both Ms. C and her analyst had to accept and face. Hence Ogden's assertion in regard to his patient that "the baby was dead, *and* the baby was alive" (p. 300, italics in original).

Ogden posits a truth that we might call *conditional:* "The truth of each component of this emotional situation was real only when in dialectic tension with its counterpart" (p. 300). And, more to the clinical point, he asserts his belief that

> If I were to have sided with one component or the other ... I believe the patient would have felt that I was afraid to know who she really was at that moment – a mother who loved her baby and a mother who was unable to love her baby.
>
> (p. 300)

Ogden also offers a comment on the very unique, very precious, and sometimes strange-seeming domain of psychic reality, when he wonders to whom these feelings belong:

> Ms. C and I were experiencing a wide range of deeply felt emotions ... the origins of which were unclear; were they my feelings or were they the patient's feelings, or were they those of a third subject that was the unconscious creation of the two of us ...? Probably all three, in ever-shifting proportions.
>
> (p. 300)

Here, too, the reader can feel the once seemingly obvious and solid ground beginning to shift. If the analyst's role includes helping truths emerge through the use of construction, to whom will they belong? How do we escape the dilemmas of suggestion and compliance? Is there a line that exists and can be drawn between justified belief and opinion, selected fact and overvalued idea? Perhaps a philosophical vertex will prove useful here.

## Truth, philosophy and the arts

Turning to *Stanford Encyclopedia of Philosophy* (2013), we learn that truth is one of the central subjects in philosophy. It is also one of the largest. Truth has been a topic of discussion in its own right for thousands of years …. The problem of truth is in a way easy to state: what truths are, and what (if anything) makes them true. But this simple statement masks a great deal of controversy. Whether there is a metaphysical problem of truth at all, and if there is, what kind of theory might address it, are all standing issues in the theory of truth. As confirmation, the encyclopedia then lists many different philosophical theories about and formulations of the meaning of truth and plunges us into deeply complex discussions of such things as correspondence theories, coherence theories, pragmatic theories and pluralistic theories.

Clearly, the investigation that we have embarked on is far more complex than a cursory first glance has suggested. In Chapter 4, we discussed the story of Picasso and his portrait of Gertrude Stein (1990). Might the arts offer further clarification?

- Film director Werner Herzog began his documentary, *Lessons of Darkness*, about the oil fires in Kuwait that followed the first Gulf War, with what turned out to be a spurious quotation from the philosopher Blaise Pascal: "The collapse of the stellar universe will occur – like creation – in grandiose splendor." When the false attribution was noticed, Herzog later explained,

  > The words attributed to Blaise Pascal which preface my film *Lessons of Darkness* are in fact by me. Pascal himself could not have said it better. This falsified and yet … *not* falsified quotation should serve as a first hint of what I am trying to deal with …. To acknowledge a fake as fake contributes only to the triumph of accountants. Why am I doing this, you might ask? The reason is simple and comes not from theoretical, but rather from practical, considerations. With this quotation as a prefix, I elevate [*erheben*] the spectator, before he has even seen the first frame, to a high level from which to enter the film. And I, the author of the film, do not let him descend from this height until it is over. Only in this state of sublimity [*Erhabenheit*] does something deeper become possible, a kind of truth that is the enemy of the merely factual. Ecstatic truth, I call it.
  >
  > Herzog (2016)

- Author David Vann (2010) recalled, "I had this class once with Grace Paley in which she told us that *every line in fiction has to be true*" (p. 3, italics added).

Fiction, of course, is by definition "not true," and yet what is more "true" in the sense of being "true to life" than *Macbeth* or *King Lear*? What is the truth of a poem – especially if we look at its emotional impact, beyond its ideational content? And what are we, as analysts, to make of the truth of the unconscious or of psychic reality, those ineffable realms that are of the greatest concern to us and to our patients?

Returning to our starting point, we can see that the penumbra of associations that surrounds, accompanies, and influences our use and sense of the word, *truth,* tends toward binaries and the absolute, while truth itself may be more like Heraclitus' river.

## Psychoanalytic truth, emergent truth

In common parlance, something is either true or false, right or wrong, correct or incorrect. Psychoanalytic truth, however, the "truth" of psychic reality, like that of poetic truth, aesthetic truth and ecstatic truth, may be of another order. If we agree with Bion – and a broad range of philosophers, from Plato to Kant and beyond – that raw existential Experience, "capital E" Experience,[8] can never be fully known, then all truths, especially unconscious truths or those that partake in or follow from unrepresented states or reflect psychic reality, are apt to be partial or incomplete. They are emergent and therefore ineffable, in search of representational expression rather than fully formed and disguised or hidden, and so not capable of being spoken unless or until they undergo some form of transformation. When they do achieve representation and can be put into words, they remain approximate descriptions of phenomena rather than a complete rendering of the thing-in-itself.

Bion's (1970) examination of the distinction between **O** and **K** – that is, between ultimate or raw existential reality and the portion of that ultimate reality that can become known to us – alerts us to the fact that there may be different forms and levels of truth and different metaphors, dialects, idioms and levels of ideational saturation through which these truths may be expressed or the terms within which they may come to be known.[9]

---

8 See Chapter 4.
9 Ferro's (2002) Field Theory offers many examples of the way that various "dialects" of description can serve as suitable containers and forms of expression for the "truth" of underlying emotional qualities.

In relation to the analytic situation, the (repressed) hidden truth that is one-half of a binary (that is, true and not false), fully formed and discoverable, may best correspond to the truth of Freud's dynamic unconscious, reflecting his topographical theory at the point at which representations have been formed to contain and express an emotional charge. It is what we know, but what we cannot let ourselves know or do not consciously notice that we know. Hal Boris (1972) once said that in order to repress something we must always remember what it is that we are supposed to forget! This truth is the truth of the archeological metaphor, the dynamic or repressed unconscious, represented mental states, and the treatment of the organized, neurotic sectors of the mind in conflict (Levine, 2012).

But as we have seen in previous chapters, the saturated, formed, and hidden truth of repression, representation, and neurosis is not necessarily the only or central truth relevant to the analytic encounter. This awareness has been accompanied by a shift in our understanding of the aims of analysis. We have become less *exclusively* interested in helping analysands find the formed, pre-existing truths that they have not allowed themselves to know, and equally interested, and sometimes more so, in helping patients develop the capacities that would make the discovery/creation of the truth – indeed, knowing itself – possible.

This shift in the aims of analysis, from the recovery of repressed thoughts to the development of the capacity for thinking, from "a metapsychology of contents to a metapsychology of process" (Roussillon, 2014), was illustrated in Chapter 3 as we considered certain ideas and assumptions in Freud's (1937) paper on constructions. While the latter presages a shift toward a more fully intersubjective view of the analytic process and relationship (Levine, 2011a, chapter 3), for the most part, it has nevertheless been read to imply that the aim of construction is the positing of actual but unremembered childhood experiences – that is, construction attempts to get at the "truth" or probability (Collins, 2011) of what actually happened as event, wish, or fantasy.

The potential problems of suggestion and compliance that this might entail are, in my view, too easily dismissed. Once we recognize that we must rely on the analyst's creativity and construction in the form of intuition, we are in danger of submitting to the forces of countertransference, suggestion and compliance. Does Bion's (1970) focus on **O**, ultimate reality, its distinction from **K**, that part of our reality that is knowable, and his introduction of the terms *becoming* and *at-one-ment* complement or begin to replace the analyst's *insight into, understanding, realizing,* and other forms of *knowing* and *knowing about* the factual truth of real events, concrete and psychic?

Bion's terms do imply a change of existential state on the part of the mind of the analyst that is promoted and made possible by the analyst's reverie.[10] It is the latter that enables the analyst to be open to and to absorb the patient's projections, allowing these projections to "sojourn" (Bion, 1958, p. 146) within the psyche and personhood of the analyst long enough for them to be worked on by the analyst's alpha function and transformed into something that can be either *thought with* or *thought about* by the analyst. This transformed something can then become the basis for an alteration or shift in the analyst's listening stance, style, tempo, pace, intensity or other quality of intervention, or of a more saturated and specific interpretation based not on the analyst's knowing "the truth" about the patient, the analytic situation, or the analytic relationship, but rather on what the analyst may *believe* to be the truth – intuiting or conjecturing – at that particular moment. Hence, the paradox – of (ill) timing and *après coup* – that a factually correct intervention may interrupt analytic process and psychic growth, while a well-meaning but incorrect (false) interpretation may lead to a new experience or new thought that opens the mind to true discovery.

## Suggestion and compliance

These formulations have been found by many analysts to be clinically useful, particularly in the treatment of non-neurotic patients and areas of the mind (e.g., Botella, 2014; Botella and Botella, 2005, 2013; Ferro, 2002, 2015; see also Levine, 2012, 2015b). They also preclude certainty as to what is true or where that truth lies, thereby returning the issues of compliance and suggestion to the forefront of analytic concern.

Although Freud never used the word *intersubjectivity*, I believe that a dawning recognition of the inherently intersubjective nature of the analytic enterprise was a truth that ultimately came to haunt Freud. This explains his repeatedly returning to the 1937 paper on constructions, which contained the seeds of the assertion that it was not only what was true (in the sense of being uncovered from hiding) that counted in analysis but also *what came forth as secondary revision (nachtraglich) or was created and cocreated in the analytic situation for the very first time, which could also prove to be decisive*. This tilt toward the importance of and reliance on *de novo construction* rather than discovery valorizes *emergent truth*, exposing the inherent transitional nature and subjective and intersubjective roots of the "truths" encountered in many successful analytic treatments. And subsequent experience with more severely disturbed patients, leading to formulations concerning the less verbalizably structured, non-neurotic portions of the mind, have only further underlined their importance.

---

10 The Botella and Botella's (2013) description of *regredience* provides a similar view within a different, but I believe analogous, conceptual model. See also Botella (2014).

We have seen that Roussillon (2011) argued that "meaning is ... more produced than revealed" (p. 53), and that this production often requires the active participation of the analyst. I would take Roussillon's conclusion even further by pointing out that the singular quest for an unchanging, interpretive truth of yesterday has been broadened to include the creation and co-creation of the emergent truth of today – and even tomorrow's truths, which may not yet have come into being (cf. Picasso and Gertrude Stein).

To put the matter in still another way, the "factual truth" of an analyst's intervention may be necessary, but may not in itself prove sufficient to produce a necessary or desired transformation in the patient's psychic state or development. The goal of that intervention, should such goals prove necessary, might be stated as twofold: "to say something that feels both true to the emotional experience of any given moment of an analytic session, and that is utilizable by the analytic pair for psychological work" (Ogden, 2003, p. 593).

It is the processual, potentially transformative dimension to the patient's encounter with and recognition of truth, uncovered or created, on which the therapeutic action of psychoanalysis often stands. As Bion (1967) noted,

> In any session, evolution takes place. Out of the darkness and formlessness something evolves …. This evolution is what the analyst must be ready to interpret.
>
> (p. 18)

And that interpretation, in turn, will produce further evolution, *ad infinitum*.

Is it, then, the process and what it gives rise to that is of importance, beyond the static moment of any statement's factuality? How often do we find that an interpretation an analyst offers because he or she believes it to be true, and that the patient feels is not correct, turns out to be useful because it helps the patient feel or see something, or put something into words, that the patient then deems to be true but had not quite noticed or articulated before?

This change in the orientation and understanding of therapeutic action and analytic process has also altered and deepened our understanding of interpretation, which no longer has an exclusive emphasis on uncovering or decoding. Just as Freud has helped move the goals of analysis from "making the unconscious conscious" to "where id was there ego shall be," Bion, Ferro, and others have led us even further to create the conscious and the unconscious from the formless void of the unrepresented. Thus, Capello (2016) has written,

> An interpretation can be said to work well not insofar as it discloses a hidden ultimate truth about the patient, but insofar as it can be used

by the latter as a tool to build a more sustainably multilayered point of view on his reality (internal and external); a point of view, in other words, that allows him to create new, more meaningful stories – stories that do not merely reflect a rational or operational way of thinking, but which resonate with emotions in relation to which the patient can increasingly afford to feel more alive without the need to split them off or deaden himself to them.

(p. 472)

In regard to truth and the analytic process, an emergent truth may sometimes take precedence over a hidden, unnoticed, or forgotten "fact." It is for this reason that Green cautioned that sometimes questions of vitality – which in our current context may relate to the truth of what has occurred but has not yet been experienced (Winnicott, 1974), or even what has not yet occurred – must preempt those of "factual truth" of the moment. Green (2005a) wrote,

> Sometimes, paradoxically, it will be less damaging to the process to allow a lively countertransference reaction to be expressed, even if negative, in order to gain access to the internal movements animating the analyst. These are all evidence of … spontaneity … having more value for the patient than a conventional pseudo-tolerant discourse which will be experienced by the patient as artificial and governed by technical manuals.
>
> (p. 35)

## (In)Conclusion

Bion (1962b) asserted that "In psycho-analytic methodology the criteria cannot be whether a particular usage is right or wrong, meaningful or verifiable, but whether it does or does not promote development" (p. ix). In one of his Tavistock Seminars, when he was asked if there was a psychoanalytic way to the truth, Bion replied, "None whatever." And he cautioned that

> Psychoanalysis is only a technical instrument, something we can make use of for any purpose we want – to make confusion worse confounded, or to mislead or deceive people, and so on …. The profound question … is the problem of whether the person who is searching for the truth is genuinely trying to arrive at the truth, or is a fake, an artificial representation of a seeker after truth. It is a very difficult question to answer.
>
> Bion (2005, p. 87)

Still, in his tenth São Paulo lecture, Bion (1980) reminded us that

> It is questionable whether any patient ever comes to a psycho-analyst unless they feel the situation is desperate; it is usually a last resort when everything else has failed. So in spite of appearances to the contrary the whole weight of the experience when a patient comes to an analyst suggests that the patient himself feels that he needs a powerful injection of truth even though he may not like it.
>
> (p. 126)

Reflecting on our innate discomfort and even hatred of any reminders of our own ignorance, and how little of the truth of life any of us may truly come to know, Bion (1976) seemed to question the entire enterprise of psychoanalysis when he mused, "What if the whole of psychoanalysis turned out to be one vast elaboration of a paramnesia, something intended to fill the gap – the gap of our frightful ignorance?" (p. 244).

Is the whole – or large portions – of psychoanalytic thinking merely a bedtime story for analysts and their patients, and, like all bedtime stories, is it meant to calm and reassure us in the transition from one psychic state to another? For children, the sometimes terrifying chasm that must be bridged is the separation and aloneness of the transition from wakefulness to sleep. Perhaps for analysts, it is the transition from consensually verifiable social reality to the psychic reality of the analytic process; from **K** to **O**; from separation of self and object to intersubjectivity; from the wakefulness of negotiating the "real world" (so called) to the oneiric state of free-floating attention and reverie without memory and desire.

Where, then, does all this leave us in regard to the question of truth and psychoanalysis? I am afraid that we may be left with the dizzying perspective of standing on oscillating, ever-shifting ground. And yet, it *is* the ground on which I believe, as analysts, that we must stand. As Bion (1979) put it, all that analysis can ever do is make the best of a bad job. We have no recourse other than doing what we can, with the means that we have, in the situation that we find ourselves. And so we go on ….

# Chapter 6

# The analyst's authority

## Suggestion, seduction, compliance and influence[*]

> We have these preconceptions that there is some sort of authority, a father or mother, who knows the answer. The aim in analysis is to make that point clear, not so that you can go on feeling how important that person is for the rest of your existence, but because you can then discard it and make room for whatever ideas you might want to express yourself.
>
> Bion (2005b, p. 68)

## I

Throughout the history of psychoanalysis, the subject of the analyst's authority has been intimately connected with problems of suggestion and compliance. Initially, Freud (1905a, 1905b) felt the need to show that symptom relief brought about by analytic therapy had a different mechanism of action and was more long-lasting than the temporary suppression of symptoms caused by hypnotic suggestion. Then, as he became concerned with the uncovering of hidden psychic contents – for example, forbidden wishes and repressed traumatic memories of childhood – authority and suggestion appeared in Freud's response to charges that the repressed memories and conflicts relating to childhood sexual and aggressive wishes that analysts were discovering in their patients were false; the result of the analyst's authority and influence, real or imagined, and the patients' wishes to believe that they were in the hands of a benevolent and powerful parent figure.

With the discovery of the transference (Freud, 1905c), suggestion and compliance reappeared in a more positive light as important components of the motivational system that helped patients persevere in treatment in the face of anxiety, conflicts and resistances. Freud (1925a) argued that rather than being used for the suppression of symptoms or the implantation of false memories or ideas, suggestion in analysis "is used instead to induce the patient to perform a piece of psychical work – the overcoming of his transference-resistances – which involves a permanent alteration in his mental economy" (pp. 42–43).

---

[*] An earlier version of this paper was given at the EPF meetings in Berlin, Germany, March 2016.

DOI: 10.4324/9781003171331-7

Earlier, Freud had tried to reassure critics that any suggestion made by the analyst to a patient would not be a problem, as suggestion,

> only affects ... [the patient's] intelligence, not his illness. After all, his conflicts will only be successfully solved and his resistances overcome if the anticipatory ideas he is given tally with what is real in him. Whatever in the doctor's conjectures is inaccurate drops out in the course of the analysis; it has to be withdrawn and replaced by something more correct.
>
> Freud (1961–1917, p. 452)

As further safeguard, Freud (1917a) declared that any premature or "easily won successes" due to suggestion would be countered by the analyst's,

> constantly resolving the transference on which they are based.... At the end of an analytic treatment the transference must itself be cleared away; and if success is then obtained or continues, it rests, not on suggestion, but on the achievement by its means of an overcoming of internal resistances, on the internal change that has been brought about in the patient.
>
> (p. 453)

By the time Freud (1937) wrote his Constructions paper, however, he felt the need to return to the questions of suggestion and compliance, because his clinical experience had forced him to acknowledge that not every analytic cure was the result of the recovery of previously repressed childhood memories.

> Quite often we do not succeed in bringing the patient to recollect what has been repressed. Instead of that, if the analysis is carried out correctly, we produce in him *an assured conviction of the truth of the construction* which achieves the same therapeutic result as a recaptured memory.
>
> ibid. (p. 266, italics added)

That is, in some instances, the analyst's construction – a *plausible conjecture* of what might have occurred in actuality or in the mind or imagination of the patient as a youngster – must stand in dynamically for – and serve the same psychic purpose as – an actual recollection.

As noted in Chapter 3, Freud was not talking about the analyst's intuiting an actual occurrence that was not being remembered by the patient – that kind of intervention would be a *re*-construction – but rather proposing something that made sense as a plausible possibility and that allowed the patient to develop a *conviction of possible meaning*. It is here that our problems return full force.

Most contemporary analysts would agree that the transference – and the so-called distortions of reality that can inevitably follow in its wake – can never be *fully* resolved or eliminated. When dealing with the unconscious, the patient's wish to please or the implantation of false memories and connections remain as ever present hazards. And perhaps most important of all, "conviction" like any other psychological state, is always potentially subject to the vagaries and demands of unconscious forces – desire, defense, narcissistic need, and so on.[1]

In the late 1980s and early 1990s, Paul Roazen (1995) made a careful study of firsthand accounts of patients who had undergone analyses with Freud. Significantly, these fail to mention Freud's specifically discussing or addressing and analyzing the unique and elevated status he had in the minds of his patients, many of whom traveled great distances to study and be treated at the feet of the master. Looking closely at some of those self-reports, I have speculated that this was a dimension of the transference to which Freud may not have paid sufficient interpretive attention:

> Some of the most insurmountable difficulties that Freud and his patients seemed to have faced were the transferences that resulted from the fact that treatment was being conducted by the founding father of psychoanalysis. For the majority of ... [former patients of Freud], their contact with Freud remained a high point of their lives. Many continued to bask in the light of the fact that they had known and were treated by Freud, even when – perhaps, because – the therapeutic results of their analyses were equivocal at best.
>
> Almost all of ... [Freud's patients] had interrupted their lives, travelled to Vienna and used their influence to obtain an analysis with Freud. This, too, no doubt colored their views of their experience and imposed a potential burden of idealization or entitlement on the treatment that must have been difficult to manage. ...Thus, one could sense that some of the reported descriptions of Freud reflected residues of what appeared to be persistent, unanalyzed transference idealizations, grandiosity, competitive reactions to analytic rivals or conflicts over masochism and submission to the will of the father.
>
> Levine (1997b, pp. 1316–1317)

Consequently, it is difficult to accept Freud's (1937) reassurance that the danger of suggestion being the operative force in the analyst's construction would not be a problem and that proper application of analytic technique was all that was needed to insure that, except for a waste of time and effort, an incorrect construction would not do any harm (p. 261).

---

1  See Feldman (2010) and Levine (2011a, 2011b) for further discussion.

One safeguard and qualification that Freud did introduce in the Constructions paper was the idea that the measure of the analyst's construction was not to be its manifest acceptance or rejection on the part of the patient or its historical verifiability by third parties, which in many cases proved impossible. Rather, its effectiveness was to be assessed by its impact on the analytic process. Did the latter deepen or become freer? Did the construction elicit new feelings, memories or dreams, reassessments of familiar past events or a more nuanced attitude toward important objects? And were these shifts occurring in the patient alone or concurrently, perhaps even at first, solely, within mind and feelings of the analyst?

Freud (1937) maintained the view that in regard to the significant facts of psychic experience,

> All the essentials are preserved; even things that seem completely forgotten are present somehow and somewhere, and have merely been buried and made inaccessible to the subject …. It depends only upon analytic technique whether we shall succeed in bringing what is concealed completely to light.
>
> (p. 260)

But we have seen that what is concealed may have lost or may never have achieved full ideational form.[2] Truth, like beauty, is often in the eye of the beholder and how it is seen or the meaning assigned to it is apt to be a matter of unconscious determination and need.

Taking all of this into account, we must wonder if Freud was too optimistic when he dismissed the potential problems of the analyst's authority in regard to suggestion. Were his assertions that suggestion only produced results of little consequence excessively colored by his early clinical experience of the long-term ineffectiveness of suggestion in hypnosis? Did his reassurances fly in the face of the implications of his own epistemological assumptions? Did omissions in his own practice indicate a possible blind spot that influenced his formulation?

When we consider non-neurotic patients and mind states, the problem is even more complicated. We have seen (Chapters 3–5) that in borderline and "limit cases" that what is at issue is the creation, co-creation and emergence of plausible truth and meaning that give suitable ideational form to previously unsaturated, inchoate feeling states. These movements deserve equal consideration to that of the uncovering of psychic elements that are hidden, but organized around verifiable historical truth. When the analyst participates in dialogical processes that assist the patient in

---

2 Chapters 4 and 5.

this way, it is impossible to say to whom the resulting mental content "belongs," even when formation of the latter is initiated and takes place in the mind of the analyst.

The stimulus for its creation – an act of figurability (Botella and Botella, 2003) – is the unconscious absorption of the patient's projections (a kind of unconscious trial identification of the analyst with the patient), which stimulates the analyst's alpha function to perform the transformation of the patient's previously inchoate sensorial material from beta to alpha. The "place" of that absorption, the "hook" on which the analyst's receptivity rests, involves the analyst's capacity to resonate emotionally with some pole or position of the patient's conflict or to be drawn toward an analogous inchoate area in his or her own psyche. This place of resonance within the analyst is the emotional "stem cell" of what, if it proves helpful, may eventuate in and be described as the analyst's receptivity or intuition or, if it proves obstructive, the analyst's countertransference.[3]

In the best of cases, once that absorption, resonance and act of figurability is accomplished and the analyst has formed a representation of something that had previously been ineffable or inchoate, and then "re-presents" this to the patient verbally in the form of an interpretation, then the two are in the same relation as Winnicott and the infant, when both are looking at the reflex hammer held up in the visual field between them.

The object – hammer or interpretation – may not have the same meaning or connotations for each of them, but at the point of mutual engagement, it is, from an intersubjective vertex, an object in transitional space. It is impossible to say to whom the psychic element newly created now belongs. Depending on one's perspective, it may be seen to belong to either or both parties in the dyad and can have different meanings or connotations for each.

Once the patient "makes the interpretation his or her own," it becomes psychically "true" – or "useful" – and the question of its origins or to whom it belongs becomes secondary or moot. Perhaps, then, there is no clear or absolute dividing line between selected fact and overvalued idea, between countertransference and subjectivity, and analysts must live with an indeterminacy of aim that abandons an absolute dependence on correspondence with historical truth and moves toward a more relativistic, utilitarian position in regard to their interventions.

These considerations do not free the analyst from the time-honored responsibility of raising questions with our patients about whether or to what extent they may be complying with what they consciously or unconsciously imagine that we want or expect from us. Nor are we absolved

---

3  See Levine (1997a).

from the obligation to consider whether or where a line may be drawn between creation, acceptance or discovery of the patient's true self versus coercion, seduction and impingement deriving from the patient's transference and compliance with the analyst as authority – Lacan's *sujet supposer savoir* – or from the analyst's countertransference need to banish the agony of uncertainty and not knowing by the creation of a paramnesia meant to fill the gap of his or her ignorance.[4] Rather, they raise the possibility that *a categorical determination in regard to the boundaries of the analyst's influence and authority in such situations may be impossible to make.*

This view is in accord with that of Donnet (2009), who recognized that

> ... [T]he question of suggestion continues to impose itself at the very heart of interpretation. Is the analyst not in the position to substitute himself for primary objects in order to make up for a deficiency, which the increasingly decisive importance attributed to the object, or the reference to the primacy of the other, makes obvious? Is there not a temptation here to see the analyst as implanting a sort of psychic prosthesis?
>
> (p. 12)

Donnet's response to these questions is that the tensions produced are *precious ambiguities* inherent in the dialectical dimension of analytic theory and practice and lie at the foundation of the analytic method; ambiguities that we cannot – and really should not – ever fully resolve.

This lack of resolution implies that there is always some degree of risk involved that the conceptual expansion of the analyst's countertransference or subjectivity will be overvalued and even turned into a fetish (*un subjectivité technique*).[5] This must be balanced against an equal risk of failing to help catalyze representational movement within the psyche of a patient in need of developmental assistance. Both the dangers and the possibilities are inherent in the analyzing situation.

Consequently, rather than coming down on one side or another, Donnet (2010) urges us to hold fast to the dialectical dimension of the encounter.

> If I talk about the *adventure* of the method, it is in a positive sense; I share this adventure, and thereby I accept the risks.
>
> Personal communication (my translation)

---

4 "What if the whole of psychoanalysis turned out to be one vast elaboration of a paramnesia, something intended to fill the gap – the gap of our frightful ignorance? (Bion, 1976, p. 244).
5 See also Kahn's (1918) critique of the overvaluing of empathy in the so-called post-modern analytic theories.

He further states,

> If it happens that in this adventure, the pattern you mention [i.e., the analyst's participation in an intersubjective process (e.g., alpha function) that catalyzes the patient's psychic movement towards representation of previously unrepresentable contents] is sometimes "excessive," there is nothing to deplore. We often see patients who are at the same time improved and provided with a false analytical self or an alienating identification. It is worthwhile to look closely at these situations, as it is always difficult to isolate in the process that which reflects a successful return to a represented scene from the dynamic depths and that which reflects the deep silence of the analyzing situation.
> 
> Personal communication (my translation)

Donnet's view seems to be at odds with that of Laplanche (1994, 1998), for example, who seemed committed to the view that psychoanalysis was an anti-hermeneutics and that after the "dissolving" produced by analysis, the subsequent construction must always be left up to the patient to accomplish. In contrast, Donnet (2010) suggests that sometimes an analytic "false self" may be better than whatever preceded it and is the best that we can do. The "logic of the encounter," then, remains enigmatic and deeply "undecidable." Attempts to formulate a concretely reparative dimension to the analyst's role in relation to early infantile trauma reflect a difficulty in accepting the limits of what is knowable within the method.[6]

Returning to Freud, we have seen a basis for this formulation and line of reasoning in the assertion that in melancholia the "shadow" of the lost object falls on the ego (Freud, 1917, p. 249; also Chapter 4). We have noted that if the ego (or the self), itself, is a precipitate of abandoned object relations (Freud, 1917a, 1923), then the shadow of the object is intrinsic to and remains ensconced within and perhaps fundamental to the construction of the self. To what extent then, do processes of subjectivization – in life as well as in analysis – ever fully free themselves from the imprint of the object through which developmental steps and psychic internalizations are catalyzed and take place? Does introjection and identification ever escape a remainder of imitation?

It is useful here to recall what we had learned previously (Chapter 4) from Roussillon (2011), that the self is "constructed in accordance with the nature and type of adjustment and mirroring that the primary object proposes" (p. 139).

---

6  See Chapters 4 and 5.

> [The] object's mediation is ... a necessary element in primary narcissism, which entails the kind of primary identification that immediately brings the "shadow" of the object into the construction of the subject and into the process of subjective appropriation that lies at the heart of it.
>
> Roussillon (2011, p. 31)

To the extent that development of the psyche within the context of the analytic relationship will follow in the same paths as infantile psychic development, then the "shadow of the psychoanalyst falls on the analytic process and treatment, ... and, with it, the shadow of all the objects that have contributed historically to constructing the self's mental apparatus." (Roussillon, 2011, p. 52). It is the oscillation and resonance of the actuality of the reactivation of psychic developmental processes and their symbolic re-accessing of earlier developmentally traumatic situations that allows construction and attention to the here-and-now of the total transference situation to assume such centrality and importance in the cure.

## II

Having begun by addressing the complexities and inherent dangers that accompany the powerful possibilities of the analyst's participation in the analytic process, I would like to sound a more positive note. I believe that there *is* a legitimate, *actual* component to the authority of the analyst that is different from that ascribed to the analyst by the patient's transference perception, the analyst's countertransference or the cultural idealizations and misattributions of the role of the analyst that may still persist. (The latter include assumptions such as these: that the analyst can have a better sense of reality than the patient, can know "the truth" of what the patient unconsciously thinks or feels and can know what life decisions are best for the patient or how life should "correctly" be lived.)

The actual authority of the analyst lies not in a superior knowing of specific contents – all interpretations are prefaced by an implicit Bionian caveat: "I can't tell you what is true, but only what I believe to be true in the hopes that you might find it useful or of interest") – but in *the analyst's ethical commitment to function in the service of the patient's analytic/developmental needs*, in *being the transmitter of psychoanalytic values and being the guardian and regulator of the analytic process*.[7] In regard to the latter two functions, I would like to begin with a personal story.

---

7  The ethical responsibility of the analyst is taken up by Chetrit-Vatine (2004) in her discussion of the work of the philosopher, Levinas, and his concept of "responsibility to the other."

During my analytic formation, I had the good fortune of having for my personal analyst, Elvin Semrad, someone who embodied the principles that I am expanding on today. He was not averse to challenging, confronting, cajoling or catalyzing things when I suppose he felt they needed his input, but he was also able to spend long periods of time in silence. One day, when I was complaining to him that he wasn't offering me the kinds of interpretations that I was reading about in Freud's case histories he said to me, "In an analysis, you help a fellow to free associate and then you get out of his way" (Semrad, 1973, personal communication).

Over the years, I have found this to be an excellent piece of advice for the analysis of neurotically organized patients who can tolerate frustration and have – or can develop – some capacity to think, free associate and reflect on the thoughts, feelings and actions of themselves and others. In those treatments, it has stood me in good stead as a psychoanalytic value, one that I have tried to convey to patients through the living out of my role in the analysis, and as a regulatory proposition in regard to the analytic process.

But what about the rest of the patients – often the majority in my practice – or the times that what may superficially appear to be free association proves relatively meaningless or thought is not so much "defended against" but is impossible? It is then that abstinence and neutrality must at times and in some way give way to spontaneity, activity and intuition (see Levine, 2012; also Chapters 3 and 4). It is then that how to separate analytically informed action and intuition from wild analysis and countertransference imposition returns as central questions. Whatever the answer offered by one theory or another, I believe it must be something that takes place within the dual "containers" of "ethical responsibility to the other" and a theory that offers a legitimate *psychoanalytic* rationale for what the analyst proposes must be done beyond the standard classical technique, which has proven so useful for the treatment of neurotics.

We have earlier seen that Green (2005a) noted the,

> dispersion, or even fragmentation of psychoanalytic thought into many opposing theories (ego psychology, Kleinism, Lacanism, Bionian, Winnicottian and Kohutian, etc) ... all [of which could] be interpreted as attempts to propose a solution to the limitations of the results of classical treatment.
>
> (p. 47)

I have noted the conflict or even the despair that analysts feel when their theory does not extend to the kind of patients or clinical problems that they are faced with or the guilt and uncertainty they feel when they find themselves doing things that they and their patients may find helpful, but which seem to them to fall outside the scope of what they understand or assume is "analytic" (Levine, 2010a).

It is for this reason that I have argued in favor of the expansion of analytic thinking by articulating a two-track theory of therapeutic action (Levine, 2010a) that will extend to patients and situations that are "beyond neurosis" (Levine, 2014). In so doing, I emphasized that the *analytic process must often begin and be maintained for long periods of time within the person of the analyst* (Levine, 2010a). This means that the analyst is the guardian and regulator of that process within him or her self, as well as between analyst and patient.

One additional source of transference perceived authority of the analyst that I have not yet mentioned is the question that patients often implicitly ask of their analysts or themselves, consciously or unconsciously: "What does the analyst want of me?" The latter may come to the fore explicitly in the preliminary phases of the dismantling of certain pathological organizations and analyses of borderline states.

The answer is complex, because from one perspective, "without memory or desire," the answer is "Nothing." But this answer is from the perspective of specific outcomes. At the same time, however, from the perspective of *process*, the answer might be,

> I would like for you to develop an analytic function and capacity so that you might better find out who you are and what you, yourself, desire. Then it is up to you to decide what if anything you wish to do with that information.

Part of the complexity, is that in desiring the latter, the analyst does not require that the patient cooperate or "form a therapeutic alliance." That is up to the patient to decide ….

## III

For example, Prof. W is painfully describing how she cannot mourn, grieve, forgive or move on from various traumatic injuries, terrors and hurts and so cannot make use of my interpretations, even those that she acknowledges are or might be accurate descriptions of her internal world and functioning. "What do you expect me to do with that information?" she asks, both as defensive challenge (assault) and, I believe, in honest confusion.[8]

She has been describing her explosive rage at her children, who she also dearly loves and I have just interpreted her envy of and destructive hatred of them. She truly wants to be a better mother to them than she felt her

---

8 The question might also actualize a situation of incomprehension that was at the heart of a traumatic misalignment and lack of maternal receptivity that existed in her earliest life.

mother was to her, but she is envious, because they are getting the mothering from her that she longed for and never felt she got from her mother. Thus, she rails against them for being "spoiled," "entitled," "wanting to get a free ride," and so on, all of which I have been showing her also seem to reflect *her* (neurotic) desires – hidden from herself, because they are so unacceptable, seem so passive and hated, only expose her to the helplessness and humiliation of acknowledging needs that over and over again she feels remain thwarted, ignored or unfulfilled, and remind her of past pain, all of which makes her feel worthless, abandoned and enraged, and so on.

I tell her that I think she is having a hard time with the feelings that my last comment seems to have aroused in her, and I add that what perhaps she will be able to someday do with what I point out to her, if she feels it is useful or correct, may be to stop and think about what I have said. If she does recognize such a conflict within herself, she can try to decide which side she will try to come out on in relation to it. She may not yet be able to change how she feels – hopefully that may come later – but she certainly can try to fight with herself to change how she behaves with her children.

In addition, I say, if what I am saying about her envy seems correct, perhaps she can begin to recognize the feeling when it starts to surface and use it as a signal to try to stop venting her rage and reflect and associate, to see what she is feeling and what is going on inside herself. If she can do that and we can look at it together, then we can try to see where it will lead and what will happen next.

What I am trying to do is walk a fine line between not being the arbiter of "truth" – I do not tell her what she feels or what she should do or what *is* so, but rather *what I believe to be so* in the hopes that that might prove of interest or use to her. (This is Bion's famous, "I tell you how I think I do analysis, …" and it is Winnicott and the reflex hammer in the consultation with an infant.) Her response is that although she recognizes the "correctness" of what I have clarified, she does not yet know what to do with that information, how to take the next steps. It is still all a matter of intellectualized knowing to her.

Now, one could assume that this is a false or deceptive statement on her part – that it serves defensive, aggressive or evacuative ends, conscious or unconscious – and is therefore just another move in a familiar (classical) context. Or, we can take literally, that she truly does not yet have the capacity to function in this way and so does not really know what to do with this interpretation. That is, she cannot yet hold herself back from hostile action or initiate or carry out a form of considered, reflective thinking that is a necessary prerequisite for competent analytic progress to be made. Does she or does she not at any given moment have within herself a psychic space within which the fantasy of the absent object can be maintained, thereby allowing for the delay of action and tolerance of frustration that is inherent in the capacity for what I have called "true thought" (Levine, 2010b)?

Having assumed on the basis of my intuition, her reactivity and my accumulated experience with Prof. W that this is perhaps more a situation of deficit rather than conflict, of psychic disorganization and incapacity rather than neurotic defense, I reply literally and concretely to her question with a set of "instructions" that were aimed at helping her think about the analytic process and her purported role as patient within it. This is itself a complex interaction with many levels of transference meaning: for example, Am I being like (actualizing) the wished for mother she never had? Am I trying to teach her to use her psyche to delay action and therefore favoring containment over impulse? Would her doing so be a covert and symbolic submission to me, sexual or otherwise? In answering her "directly," am I submitting to her? Has she seduced me into "instructing her" so that she may defy me? Perhaps the answer is "all of the above." These are questions that must await further developments, can never be categorically answered and may only evoke tentative answers *après coup*.

Given what I know of Prof. W's past, I feel the "What do you want me to do with that?" addressed to me had the earmarks of a test, as well of a repetition and attempted reworking, of a known traumatic disappointment. [That is, my response offered her an interpretation *in* the transference rather than *of* the transference (Sechaud, 2008).]

As a template and an instruction for the future, through my response to her, was I actualizing the wished for mother of container/contained? In taking her question at face value and answering it, was I not gratifying something rather than asking her to wait and discover and try to see? Was this a developmentally necessary "ego need" (Winnicott, 1963, p. 86) as opposed to a symbolic instinctual gratification? Or was I joining her in a denial of her agency and intention, albeit unconscious intention, in allowing that this behavior is redolent of deficit rather than unconscious hostility?

Once more, the answers to these questions are again probably all of the above and more. I was also trying to remind her of certain *psychoanalytic process values* – for example, frustration tolerance; delay of gratification; negative capability and free association – and in doing so, attempting to fulfill my role and responsibility as *guardian of the analytic process*.

In working with patients such as Prof. W, however, there is still another consideration. Before one can support, foster or guard a psychoanalytic process, one must often help the patient develop the internal competence and capacities needed to engage in this form of psychic work. That is, in order to function effectively in an analysis, a patient must have or must develop what Green (1980) metaphorically has described as a *framing structure*. The latter is an internal psychic space that under "good enough" circumstances will appear as the result of the infant's internalization of the physical impression left on the infant by the mother's arms. In normal development,

> When conditions are favourable to the inevitable separation between the mother and the child, a decisive mutation arises in the depths of the ego. The maternal object in the form of the primary object of fusion fades away, to leave the place to the ego's own cathexes which will found his personal narcissism. Henceforth the ego will be able to cathect its own objects, distinct from the primitive object. But this effacement of the mother does not make the primitive object disappear completely. The primary object becomes a 'framing-structure' for the ego sheltering the negative hallucination of the mother.
>
> (p. 165)

Once established, this structure will allow one to,

> face waiting and even temporary depression, the child feeling supported by the maternal object even when it is not there. The framework, when all is said and done, offers the guarantee of the maternal presence in her absence, and can be filled with fantasy of all kinds, to the point of, and including, aggressive violent fantasies which will not imperil the container. The space which is thus framed constitutes the receptacle of the ego; it surrounds an empty field, so to speak, which will be occupied by erotic and aggressive cathexes, in the form of object representations .... it plays the role of the primordial matrix of the cathexes to come.
>
> However, if a traumatism such as blank mourning occurs before the infant has been able to establish this framework solidly enough, there is no psychical space available within the ego.
>
> (p. 166)

In the absence of this psychical space and the soothing, self-regulatory function that it can stand in for and support, emotional self-regulation and frustration tolerance may become impossible to maintain. Patients may become whipsawed between the two poles of fusional loss of identity and annihilating abandonment. As Green (1975) further notes, "the analyst's silence can be experienced in certain borderline situations (*situations limites*) as the silence of death" (p. 17). At such moments, the challenge to the analyst is how to use one's analytic presence – silence and words – to create, support and strengthen the existence and functional capacity of the holding structure and psychic space.

Green (1975) asserts that the analyst,

> supplements through verbalization the lack of maternal care in order to encourage the emergence of a relationship to the ego and to the object, until the moment is reached when the analyst can become a transitional object and the analytic space a potential area of play and field of illusion.
>
> (p. 17)

What I am proposing is that from this metapsychological perspective, a seemingly "instructional intervention" is an analogous supplementation to the maternal care that was presumably missing in the patient's early maturational situation and a necessary support for psychic regulatory processes. In helping to still unspeakable and unbearable agonies and terrors, such interventions can play a reparative role in resolving crises of annihilation anxiety that appear via the repetition compulsion in the here-and-now current moment of the analytic session.[9]

This is a dynamic, metapsychological description of what might look from the outside to be a supportive or instructional intervention. From another perspective, it is an attempt to help foster and transmit psychoanalytic values and induct the patient further into an analytic "culture" and process. As such, it is redolent of a kind of suggestion and reflects particular values. But these are less concerned with specific content and more about functioning, process and how to optimize one's participation in an analytic process. Undoubtedly, this is suggestion again and the analyst's authority, but in still another light, one that tries to foster psychic organization, subjectivization and agency, protect and enrich the patient's sense of autonomy and aid in the positive trajectory of psychic development, without regard or reference to specific psychic contents or life decisions.

As psychoanalysts, we must have Faith (Bion, 1970) in a process called "psychoanalysis" and we do our best to induct the patient into that process, which can eventually prove to be self-perpetuating in ways that we have (hopefully) experienced personally and believe to be useful. This inevitably requires some kind and degree of instruction and suggestion. But as I have tried to show, the latter more centrally is a matter of values and process and not necessarily specific ideational contents.

---

9 See Winnicott's (1974) Fear of Breakdown paper.

Chapter 7

# Trauma, process and representation

## I

The concept of "trauma," so central to Freud's (1895b) original formulations of hysteria, continues to occupy a problematic place in psychoanalysis. The difficulties involved are far greater and more complex than are implied in the oft-repeated – and, I think, often mistakenly polarized – debates about Freud's (1897) renunciation of the seduction theory and its implications for our understanding of the psychogenesis of pathology. Obviously, actual events that we may come to refer to as "traumatic" are significant; and their significance can be described in terms of what we hypothesize or observe to be their intrapsychic, intersubjective and interpersonal consequences.[1] Confusion about the meaning of the term, trauma, however, arises, in part, from variations in connotation and usage that exist between the domains defined in various psychoanalytic theories by the pairs internal and external; drive and reality; fantasy and reality; psychic reality and external reality and, as I shall describe, in limitations in how Freud's formulations and psychoanalytic theory have, in some places, been traditionally viewed.

A further difficulty, at least for English speaking analysts, may relate to common parlance. When the Oxford English Dictionary (1971) defines the word, "trauma," it applies the same word to both the cause and its effects: "A wound or external bodily injury; also the condition caused by this" (p. 3387). This double referent tends toward an over-inclusive usage, a practice that analysts often follow when they employ the same word, "trauma" – or its variants such as "traumatic" – to designate:

- The noxious cause of a complex process;
- The resulting acute, internal state of being injured, helpless, terrified or overwhelmed;

---

1 On second thought, perhaps it is or was not always so obvious. A colleague once confided to me that her training analyst never once questioned her or made an interpretation about her experience as a prisoner in a concentration camp during World War II!

DOI: 10.4324/9781003171331-8

- The immediate damage inflicted; and/or
- The longer range sequelae that these earlier stages may produce.

The difficulties that can follow from this conflation of meanings are evident. It is as if an enormous rock fell into a lake producing a huge splash and ripples, which then caused long-term ecological damage and the same name was used to describe the rock hitting the water, the immediate disturbance that it produced and the eventual ecological changes that resulted. In this chapter, I will attempt to examine some of the implications for analytic process of Freud's concept of trauma when viewed from the perspective of his theory of psychic representation as it has been advanced and extended by contemporary authors influenced by the work of Bion, Winnicott, Green and the Paris School of Psychosomatics.

## II

In a classic article, Baranger et al. (1988) carefully explicate the multiple and evolving meanings that the term, trauma, had for Freud throughout his writings, as he applied it to *infantile psychic trauma* and the origins of neurosis. Shifts in meaning and usage of the word continued after Freud,[2] and, by 1967, Anna Freud cautioned that as a technical term, "trauma" was in danger of being emptied of meaning through overuse and overextension. In the same article, she referred to two different categories of psychopathology: one caused by trauma and the other due to "pathogenic influences in general" (p. 236). However, she neither illustrated the difference between these two proposed categories of experience nor specified what constituted the boundary that she felt existed between them. Was she attempting to distinguish between "pain" or "conflict" and "trauma"? Pointing to a matter of quantity? Of quality? To a moment when excess quantity produced a qualitative change?

In leaving open the question of what this distinction actually referred to, Anna Freud may have inadvertently left unanswered doubts as to whether or not, in fact, the distinction even exists. Her suggested solution to the problems surrounding the use of the term, trauma, was that it be accompanied by modifiers, such as *adult* or *childhood* trauma, *shock* trauma and *strain* trauma (Kris, 1956), *massive psychic* trauma (Furst, 1967), *cumulative* trauma (Khan, 1963) and *micro-trauma, screen* trauma (Sandler, 1967). While this may be clarifying in some contexts, I do not think it fully resolves our theoretical conflicts or addresses the fundamental problems that have inhered around the term.

---

2 The literature on this subject is enormous and I will not attempt to summarize or comment on it here.

As an example of how problematic some views of trauma have become, in a discussion of the denial and dangers of global warming and the nuclear threat, one North American colleague commented that she was taught by her supervisors that such factors in the associations of analytic patients were *always* to be seen and analyzed as displacements from internal conflicts and not dealt with as things in themselves. At the other extreme, in a paper presented at the North American Celebration Centenary Conference of the IJP, Greenberg (2019) suggested that

> there has been a broad recasting of psychoanalytic developmental theory in a way that emphasizes the impact of what has happened to, or been done to, the child in contrast to the conflicted experiences that are inevitable as the child attempts to organize and navigate a way through the complex, confusing, and constantly changing world… the emphasis has shifted from a focus on intrapsychic conflict and its attendant fantasies to what has become known as "developmental trauma.
>
> (p. 1145)

Needless to say, I find the either-or extremity of these positions problematic and puzzling. The external events and their consequences that we come to call "traumatic" – for example, the threat to life and economic hardship caused by the recent COVID-19 pandemic – have meaning and significance in their own right. Given the opportunity for sufficient psychic elaboration and working through, these actual events become (*après coup*) associated with and containers for significant internal, often previously unrepresented, catastrophic threats, emotional upheavals and disruptions.

While Greenberg's assertion may be regarded by some as a regional view seen from the perspective of a North American analyst who comes out of an interpersonal/relational background, it does capture a certain current of contemporary analytic thinking – the kind of thing that has a tendency to persist and can work its way into the general fabric of analytic thought throughout all the regions. And it raises questions that are worth considering no matter what analytic region, language group or theoretical orientation we find ourselves embedded in. Are there specific classes of patients who will require significant revision in analytic technique

> because they have been made more vulnerable than other people as a result of developmental trauma [?] …. [A]re there times when we must modify technique because we are encountering areas in which the developmental trauma … [outweighs] some other dynamic process that we believe should be treated in a different way?
>
> Greenberg (2019, pp. 1145–1146)

And if the latter is the case, does this modification and "different way" inevitably require that we must move beyond the domain of psychoanalytic understanding and treatment and search for some other modality?

## III

While the circumstances and aftermath of trauma may require *variations* in the assumptions pertaining to the classical analysis of neurosis in regard to understanding, listening stance, timing and technique, I believe that as many analysts have increasingly recognized the value of adding a metapsychology of process to a metapsychology of content (e.g., Roussillon, 2014),[3] our field has been evolving a broader and more comprehensive *psychoanalytic* understanding of trauma and its psychic consequences. This can allow us to recognize, understand and address these problems *clinically* and *psychoanalytically* from within a consistent and coherent theory of psychic development, therapeutic action, analytic process and technique (Levine, 2012). From this perspective, the seeming dichotomy between what we might call "drive/fantasy/wish related pathology" and "trauma related pathology" appears to be a false one. It has resulted in large part from a limitation in our application and development of analytic theory, as we have tried to understand and treat non-neurotic mind states and conditions. Recall, for example, Freud's pessimistic assumption that the narcissistic neuroses were not amenable to psychoanalytic remediation. The inevitable restrictions in listening stance and technique that followed have erroneously implied for some that analysis was not the most appropriate or suitable treatment for post-traumatic pathologies and states.

The issues may become a bit clearer if, instead of talking predominantly or exclusively in terms of traumatic *events* and the distorted perceptions, interpretations and psychic *contents* that this can produce, we try to specify something about the vicissitudes of psychic *process*; about the capacity or incapacity for and strength or weakness of transformation and representation, for historicization, subjectivization and passivation, for objectalization and disobjectalization, for thinking, meaning making and their disruption or absence. That is, to speak about capacities and incapacities, disruptions, disorganizations and degrees of failures of psychic processes as they occur and exist intrapsychically and most importantly as they may occur and exist intersubjectively within the analytic relationship and situation. To do so has its own long history in psychoanalytic thought.

Traditionally in psychoanalysis, at its most general level, trauma has been described in terms of the disruptive effects of excess excitation on psychic

---

3 In a comment from the floor at the 2014 French Language Conference in Montreal, Roussillon said, "What we need is a metapsychology of process rather than a metapsychology of content."

functioning and development and its impact on the mind's capacity for emotional containment and the creation of representations, symbols and affective and associational links between ideas. Trauma, in the form of failure of adequate environmental provision in the earliest phases of development, tends to favor instinctual defusion and to some authors the strengthening or accentuation of the death instinct as evidenced by the many clinical manifestations of the repetition compulsion (Freud, 1920). A traumatized psyche may demonstrate difficulty in performing the processes needed for psychic elaboration and linkage of sensorial experience: dreaming dreams, thinking thoughts, modulating tensions and extracting from and assigning personal meaning to the raw, factual "data" of existence.[4]

Many theories attempt to describe how the regulatory capacities of the mind originate, evolve in the primary object (mother-infant) relationship, can be traumatically disrupted and may subsequently be restored, strengthened or acquired for the first time in a successful analytic therapy.[5] While terminology may differ, what seems constant across different formulations are the binary choice points: equilibrium or chaos; representation or psychic voids (de-cathexis); development or stasis; contained anxiety that signals and directs homeostatic regulation or unbound anxiety that reflects and produces further disruption and trauma.

As an additional caution, we must also remember that trauma per se is not a monolithic entity. Human experience, even of the same or similar events, – for example, war, genocide, torture, rape, childhood sexual abuse, early parental loss, neglect or mis-attunement – is context dependent and highly subjective. The forms in which trauma may appear, its impact and its outcome, are expectably diverse and highly variable. The events, processes and consequences that are referred to as "trauma" or "traumatic" are as varied as the ages, developmental levels and mental capacities of those who are affected. Responses to potentially traumatic events are individualized, highly subjective and influenced by the responses or lack of responses by one's familial and societal surrounds. It is therefore confusing – perhaps even impossible – to try to talk generically about "trauma" or categorically about any given trauma or class of traumatic events, as if or with the implication that one was speaking about unitary phenomena with specifiable, generalizable characteristics.

From a clinical perspective, perhaps the most one can do in talking about categories of trauma is to discuss the various challenges that a given set of potentially trauma-inducing circumstances might pose for an individual and then look at each individual's highly subjective mode of experiencing and responding to those challenges and the supports offered in any instance by the specific familial, social or cultural surround. Each set

---

4 See, for example, Bion (1962b, 1970), Green (2005a), Winnicott (1974)
5 See, for example, Levine (2020).

of experiences that will be qualified as "trauma" that any of us undergoes will, to some extent, be understood and integrated into our particular subjectivities according to our unique, subjective organizations of self, understandings of and position in the world.

## IV

For Freud, the term, trauma, was associated with something that was an excess of unrepresented, unbound "force" (e.g., internal drive pressure or external threat) that overwhelmed, *disorganized and disrupted psychic functioning*. He stated this definitively in Beyond the Pleasure Principle (Freud, 1920), linked it to the death instinct and repetition compulsion and re-affirmed it in The Ego and the Id (Freud, 1923) and in his later writings. Earlier, Freud (1914) had connected the repetition compulsion to the dynamic unconscious, and talked about it as a way station toward and defense against the recollection or recognition of unacceptable, anxiety producing *representations* (memories, fantasies or wishes). At this stage, he seemed to be focusing predominantly on neurosis and the question of under what circumstances would which ideational contents (representations) be acceptable to consciousness.

By 1920, however, Freud was increasingly concerned with conditions and mind states that lay beyond neurosis. Thus, he expanded on his earlier explanation of the repetition compulsion to include considerations that reflected the de-fusion and accentuation or strengthening of the death instinct. These processes produce an unbound, "overflow" of uncontained force in the psyche that lies beyond representation and verbalization and finds discharge and evacuation through the action of repetition.

Even in his early formulation, Freud implied that the repetition compulsion often included a potentially reparative dimension. While the circumstances it reproduced were often painful, they could be seen to offer a kind of proto-containment that attempted via action and discharge "to control and lessen unpleasant or traumatic experiences" (Potamianou, 2015, p. 945).[6] In Moses and Monotheism Freud (1939) added the possibility that an immature or severely overwhelmed ego might be unable to muster even this degree of response (p. 76). When that is the case, "nothing is repeated and nothing is remembered, the ego's organization is conditioned by avoidance processes that may develop into inhibitions and phobias" (Potamianou, 2015, p. 945).[7]

---

6 This intimation was taken up by Winnicott (1974) and implicitly Bion (1962b, 1970). It has begun to be developed more centrally by contemporary authors such as Bergstein (2019), Eekhoff (2019) and Eshel (2017), each of whom sees the possibility of an unconscious plea for intersubjective psychic regulatory assistance in the compulsive repetitions.

7 See, for example, Green's (2000a) Central Phobic Position.

Stepping back to look at the *process* of trauma, Scarfone (2017) writes,

> In the most general sense, *trauma* is a tear, a breach: you start with a more or less unified surface that is then shredded by the force of an impact .... Trauma ... does not describe simply a loss of continuity in the surface of the body or of the mind; rather it initiates various degrees of disorganization with what the surface both contains and keeps *operational* .... [Thus, ] the breach in the protective shield [that Freud (1920) described] not only damages the continuity of the surface but, more important, it also causes various levels of disorganization in the workings of the apparatus – i.e., its capacity to process and bind the quantum of further excitation.
>
> (p. 23, original italics)

Put simply – although it is anything but a simple matter of theory, practice or personal experience! - what is at issue is whether or not or the degree to which the raw existential "facts" of one's experience and existence can be psychically worked on and made meaningful in terms of one's identity, personal narrative and life trajectory.

*The events to which we ultimately will refer to as "traumatic" disrupt and disorganize the psychic processes through which meaning making occurs.* They "paralyze the psychic apparatus, leaving it deficient in elaborative possibilities and exposed to overwhelming anxieties" (Potamianou, 2015, p. 946). They also exceed the capacity of one's familial or cultural surround to provide sufficient attenuation, containment and redress needed to mitigate the effects of the disturbing events.

It is the "elaborative possibilities" of the psychic apparatus that prove essential for making sense of our experience: "making sense ... means creating meanings that are *one's own*, and are thus the most precious possessions in that they structure the subject's individuality" (Scarfone, 2017, p. 38). The psychoanalytic theories with which many contemporary analysts have come to describe these processes are closely related to Freud's theory of representation (Chapter 2; also Levine, 2012, 2014; Levine et al., 2013) and the vicissitudes and gradients of transformational movement from unrepresented to represented mental states.

## V

It remains an open question as to whether or to what extent trauma of some kind lies at the heart of *every* process that we view as pathogenic. Do the feelings of helplessness and agonizing despair (Potamianou, 2015) that we associate with the untoward events that we qualify as trauma produce a separate category of psychopathology that is different from conflict driven neurosis? Or is the seeming distinction between the two categories only apparent? Does every neurotic conflict begin, for example, with a micro-trauma and is any apparent distinction between the two categories trauma/conflict simply a matter of the *quantity* of disorganization produced?

Recall that Freud (1915–1917) suggested that a kernel of actual neurosis might lie at the heart of every neurotic conflict and in his Introduction to "On the psycho-analysis of war neuroses" (Freud, 1919), he made the astonishing, often overlooked assertion that "we have a perfect right to describe repression, which lies at the basis of every neurosis, as a *reaction to trauma* – as an *elementary traumatic neurosis*" (p. 210, italics added).[8] Taken together, do these statements imply a perspective from which what we may ordinarily think of and describe as "trauma" and "conflict" have a level or degree of sameness or continuity?

The designation "actual neurosis" implies some form of unrepresented state (Levine et al., 2013). That is, an absence or "different state"[9] of psychic organization than one marked by the capacities for psychic linkage and elaboration, containment, representation, symbolization, full ideational saturation, and so on. The existence of an actual neurosis at the heart of every psychoneurosis may also imply that psychoneurosis cannot be thought about or described solely in terms of organized, ideationally saturated, unacceptable, anxiety producing desires being barred from consciousness. Botella (2014) suggested that

> every psychic structure, even that of an oedipal neurosis, if it is explored far enough, will touch on certain psychic zones involving traumatic experiences which have not been represented, thought, and registered in memory but which nevertheless form part of each of us.
> (p. 916)

Designating repression as "an elementary traumatic neurosis" implies that Freud thought of repression not only as an ego mechanism of defense, but as "a *reaction to trauma* and therefore a breach in the ego" (Scarfone, 2017, p. 36). Thus for Freud, at least in the 1919 paper, pathogenesis cannot be simply parsed into categories such as internal cause versus external cause or trauma versus fantasy. And in noting that "traumatic, penetrating, and unravelling phenomena, usually associated with disorganization, are always present in psychic organization," Scarfone (2017) reminds us that "As a feature of Freudian thinking, trauma was not a momentary concept quickly overshadowed by the constitutional model of the drives" (p. 25).

---

8 I am indebted to Scarfone (2017, pp. 33–35) for calling this to my attention.
9 I leave open the question as what a "different state" might be or how it might be conceptualized, much as Bion left undefined the exact nature of terms such as alpha function or beta-element.

From the Project (Freud, 1895a) onward, Freud emphasized and struggled to articulate the central role of the psyche in binding, containing and transforming excess, unpleasant or unwanted "excitation," in the form of affect, emotion, impulse or drive. This was as true of his initial theories of abreaction, childhood seduction and dammed up libido as it was in his final theories that pitted the binding power of Eros against the unbinding power of the death instinct.

Bion (1962a) argued that both perception and "thinking" were continuously evolving functions of the personality and sought to examine the factors that contribute to their development and use. In his lectures and supervisions (e.g., Bion, 2005a, 2005b), he often suggested to audiences that the psyche was a relatively recent evolutionary acquisition that evolved in order to help cope with emotions, perceptions and sensations; that is, to cope with the problem of being sensate and being aware of what it feels like to exist. Influenced, in part, by his experiences as a tank commander in the World War I,[10] Bion believed that raw existential experience was potentially traumatic and required psychic work to contain its inherently toxic effects. This view, which was analogous to and an extension of Freud's insistence that the drives made a demand on the psyche for work, was inherent in and elaborated on in Bion's theories of thinking, transformation, alpha function and container/contained.

Botella (2014) reads Freud's (1933, p. 29) revised theory of dream work as reflecting Freud's understanding that "a primordial function of psychic life [is] to create representations permitting ... hitherto unrepresented trauma to be integrated within ... representational networks" (Botella, 2014, p. 915).

In earlier chapters, I have explored the role of construction in the analytic process (Chapter 3) and described "the representational imperative" (Chapter 4) to indicate the essential role that psychic elaborative processes play in emotional regulation and homeostasis. These are just some of the analytic theories that indicate that what we eventually call trauma is determined by the relative strength and balance of the ongoing struggle to contain, "de-toxify" and "metabolize" raw existential experience – the inevitable consequence of being sensate and alive in the world.

## VI

In regard to clinical praxis, I believe that the key element for a theory of pathogenesis and mental functioning is not the either/or of "external"

---

10 For extended studies of this connection see Souter (2009), Szykierski (2010), Brown (2012) and Tarantelli (2016).

versus "internal" causation or "trauma" versus "drive." Instead, it is an appreciation of the ways in which the raw data of existential experience is or is not transformed into meaningful psychological experience and then lived out within the immediate here-and-now of the analytic situation, no matter where or from what substrate that data may originate. Thus, in assessing the consequences of any experience or interaction, trauma can be measured by the extent to which various psychic processes referred to as cathexis (Winnicott, 1971), containment (Bion, 1970), objectalization (Green, 2005a), symbolization, figurability (Botella and Botella, 2005), representation (Levine et al., 2013) and other denominations of mental processing (Marty, 1976, 1980) are disrupted or prevented from developing.

Where psychic development and functioning remain robust, these progressive, homeostatic psychic processes can proceed more or less autonomously. When weakened, disrupted or absent due to constitutional factors or untoward external situations and problematic object relations – that is, what we may later call "trauma" – intersubjective assistance in the treatment situation becomes increasingly essential. This assistance may take the form of interpretive constructions, narrative co-construction (e.g., Ferro, 2002) or intersubjective, homoeostatic regulation, such as Bion (1970) described in his theory of alpha function and container/contained.

With patients who fall outside the category of neurosis, in order to facilitate the necessary therapeutic movements, analytic interventions must be flexible, intuitive and prepared to go beyond the confines of the assumptions of classical technique:

> Confronted with a wide range of disorders that are nowadays no longer centered around desires and prohibitions, but include voids in objects, gaps in identity formation, compulsive repetition of elements of reality in daily life or in dreams, analysts have to consider a broad horizon of psychoanalytic praxis that corresponds with inevitable changes in the use of the classic psychoanalytic technique. They have to work not only on repressed material but on obliterations, erasures and ruptures that indicate defects in mental functioning and massive reductions in mental processing.
>
> Potamianou (2015, p. 958)

In these instances, the repetition compulsion may be driven by and reflect the unstructured unconscious rather than the dynamic unconscious. Its phenomena, which take place under the aegis of the death instinct, include such things as de-cathexis (Winnicott, 1971), the destructive pole of the work of the negative (Green, 2005a), operational thinking (Marty, 1976), "black holes" and "psychic voids," and may not be a mid-way form and way station of organized, structured but repressed desire or memory. That is, compulsive repetition may signal the active presence of a blind – and "thoughtless" – repetitive *action* driven by *unrepresented* forces. In addition to defensive and aggressive ends, this repetitive action may contain a desperate plea for intersubjective assistance in dealing with and helping to relieve primitive agonies.[11] Clinically, this may require the assistance of intuitively derived, interpretive constructions (Chapter 3; Levine, 2011a).

In regard to the latter, Bergstein (2019) following Bion writes of the healing, structuring, "bridge building" role played by the analyst's constructions in the process of analytic remediation and repair:

> the curative aim of construction is not so much discovering or conjecturing 'facts' – e.g., what happened in utero or in the pre-verbal period of life – but rather creating a 'thought container' for that which seems unthinkable, thereby "linking states of mind which seem unbridgeable and even unreachable... generating motion between different parts of the psyche, for transforming *barriers* within the mind into *caesuras* (i.e., breaks after which there is continuity), and for incorporating and integrating different parts of the Self, even those seemingly inaccessible ones.
>
> (p. 29)

Similarly, Potamianou (2015) offers that

> By converting energy charges that evade figuration, the analyst's constructions disengage the patient's thinking from encapsulations and open the way to the recovery of memories or to the emergence of convictions that concern a newly constructed past. Sensations and somatic events become part of a psychic text that is integrated into a myth-historical narration woven during analytic work.
>
> Potamianou (2015, p. 961)

She further adds,

> If the analyst succeeds in giving to the compulsive repetitions the meaning of an enactment in the transference, as well as that of a wish rooted in the past/present relationship of the analytic couple, then this fatal destiny in human history may serve as an agent of change.
>
> Potamianou (2015, p. 962)

---

11 See also Roussillon (2011) and his formulation of the signal function of the drives.

These comments resonate both with Bion's (1970) assertion that the analyst must do more than just recognize and "know" the patient's difficulties; must, in some way, become "at-one-with" the patient's annihilation fears and primitive agonies and with the logic of Winnicott's writings on regression to dependency as exemplified in his (1974) Fear of Breakdown paper. In the latter, Winnicott emphasizes that the *analyst must unconsciously fail the patient* – unwittingly contribute to the production of an *actual* micro-trauma in the here-and-now – in the ways in which the patient needs him to, so that an attenuated version of what once occurred prior to the formation of an integrated and organized infantile self could then be experienced in the transference under the aegis of the patient's unconscious omnipotence and therefore achieve figurability (be represented in the mind) and "suffered" for the first time as Bion (1970) might say, as personalized, subjective experience, that can eventually be mourned and worked through. All of this seemed to have been implied but was not elaborated on by Freud (1912) in his papers on technique, when he said in regard to the analysis of the transference, that one cannot slay the enemy in effigy or in absentia.

But to speak of the analyst's "constructions" and "transference interpretations" evokes connotations of the semantic dimension of words. Sometimes, the analyst is confronted with the *non-repetitive consequences of trauma* (Freud, 1939); patients whose deadened ego has been so disabled that it cannot muster the response of repetition. In such cases, there seems to be only deadness or a void: a seeming absence of transference, feeling, action or repetition, except for inertia, nothingness, deadness and boredom. Then, prior to or in addition to their lexical value, it is the "physicality" and emotion, the affect and action dimension of the analyst's words (Chapter 9), that may be required to engage and "prime the pump" of the patient's psyche.[12]

Recall that Bion (1962b) suggested that in regard to the psychotic portion of the mind, patients cannot describe their situation in words, but instead have an unconscious "capacity for evoking emotions in the analyst" (p. 24). This includes emotions of nothingness and voids. It places a heavy burden on the analyst's countertransference and intuition for sorting out what is or might be being communicated in the seeming absence of communication and meaning and how it is to be understood and possibly used in the analysis.[13]

Bergstein (2019) offers us still another valuable insight into these situations when he reminds us that "The paradox of nothingness is that

---

12 For an example, see Chapter 8.
13 See Eekhoff (2019) for further discussion and illustration.

it is full of desire, a desire to communicate, but it can appear that the subject communicating nothingness in the transference wants nothing or wishes to nullify what there is" (p. 113). He adds that these are experiences that cannot initially be verbally communicated or dynamically interpreted. They "must first be lived, sometimes for the first time, in the here-and-now of the analysis" (p. 137), often by both analyst and patient.

As a final note, Anne Alvarez (2012), who has worked extensively with autistic and developmentally disturbed children, but whose conclusions are equally applicable to all kinds of non-autistic adult patients whose problems are beyond neurosis, has argued that some traumatized patients are less hiding than lost (p. 2) and require "reclamation" – a call back to life and relating. They are unable to use or profit from a "why" interpretation (an explanation that offers alternative meanings) or a "what" interpretation (a description aimed at enlarging meanings). What they need is a vitalizing "Hey!" intervention, one that offers and insists on meaning as something that can and does exist and that matters) (p. 3).

Many of these are patients who suffer the trauma of adverse biological endowment and/or severe environmental misattunement or abuse. Whatever the combination of etiological circumstances, the result is a massive withdrawal and "a chronic apathy about relating, which goes beyond despair" (p. 13). They may be more "undrawn" than withdrawn. Their analysts not only have to point out their lack of interest in objects and the world, but also sometimes find ways to attract and hold their interest (p. 25). Their inner and outer worlds may seem "desertified"; objects may be "experienced as uninteresting, unvalued (not devalued), useless, possibly mindless" (p. 10). These patients may feel so hopeless, withdrawn, defeated or neglected that they have no interest or hope of being able to attract and hold the interest or love of an object. Consequently, they "may need to be helped to be able to feel and to find meaning…. then, feelings can begin to be identified and explored; eventually, explanations, which bring in additional meanings, may be heard and taken in" (p. 11).

Put another way,

> long before certain patients process their hatred and find their capacity for love, they may have to develop the ability to be interested in an object with some substantiality and life. Something and someone has to matter. This is work at the very foundation of human relatedness…. Once this is achieved, the work can move to higher levels, sometimes in the course of a single session.
>
> Alvarez (2010, p. 875)

Alvarez suggests that the "Hey!" interpretation is analogous to the kind of work that the mother of the neonate must sometimes do to call the infant into engagement and life.

## VI

To summarize:

Raw experience must be transformed and "translated into [a form that has the potential for] verbal speech in order to insure continuity in the mind" (Roussillon, 2011 p. 116). When this transformation occurs, "words will begin to be associated with internal states and, therefore, replace to some extent the narrativity of gestures and of actions of thing-presentations and affects" (ibid., p. 116). The latter never fully disappear, but become subsumed in qualities of speech, such as prosody, tone, rhythm and intensity of speech, that provide emphasis, and embody (literally, as well as figuratively) action and affect beyond symbolical meaning. Their internalization and transformation are dependent on the actual quality of interactions with external objects.

The capacity to transform the inchoate raw data of experience into psychologically representable (mentalizable) elements is a major goal of psychological development, the essence of "successful" human mental activity and at the heart of the transformational aims of the psychoanalytic process. From this perspective, what matters is not where the stimulus (excitation, drive derivative, bodily sensation, fantasy, affect, tragic event, memory, etc.) originates – "inside" or "outside" – but whether, how and to what extent it is processed by the mind and then how it is or is not used in a creative way in relation to the other.[14]

What earns the designation, "trauma," is that which outstrips and disrupts the psyche's capacity for representation. Under such circumstances, emotions and raw sensation cannot be channeled by being bound to thoughts, and causes affects storms and seeks discharge in action. That which cannot be represented – thought about or contained within the mind – cannot enter into one's subjectivity or a reflective view of one's personal history (e.g., Winnicott, 1974). Absent the potential for mental representation, these events and phenomena are "historical" only from an external, third-person perspective. Until they achieve representation and are mentalized, they remain locked within an ahistorical, repetitive process as potentials for action, affect, somatization and evacuation.

---

14 This, of course, implies also implies the freedom to "not communicate" in order to preserve one's integrity and potential for future creative manifestations (Scarfone, 2005).

Processes of figurability (representation) may be carried out alone or intersubjectively with the assistance of external objects. *Failure to sufficiently do so leads to varying degrees of micro- and macro-traumatic states that are the precursors and cause of psychopathology.*

We might call the more ordinary of these states the "traumata of everyday life" and note that to the extent to which they do catalyze representation and psychic elaboration they stimulate psychic growth.

When elaborative psychic processes are "successful," affect is bound to thought, anxiety is kept at the level of the signal or stimulus to work, including the work of strengthening and developing psychic regulatory processes. When they are unsuccessful, then the anxiety signal builds in strength until it crosses a threshold and, like a river overflowing its banks, reaches at least micro-traumatic proportions.

A relative insufficiency of representational and psychic elaborative processes leaves one susceptible to micro- and macro-traumatic states that can be described in economic terms as the overwhelming of the individual's stimulus barrier, ego defensive capabilities or capacities for emotional homeostasis. Alternatively, these states may be described in terms of the helplessness that follows from being overloaded with pre- and proto-mental elements that cannot be sufficiently transformed into the precursors of thought, cannot be contained within the mind and are fit only for denial, evacuation, somatization or characteropathic enactment (Ferro, 2002).

When these states are inadvertently produced or felt to recur by the patient within the setting of an analytic relationship, when the analytic relationship becomes in essence the source of a potentially micro-traumatizing experience in the transference, then the analyst has the opportunity to *act analytically in the present* to help the patient restore emotional equilibrium, understand and put into words the sequence of events that brought the relationship to a potentially disruptive head and thereby serve as a "new object" in the face of an all too familiar, potentially traumatic interaction. The process I am describing was alluded to by Freud (1912) in his papers on technique, when he said that enemies could not be slain in absentia or in effigy and by Winnicott (1974), who said that what had once been experienced by the infant in a state of helplessness had to be reexperienced and worked through in the transference under the aegis of the omnipotence of the patient's self.

## Chapter 8

# Making the unthinkable thinkable

## Autism, ASD and representation

**I**

The genius inherent in Freud's initial formulation of psychoanalysis was his discovery that the manifest content of everyday discourse and experience was a potential indicator of unconscious meanings related to significant psychic conflicts. These hidden meanings were pre-existing (i.e., already represented by more or less fully formed, potentially verbalizable ideas in the mind), could reveal themselves through slips of the tongue, jokes and dreams – the latter anointed as "The Royal Road to the Unconscious" – and, most important of all, they determined and made sense of what otherwise seemed to be "irrational" neurotic symptoms. In essence, to those who could begin to hear and discern these meanings, the symptoms of neurosis offered a continual, disguised, symbolic discourse about unacceptable or problematic desires, fantasies, fears and childhood trauma, the psychic conflicts they produced and the defensive responses that they elicited. The aim of treatment was summarized in the expression: "Making the Unconscious conscious."

The assumption that there was intention, motivation and significant, already formed hidden and unconscious sense and meaning that could be hypothesized about and discovered in hysterical symptoms, obsessive thoughts, compulsive acts and paranoid suspicions lay at the heart of Freud's first topography (the "topographic theory"). The latter is a theory about representations: specific ideational elements (wishes, desires, perceptions, fears and fantasies) that are saturated in regard to meaning, capable of being more or less fully described in words, possessing potential symbolic value and able to be strung together in the patient's discourse to form chains of signifying associations. It is a theory that has proven – and continues to be – of enormous value in guiding the understanding and classical treatment of neurosis and the neurotic sectors of the mind. (I am using the term "neurosis" here to imply representation and a higher level of psychic structural organization in which unconscious conflict between internal objects (which are represented entities) is a significant factor).[1]

---

1 See also Chapter 2.

DOI: 10.4324/9781003171331-9

However, Freud's deepening clinical experience – with problems presented by narcissism, trauma, unconscious guilt, negative therapeutic reactions and the various phenomena that he would categorize as lying "beyond the pleasure principle" (Freud, 1920) – led him to hypothesize the death instinct and propose his second topography, the so-called structural theory (Freud, 1923). While the North American ego psychologists emphasized the implications of the latter for defense analysis in the treatment of neuroses, Andre Green (2005a) explored its implications for the understanding and treatment of those conditions, mental states and diagnoses that lay beyond neurosis at or beyond the limits of what was once deemed to be classically "analyzable." In particular, Green noted that Freud's theoretical shift marked a change from a theory centered on psychic contents (ideational *representations*) to a theory about the movements needed to tame the unstructured, not yet represented aspects of *the drive* – that is, emotion, impulse and somatic discharge – within the psychic apparatus. Thus, the aim of analytic treatment shifted to, "Where Id was, there Ego shall be," with the important proviso that the drive now was not only a problem *for* the Ego but *within* the Ego.

Throughout this book, we have assumed that the capacity to create psychic representations has been seen not as a given, but as a developmental achievement. Its absence, weakness or failure can leave one at the mercy of "unrepresented states" (Levine et al., 2013) and "psychic voids" (Green, 2005a). These formulations challenge "the fundamental credo of psychoanalysis that psychological states are full of meaning" (Alvarez, 2019, p. 867) and imply that in many important instances, *meaning is something that is yet to be created* rather than uncovered or discovered.

Unrepresented states and psychic voids reflect registrations and events of the pre-verbal period, the sequelae of massive trauma and the deeper strata of the id. They are assumed to underlie and contribute to the diagnoses of autism and ASD, as well as other non-neurotic conditions, such as psychosomatic disorders, addictions, perversions and primitive character disorders. The affects that unrepresented states produce or are associated with are often those of terror, emptiness, annihilation and despair. As Alvarez (2019) has noted, to speak of "the unrepresented" offers a potentially new paradigm that "involves the inclusion of psychoanalytic inquiry and attention to the existence of empty meaningless states, and then to the question of their treatment" (p. 878).

Given the organization of the psyche – with an unstructured as well as a dynamic unconscious; with psychotic as well as neurotic parts of the mind; unintegrated as well as integrated areas; unrepresented areas of more or less "force without meaning" as well as represented states of specific ideas linked to affect – we should expect to find that to some degree, unrepresented and unintegrated states are universal and will exist and be encountered in all of us. Consequently, the opportunities and challenges presented by the understanding and treatment of autism and ASD may offer us metaphors and clues that may be relevant to aspects of the treatment of all patients, no matter what their dominant diagnoses may be.

## II

The idea that raw existential Experience begins with a pre-psychic or proto-psychic registration that does not yet qualify as being a psychic representation in Freud's sense of the term assumes that both drive movements and the products of perception begin as sensory events – raw "facts," somatic registrations or sensations – that must then be transformed in order to become representations and be made psychic. (Think here of Bion's (1962b) description of beta elements needing to be transformed by alpha function to become alpha elements in the construction of the mental apparatus and the containment of thoughts.) The results of that transformation (which includes the production of what Freud called "derivatives of the drive") will appear in one's mind and/or experience as either – or some combination of – affect, impulse to action, somatic discharge or representation. The latter, representation, is the potentially most "successful" end product of transformation and the most adaptive form of containment for what otherwise would be potentially disruptive excess excitation. (Think here of Freud's (1920) theory of trauma, which he defined as disruption of psychic regulatory processes, and sublimation, where the unruly and peremptory, potentially disruptive force and energy of the drive is harnessed, channeled and transformed into artistic or otherwise culturally valuable creations).[2]

As contemporary psychoanalysis has been working through the clinical significance of Freud's second topography, we have increasingly found ourselves considering the implications, results and need to remediate the effects of psychic *deficits* as well as conflicts. These have been understood as some combination of the failure of a necessary environmental provision on the part of the primary (maternal) object and/or a constitutional inability of the infant to make use of what for another child would be a "good enough" bit of mothering. Put another way, our attention has been turned to all that is pre- or proto-psychic; all that is emergent or still potential in development, unsaturated in regard to ideation and meaning, not yet fully formed and that requires dialogical and intersubjective containment and transformation in order to be "metabolized" and expressed. Here, the implications of Winnicott's famous dictum that "there is no such thing as an infant"[3] and Bion's theory of thinking (1962a), de-

---

2  See Chapter 7.
3  Discussion at a Scientific Meeting of the British Psycho-analytical Society, *circa* 1940. Referenced in Winnicott (1960a, p. 39, footnote 1).

scription of alpha function and container/contained (1962b) and his insistence that the development of the mind is a two-person creation are most relevant.

One consequence of this change in theory is that analysts have increasingly come to recognize the importance of understanding, formulating and learning to clinically catalyze the processes through which the self is vitalized, representations are formed and psychic regulatory processes are strengthened and created. As I have argued throughout this book, as they have done so, they have embarked on a change in emphasis – although *not* a move completely away from – the analysis of contents, that is, ideas and representations, a predominant focus on the recovery of repressed childhood memories, the healing of splits, the uncovering and discovering of hidden feelings, thoughts, phantasies and desires. We now find ourselves increasingly concerned with the problem of how to accomplish an analytic work that helps strengthen and sometimes even helps create for the first time, the development and/or strengthening of psychic capacities and processes that underlie and ensure the instruments for thinking, dreaming, emotional regulation and object relating.

The latter statement applies to some extent to all patients, but becomes increasingly relevant as we address the less organized, more primitive or archaic, more traumatized aspects of the patient's mind and experience. One of its clearest iterations appears in Winnicott's later work – for example his 1974 Fear of Breakdown paper – where he emphasizes that the analyst must unconsciously fail the patient – contribute to the production of an *actual* micro-trauma in the here-and-now – in the way in which the patient needs him to, so that an attenuated version of what once occurred prior to the formation of a constant and organized infantile self could then be experienced in the transference under the aegis of the patient's unconscious omnipotence and therefore "suffered" for the first time as personalized, subjective experience and worked through.

Analogous formulations are those of Pierre Marty (1980), one of the founders of the Paris Psychosomatic School, who insisted that somatic symptoms, unlike hysterical symptoms, were without psychic representation and inherent personal meaning. He viewed them as inherently opaque and asymbolic and suggested that they only acquired signification and unconscious "meaning" *après coup* in the course of an analytic treatment. Michel de M'Uzan (1984) spoke of patients that he called "slaves of quantity," because their symptoms were economic overload phenomena that occurred without unconscious motivational intent or symbolic meaning. And Jean Laplanche (1987) implied that there was an unrepresented, non-specific ideational component inherent in the untranslatable residue of unconsciously transmitted sexual desire that initiated the infant's psychosexuality in the "fundamental anthropological situation."

The point I wish to emphasize is that contemporary psychoanalysis has generated a number of theories of deficit (unrepresented states that require transformation in the service of psychic development, regulation and homeostasis) and assumed that deficits and voids can weaken and traumatize the psychic apparatus. These present clinicians with the challenge of how to deal with patients whose treatments do not conform to the expectations of classical analysis and may require modifications in theoretical understanding, listening stance and analytic technique.

With all of this in mind, I would like to now consider the questions of autism and autistic spectrum disorder and autistic enclaves, nuclei and defenses in otherwise non-autistic patients. This will lead us to the work of Frances Tustin (1986, 1992, 1993) and the many authors she has influenced.

## III

I would like us to begin by considering not the aetiology of autistic states and pathology, which I assume will vary and will entail some combination of constitutional and environmental factors, but the existential problems faced by autistic patients and their analysts. What is the psychic capacity and experience of self and other like for an infant or child that we will come to diagnose as being autistic or having an ASD? What is their capacity to engage in more normal developmentally facilitating relationships and activities and make use of the resources that their environment may afford them?

Perhaps it is axiomatic to begin by noting the oft encountered, weakened sense of the existence of other people and of one's own self in autistic and ASD patients and their impairments in vitality, object relating, symbolic capacity, language and imaginative play. Alvarez (2012) reminds us that faint or disordered signs of relatedness or object seeking may nonetheless be present in autism and early developmental disturbances: "even autistic children look for something without knowing what they are looking for, but recognize it when they get it" (p. 134). She further has learned that if this faint searching is recognized and responded to, it may be amplified:

> Regardless of aetiology, ... a disorder of the capacity for social interaction may require and benefit from a treatment which functions via the process of social interaction itself. Such a relationship will need to take account of the nature and severity of the psychopathology and the particular developmental level at which the non-autistic part of the child is functioning.
>
> (ibid., p. 167)

Another vital issue in these patients, one that lies at the root of all psychic development, is the question of how one deals with the inevitable emotions of frustration and pain. For the infant, such "dealing" requires and "involves the capacity for shared experience, and for making contact through interaction with the mind of another. Through this contact one begins to sense the possibilities opened by such shared experience with a live-minded subject" (Eaton, 2011, p. 41). But for some infants, this capacity for shared experience cannot be taken for granted. The object may be or may be felt to be inaccessible or unreachable, traumatic rather than containing. There may be an actual failure of environmental provision on the part of the object or some constitutional inability of the infant to make use of what is being offered.

Whatever the case, the infant may begin to withdraw from object contact or may never emerge from an inherently encapsulated, auto-sensuous state, discouraging his or her objects and setting in motion a series of responses and failures in development that lead to an autistic presentation. How do we understand the latter? To what extent is it a self-protective defense (a psychic retreat) or a quasi-reflexive biological, homeostatic reaction? What, if anything, lies behind the auto-sensuous world of the autistic infant? Is it a "bad object," a "no-thing" (Bion 1970) or a void? Does a bad object defend against a "no object"? And is a "no object" an object or a void? Does an unrepresented or unintegrated part lie behind the autistic part? (Alvarez, 2019).

Autistic maneuvers and defenses are often resorted to in the face of catastrophic fears of annihilation due to endless falling, spilling, tearing apart or tearing away. To what extent do these anxieties reflect organized unconscious phantasies? Or are they the affects associated with the individual's approach to the "black holes" and "voids" of unrepresented and unintegrated states?

Power (2017), following Tustin, summarizes the problem as follows:

> the infant fated to become autistic is exposed *prematurely*[4] to recognition of the mother as a physically separate object and because this recognition is experienced as developmentally premature (from the standpoint of the infant's experience) it is felt as a violent rupture of the physical intactness of the infant itself, opening a hole through which the infant's existence can pour out never-endingly. Tustin's image for this process, again from the infant's perspective, was that the removal of the nipple tore off with it the infant's mouth. That is to say, the shock of prematurely recognizing physical separateness

---

4   The extent to which this recognition is premature is determined by both constitutional hyper-reactivity and environmental factors.

(metaphorically, the removal of the nipple from the mouth and the physical space between infant and mother created by this action) is experienced by the infant *somato-psychically* (a physical tearing of the nascent self through which existence spills out). Part of the traumatic impact of this experience stems from what is *not* experienced—the infant fails to subjectively appropriate possession of an orifice with which it can, increasingly under its own control, regulate movements into and out of itself in congress with the object world.

Without this sense of voluntary closing and opening, but with a sense of traumatic injury instead, psychic emergency measures ensue aimed at plugging this "black hole". It is the objects and actions clung to and repeated as emergency measures and attempts at repair that Tustin called "autistic objects" and "autistic shapes." Both terms denote a *turning toward sensory experience as a means of blocking the wound and providing a seal to protect the endangered self.* Along with attempting to plug the black hole, these sensory preoccupations psychically obliterate the awareness of separateness and in this way they substitute for object relatedness rather than promote it. Thus, unlike transitional objects, autistic objects and autistic shapes do not facilitate a path toward object relations, but instead block or even erase this path. Said more simply, in Tustin's view the autistic object or shape substitutes for the object rather than fostering its gradual and tolerable recognition as separate, thus derailing the development of true object relatedness that would follow on from this evolving recognition. With respect to the object's absence, in these states faith in the object withers and hopes for its return vanish.

The process described by Tustin subverts the development of thought, representational capacities and symbolization, because it short-circuits the ability to recognize and tolerate the absence of the object and the frustration that accompanies this absence. There is no representation of an absent other, not even an hallucinated other; and consequently no mental evolution toward a capacity for bearing absence via recourse to phantasy and thought. In Winnicott's terms, there is no transitional space within which objects can be found/created. As others have pointed out this short-circuiting of the processes for thinking leads to a flattened psychic spatiality, a spatiality that tends toward the two dimensional and away from the growth of an internal space in which phantasy and thought can gestate. There is an atrophy of identificatory processes such that adhesive pseudo-relatedness dominates and mimicry and various forms of adopting physical/sensory aspects of the other are prominent.

(pp. xxi–xxii)

To this description, I would add a series of comments about what Alvarez has found necessary and useful in the treatment of children with autism,

ASD and various forms of borderline states, childhood psychoses and pervasive developmental disorders. As you read these descriptions, you may begin to consider how they apply to the incapacities and ego deficits of non-autistic adult patients. The common ground lies in the formulation of unrepresented states, inadequately developed regulatory capacities and the need to find ways to understand and catalyze previously thwarted vitality affects and essential ego development.

## IV

In one of her most quoted papers, Alvarez (2010) speaks about three conceptual levels of intervention:

- Level 1, most suited to work with neurosis, is the *explanatory level* – (why-because) – that offers alternative meanings.
- Level 2 is the *descriptive level* – ("whatness" – "isness," as in "You seem angry," or "That must have hurt!" etc.) – that enlarges meanings via description or amplification.
- Level 3 is an intensified, *vitalizing level* of *reclamation* – (Hey!) – that calls patients into contact and insists that something called "meaning" exists in life and between people.

It is the third level that offers analysts and therapists interpretive options and considerations that go beyond the uncovering of hidden, pre-existing meanings.

Autistic, ASD, borderline, psychotic and other patients who are "beyond neurosis" have limited ego capacity and can be too overwhelmed by despair or persecution to benefit from interpretations that seek to remove defenses against painful truths. Alvarez (2012) writes, "I learned that I needed to respond to, or even carry for them, their hopes and aspirations, and that such interventions need not encourage manic denial when thoughtfully applied" (p. 1). Put another way,

> long before certain patients process their hatred and find their capacity for love, they may have to develop the capacity to be interested in an object with some substantiality, life, or, in the case of perversion, strength and a capacity to excite in a non-perverse fashion.
> 
> (ibid., pp. 5–6)

With patients, who often dwell in states of dissociation, despairing apathy or deviant excitement, "the question arises of whether feelings or meanings matter at all" (ibid., p. 7). Objects may be experienced as "uninteresting, unvalued (not devalued), useless and possibly mindless" (ibid., p. 10). Addressing these difficulties will require work "at the foundations of mental and relational life" (ibid., p. 12) in order to treat "patients in affectless states of autism, dissociation or apathy following chronic despair" (ibid., p. 12) and neglect, patients who cannot listen or feel. At its extreme, these patients may demonstrate "a chronic apathy about relating, which goes beyond despair. Nothing is expected" (ibid., p. 13). Such patients may best be described as "undrawn" rather than "withdrawn." In their treatment, they "First.... need to be helped to be able to feel and to find meaning.... Then, feelings can begin to be identified and explored; eventually, explanations, which bring in additional, alternative meanings, may be heard and taken in" (ibid., p. 11).

In some non-neurotic patients,

> so-called 'defenses' were actually desperate attempts to *overcome* and *recover from* states of despair and terror. They carried, that is, elements of basic developmental needs: for protection, for preservation, a sense of urgency and potency, and even revenge and justice.
>
> (ibid., p. 78)

It was not enough to provide them with better object relational experiences in the analytic relationship. It was also necessary to point out that they like, need and wish for those experiences.

To some extent, feeling understood requires an expectation that such a thing as understanding exists in the mind of others and a sufficient number of experiences of having felt understood by another to make paying attention to the other to find out what they are thinking, feeling and noticing worthwhile. These are matters of experience and attention. However,

> Some children who have been rarely or never understood do not know what understanding is. The more advanced ones, when they first notice the therapist "understanding" them, often ask, "How did you know that? Are you a mind-reader?"
>
> (ibid., p. 151)

"Attention, ... before it can be held, sometimes has to be caught and elicited.... For alpha function to operate, the object has to be seen to be worth attending to in the first place" (ibid., p. 142). Consequently, Alvarez writes, "We have to find ways of helping these children to attend to us, and have to sustain their attention; ... emotionally heightened interest is central to this process" (ibid., p. 173). The analyst may have to provide something vitalizing and intensified to attract the patient's attention to the analyst as a live object, to up-regulate affect in the situation and to insist on meaning "calling the child into contact with an object, and also recalling ... [the child] to himself when there is a severe deficit in both the [child's] self and internal object" (ibid., p. 147).

Let me illustrate some of these issues with a brief clinical example.[5]

## V

In our first interviews and throughout most of his first year in three times per week analysis on the couch, Thomas dressed poorly in torn tee shirts, jeans and sandals, was barely audible and spoke endlessly about his fatigue, trouble establishing a basic routine of showers, tooth brushing, clothes washing and grocery shopping, difficulties regulating his sleep and eating patterns and so on. His speech was relatively two dimensional and flat and often evoked very little associational response. Although Thomas had been readmitted to college, he had neglected to register for courses or arrange living accommodations. So, in effect, he presented as "unregistered," isolated – the few friends he had made in his first year of college had all graduated and left the area – and virtually homeless. A good deal of our first sessions were spent with my "noticing" and talking with him about his situation, until he completed the necessary external, physical and administrative arrangements and became somewhat settled.

Thomas did not easily associate to a meaningful life history and could not generate a cause-and- effect narrative of his immediate circumstances or of what led to his flunking out of school. To what extent was this repression, suppression, defense or a weakness or absence of representation and an incapacity to produce and link thoughts into emotionally meaningful narratives?

The story that slowly emerged was that of divorced parents, whom he referred to by their first names rather than "mom" and "dad," and who he felt were remote, self-involved, inadequate as parents and paid little attention or gave little credence to his needs. He had an emotionally disturbed, dyslexic older brother, who could not adapt socially to the presence of other students at school and so was "home schooled" by mother when Thomas was about to enter the third grade.

At that point, Thomas was also removed from school and placed in home schooling "for the convenience of Michelle" (his mother), he bitterly told me. Eventually, I was able to inquire about and suggest to him that this removal isolated him from peers at a crucial period of his life – he did not keep contact or have play dates or other activities with his previous school friends – and contributed to his withdrawal and asocial tendencies,

---

5   Descriptions of this case also appeared in Levine (2020).

which included sleeping all day and staying up all night playing fantasy games on his computer. However, while such interpretations made sense to me, they seemed to mean little to Thomas and he did not elaborate on them in a more enlivened way or use them to deepen the analytic process.

A surprising feature of the first year of our work together was that Thomas was diligent about keeping appointments and always ended with a handshake. I did not comment on this, but noticed and silently wondered if he needed the concrete connection of physical touch to reaffirm something of our existence and contact; to know or signal that each of us was there.

Of course, in the first year, I tried to talk with him analytically about many things, including his present fears of not really being ready to resume school, his shame at being a much older student who had previously failed and his isolation, disappointment and bitter anger at his parents that seemed to extend to everyone and everything. Nothing seemed attractive or of real interest to him. While these interventions seemed to follow from the flow of his discourse, they did not seem to be of use to him and did not seem to deepen the process.

But I also sometimes took a more active role, when I felt he needed some concrete input or signs of being noticed and taken to be of interest by me as a potential object. For example, when his father was coming to town for a business meeting and expecting to spend the night in Thomas's dorm room – this would have displaced Thomas to an air mattress on the floor and disrupted his study schedule during exam week – I responded to Thomas's complaints – and my building countertransference irritation – by short-circuiting the more usual and expectable analytic exploration of his passivity, feelings and possible denial of anger, and so on and suggested he think about why he wasn't telling his father that this was not a convenient plan. Thomas responded by confronting his father and other, more adaptive arrangements were made.

Initially, ours was a very slow–going, deadened analytic encounter and I dealt, in part, with my restlessness or impatience with the thought that whatever else his dull recitation of sleep patterns, missed meals, unbrushed teeth, and so on might contain or imply in more classically defensive or object relational terms – for example, acting out his sense of worthlessness, identification with parental neglect, masochistic self-punishment and attack on his parents for their neglect and many other things – he was describing his trying and slowly succeeding in working out a better connection to his neglected body and working to some extent on repairing a form of body-mind dissociation (Lombardi, 2017). That is, in response to my noticing and attending, Thomas was noticing and attending to the fact of his own existence through recognition of basic bodily needs and functions.

One "fact" that persisted throughout this first year was his claim that no one at the university "interested him" or was worth trying to make friends or hang out with. Nothing in Boston was interesting enough to get him to leave his room. I say "fact," because "complaint" would imply that Thomas might hope, want or expect it to be otherwise. Although not constitutionally autistic like Alvarez's (2010) Robbie, Thomas seemed to have given up or else had collapsed into a miasmic state of withdrawal and collapse. Was he, perhaps, avoiding trying to make contact with anyone or anything, because he was so used to disappointment that he didn't believe anything else was possible for him and he didn't want to face further disappointment or had he simply given up on life and people in exhaustion and defeat?

Much to my surprise, despite the seeming emptiness of his life, inner and outer, Thomas passed his courses in his first semester and made Dean's List in his second. As he prepared for his summer break and the return to his mother's home out west – which did not include mentioning or feeling very much about the interruption of treatment and our relationship – he began to lament the fact that he would be isolated in a suburb without public transportation or his car, which he was leaving behind at school. I felt that this isolation would be a potential setback. He had begun to become interested in and excelled in one course, had been offered and accepted a small job doing research the next fall by that course's professor and had begun a project with a classmate and for the first time expressed looking forward to working with someone.

Feeling some urgency within myself at the possibility of Thomas's losing whatever small progress he had made, I expressed my surprise that he had not made plans ahead of time for something to do over the summer. I further asked why, if he had driven to school and was concerned about being shut in and isolated without his car over the summer, he wasn't driving it back home. As I did so, I had the image of a shoehorn levering a foot into a shoe and the thought of pushing a baby bird out of its nest so that it might begin to fly. He began to tell me about the trip East, how he had slept in his car, or in a sleeping bag under the stars, how it reminded him of camping out alone and on his own and how much he had once enjoyed that.

Somehow, this exchange sparked more positive feelings and a rush of associational life *in me*, as it brought to my mind memories of my own backcountry adventures out west. And I spontaneously asked if he had ever seen the big parks. He hadn't and I suggested that maybe, if he wanted to and felt comfortable, this could be an opportunity to take a more leisurely drive across country and visit some of them. He came back 2 days later and there was a palpable shift in his mood. He reported feeling excited and had done some research. He had downloaded and studied auto routes and hiking maps and decided that he would do it. Along with the decision to refuse his father and the beginning interest in the school course and project with the fellow student, this was one of the few manifest "signs of life" of our first year's work.

While it cannot be concretely demonstrated or "proven," what I wish to suggest is that the work with Thomas went on at multiple levels, one of which involved the inter-affectivity of our object relationship. That is, his desertification and need mobilized some urgency and alarm in my mind, spurred me into action and led me to the proactive intervention about his car. Thomas's response included associations about sleeping under the stars and these then triggered a cascade of memories and feelings in me about my backcountry travels. For a moment, my own endless – and often seemingly fruitless – "trekking in the desert of Thomas's analysis" was transformed in my mind – surely reactively, defensively as well as affirmatively – into the memory of camping with friends and more pleasant associations of hiking the American west. The fact that backcountry hiking was such a pleasurable memory for me must, in some way, have been communicated to Thomas in the emotion, cadence, music and tone of how I said what I said to him when I suggested he think about seeing the parks.

This surge of positive emotion in me seemed to have enlivened something in him. My hypothesis is that it was not only the semantic content of my intervention, the reasonableness of the idea of relying on his own car, but the concomitant emotions with which it came that helped jump start something in Thomas that in the larger context of our relationship and history took hold. That this was analogous to Miller's (2015) description of the need for the interested and pleasurable, emotional presence of the object that are presumed to unite with the infant's own somatic pleasure at being noticed, responded to, satisfied and cared for, in the process of creating and marking the first psychic representations.

Events in the second year of our work followed a similar trajectory where the affective presence of my interventions and interactions rather than their "analytic meaning" as content seemed to be what was key in providing a spark for orienting Thomas back to vitality and engagement with objects, the world and his own desires. Like the concrete warmth and touch of the handshake at the beginning and end of each session, the emotional quality and presence of my interventions seemed to be just as – and often more – important than the content of what was said.

By the second year of our work together, Thomas was a more enlivened and engaged patient. His speech was more discernible and emotionally inflected, his routine had become more regularized and he even began to date a girl he found interesting and attractive. He still had a tendency to lose track of himself and lapse into states of deep withdrawal, but our exchanges held more associational resonance and our work turned a bit more traditionally to the exploration of the cause and effect, object relational and emotional determinants of his ups and downs. For my part, however, I continued to allow my feelings to silently play free as I paid attention to what I felt at times was the need for me to affectively establish my presence as a noticing and involved object, allowing myself to use intuition, affect, curiosity, humor, and so on as some of the accompaniments of my analytic inquiry and interpretive presence. That is, I was aware of the need to be sure that I was as Alvarez said in relation to her patient, Robbie, "dense enough, substantial enough, condensed enough to attract his attention and concentrate his extremely flaccid mind."

Of course, unlike Robbie, Thomas was not autistic. But he was deeply disillusioned and withdrawn and the principle of how to reach and restart his emotional engagement in life presented the analysis with a similar kind of problem.

## VI

Returning to Power's (2017) essay we note that

> Non-neurotic states of mind and the mental processes that characterize them are of great interest for contemporary psychoanalysis. Weakened capacities to represent one's mental life, difficulties with symbolization, reliance on evacuation, erasure and foreclosure as well as other direct forms of discharge to manage psychic distress, and activation of annihilatory levels of anxiety, all present the practicing analyst with significant challenges in creating an analytic process, managing and maintaining an analytic frame, and dealing with the countertransference. Patients who present with these difficulties place great demands on the analyst to be a lively, engaging presence, to be flexible and spontaneous, to trust in and rely on reverie despite profound challenges to the analyst's own representational capacities, and to be willing to employ these capacities in the service of assisting patients' efforts to "weave psychic patches" in response to holes or tears in the psyche. The task nowadays is often one of helping to fill in psychic voids where representation of experience is absent or weak, and less often one of simply uncovering repressed, conflictually laden but symbolically represented content (Levine 2012; Mitrani, 1995; Roussillon, 2011).
>
> These difficulties, both conceptual and technical, are especially highlighted in psychoanalytic work with patients who demonstrate a variety of autistic disturbances, whether they are formally diagnosed as autistic or on the Asperger's Spectrum or described as manifesting autistic states or barriers (Klein, 1980; Tustin, 1986). Though the differences between these various types of clinical presentations may

be vast, important similarities arise from the fact that for each, *endogenous autosensuousness* (Tustin, 1992, p. 18) dominates mental life to an extent that mental development is endangered by the limit that sensory life places on the growth of subjectivity. Said slightly differently, in all these disorders sensory life becomes an obstacle to, rather than a springboard for, emotional growth and psychological development.

(pp. xv–xvi)

In *Learning From Experience*, Bion (1962b) asserted, "The problem presented by the psycho-analytic experience is the lack of any adequate terminology to describe it" (pp. 67–68). There is an uncertainty inherent in the infinite complexity of human development and personal relations that renders emotional truth fleeting: transient and always in transit (Bergstein, 2019, p. 4). Consequently, efforts to report or describe the *experience* of the psychoanalytic process, such as I have attempted to convey in this chapter, and the claims of psychoanalytic theories in general, inevitably challenge and may appear to fall short of our everyday views of causality and evidence. The latter are limited by and appear in a context of the three-dimensional perspective to which human consciousness is restricted, while the realm of psychic reality and the unconscious, especially the unrepresented, unrepressed and inaccessible unconscious, is multi-dimensional, perhaps infinitely dimensional (Bergstein, 2019; Bion, 1970).

Added to this fundamental limitation in the extent to which any of us may be able to come to know the domain of the psyche is an all too human foible that each of us shares. We tend to hate any limitations in what we can know and so create "explanations" that attempt to negate and deny the painful fact of our ignorance.[6]

I have tried to show how over and above any *content* related interpretations, the inter-affective, intersubjective responsiveness and vitality of the analyst seemed to play a key role in the reclamation (Alvarez, 2010) and reanimation of a deeply withdrawn, perhaps regressively un-drawn, desertified young man. The question of whether the kind of interventions described are analogous or identical to what has been proposed as essential environmental provision in the mother–infant relationship are moot and probably unanswerable.

So too the relationship between inter-affective reclamation and activation of the patient's psychic capacities for representation, symbolization, affective and associative linkage, objectalization and so on. The achievement and consolidation of each of these capacities has been described in various analytic theories as following from interactive, inter-affective and/or intersubjective relational experiences with primary objects. Each

---

6  See Chapter 3.

has been indicated as playing some role in the lifelong process of binding internal (e.g., drives and their derivatives) or external (e.g., perception and sensation) excitation and making sense of and creating meaning from one's own knowable experience. Bion's (1962b, 1970) description of alpha function and container/contained is but one of the many available theoretical formulations that attempts to put these processes into words.

In the case of Thomas, I would propose that the inter-affective and intersubjective stimulation afforded by *my* affect laden memories that underlay my question and suggestion about visiting the parks, memories that were probably defensive and self-restorative for me in the face of Thomas's barrenness and despair, as well as hopeful conveyors of my positive parental countertransference toward him, helped enliven Thomas and spark his own capacities for thinking, imagining and dreaming into action. Once his attention was attracted and the "pump" of his psychic apparatus had been thereby primed, his representational capacities could be said to have emerged or come back on line in the service of thinking through what a western trip and access to a car at home over the summer might be like for him. This restored capacity for "thought as trial action," a capacity that is heavily dependent on processes of representation and figurability, enabled him to do the research, think through the possibilities and make the actual decision to follow up on my suggestion.

The latter formulation is presented with full knowledge that it is a working – and I believe – workable – metaphor for what might take place and be helpful in an analytic interaction. As such, it is a construction or myth whose pragmatic value may or may not become apparent to other clinicians who read this based on their personal experience. My hope is that my description may remind some of you of real [analytic] life and how humans behave, the way a good play or novel might (Bion, 2005a, p. 2) and in doing so, may help you negotiate a useful path in a future encounter with a patient.

Chapter 9

# Word, body, thing
## On the movement from soma to psyche

> ...look at it from one side; there is a psycho-somatic complaint; turn it round; now it is soma-psychotic. It is the same... but what you see depends on which way you look at it"
>
> Bion (1976, p. 244)

## Defining the problem

How do we understand the body and its place in analytic theory and clinical practice? Freud linked the origin of the psyche and the birth of thought to the body, when he described how the desire for the breast in the face of hunger following the first successful feed initiated a process of hallucination (perceptual identity of the memory of the first feed) and the birth of reality testing (discrimination between perception and memory; reality and fantasy). Bion (1962b) postulated a proto-mental matrix in which the physical and mental were not yet differentiated and from which distress in either physical or mental forms could arise (pp. 101–104). Winnicott (1949) contended that "mind is ... a special case of the functioning of the psyche-soma" (p. 244). Especially at the beginning of life, "the psyche and the soma are not to be distinguished except according to the direction from which one is looking" (ibid., p. 244). Despite these formulations of mind-body unity, however, there is still a tendency for analysts to think, speak and function clinically as if they believed in a mind-body dualism.

In this chapter, I will argue that although frequently silent and often unrecognized, except for situations of extreme body-mind dissociation (Lombardi, 2017):

- The body is always tied to and present in regard to the psychic.
- Affect, emotions and impulse (actions) are the "red threads" that connect psyche and soma and continue to announce the presence of the body, as they inform, enrich, reflect and enliven cognition (ideation).

DOI: 10.4324/9781003171331-10

In this sense, in regard to the body, analysts are like Monsieur Jourdain in Molière's *Le Bourgeois Gentilhomme*, who desperately wanted to learn to speak prose and, much to his amazement, discovered that he had been doing so all along.

To illustrate the inevitable and inexorable connection between body and mind, I will examine "the word," reminding us that in addition to being a conveyer of ideational thought and semantic *meaning*, the spoken word is also a concrete physical entity, a packet of energy in the form of sound waves, and therefore a manifestation of the physical universe, of the body, a *thing*. Although we may more commonly think of the words that we speak – and the thoughts that they reflect – as that which is written on the message tied to the leg of the carrier pigeon, there is a sense in which it is as if the meaning or message of the words are inseparable from some qualities of the pigeon itself. Here, we may think of affect, volume, rhythm, tone and other "non-ideational" qualities of speech that reflect discharge and the bodily self, that reflect, transmit and induce emotion and that *act*, physically as well as semantically, on one's audience.

Seen from a biological vertex, the physical brain (body, soma) is the foundation of the mind. Brain supports psyche; but the word psyche is derived from the Greek word for *soul*. Perhaps what psychoanalysis offers us is a metapsychology of the soul. Not the soul of religious discourse, but the soulful (soul = *anima*), animated feeling of aliveness and meaningfulness that may be so painfully absent in today's patients: for example, Winnicott's (1960b) False Self, Green's (1980) Dead Mother Syndrome and the many manifestations of psychic void and unrepresented states (Levine et al., 2013) that lie beyond neurosis and that we now encounter in our consulting rooms.

Freud's (1895a) *Project for a Scientific Psychology* attempted to biologize psychological phenomena by using the (somatic) metaphor of the reflex arc and neuronal discharge to describe the management of excitation in and by the mind. In *Studies in Hysteria*, (Freud, 1895b), he reversed this strategy and gave us a way to understand the psychological determinants and meaning of certain physical acts and bodily disorders that had previously been thought of as only somatic symptoms and motoric discharge. Recall Emma's paralyzed arm or Dora's fingering her purse as she talked of her attraction to Herr K. Freud (1905c) interpreted the latter as Dora's unconsciously introducing the subject of her masturbation and commented that one's body and one's actions may well reveal what the mind cannot stand to be conscious of.

But this model of bodily "speech" and "memory" is only one side of the problem. It best relates to neurosis (hysteria) and that which is represented, symbolically linked, repressed and expressed as action, gesture and physical symptom. At the other end of the spectrum, "beyond neurosis," there is the economic problem of the unrepresented (Levine, 2012), in which a surplus of uncontainable emotion may erupt in affect storms, impulsive actions, perversions, addictions or somatic symptoms and the meaning of the eruption is only acquired secondarily, *après coup* [see De M'Uzan's (1984) "slaves of quantity," Marty et al.'s (1962) work on psychosomatics or my own work on unrepresented states (e.g., Levine, 2012; Chapters 2–4)].

## Emotion and affect – The body as fundamental to the mind

Given what we know from the neurosciences and other branches of biology, there is little doubt that thinking and the mind (psyche) are anchored in and dependent on the presence and functioning of the brain (soma). In psychoanalysis and the various psychologies, this relationship seems always to be in danger of being lost sight of. When we think of "thoughts" or "cognitive psychology," we may (mistakenly) assume something split off or separate from "feelings" or "affect." In so doing, we drive an artificial wedge between psyche and soma. To help avoid this inadvertent – and often unwarranted split – it may be useful to consider "emotions" from a psychoanalytic vertex.

Bion (1970) reminds us that "… what takes place in the consulting-room is an *emotional* situation" (p. 118, italics added). In *Learning From Experience*, he classifies the emotions as beta-elements, referring to them as "objects of sense" and placing them in a parallel position to that of other *sense impressions* (Bion, 1962b, p. 6). In so doing, he simultaneously disqualifies at least some part of "emotions" as *psychic* elements – beta-elements cannot be thought with or thought about – even as he locates another part of emotions in the domain of **K**: something that can be known (felt) and therefore experienced. Consequently, in describing affective life and experience, we need a term that can encompass something that is a psychic experience with a potentially knowable part, but is rooted in bodily sensations and in a level of inscription that is beyond sensation, full ideational saturation or accessible conscious awareness.

Aulagnier (2015) has called emotions "the visible part of the iceberg which is affect, …. a lived experience" (p. 1378). Building on this, I have suggested using the term *feelings* for the visible part or the iceberg and the term *affect* for the totality (see Chapter 4). In doing so, I wish to remind us that in regard to the domain of feelings, there is continuity between what we can experience and know (emotions; Bion's **K**), what is emergent and therefore not yet known although perhaps potentially accessible at some future time and what is and may remain ineffable and unknowable (Bion's **O**). According to this definition, the deepest part of the iceberg we call affect, is somatic; of the body; not yet named, not fully nameable (i.e., inscribed but psychically unrepresented). Our emotions demarcate and reflect something that forms a continuous bridge between soma and psyche, body and mind.

The story, however, is even more complex, because it cannot be fully told without considering our objects. Jacques Press (2016) writes,

> … affect always forms a complex network that directly or indirectly involves both the individual's representational system and his object and body, and cannot be described other than in the context of this network.
>
> (p. 99)

This view, that there is *a network of affect linking ideation, object and body*, concurs with that of Aulagnier (2015), who described the impact of emotion and affect on the body of *both* subject and object.

> Emotion [reflects and] modifies the somatic state, and it is these perceivable somatic bodily signs that move the person who witnesses them, triggering a similar modification in his or her own soma … Emotion thus makes two bodies resonate with each other and imposes similar responses on them. The body of one person responds to the body of the other, but as emotion concerns the I [self], one can also say that the latter is *moved by what the body allows it to know and to share of the other person's bodily experience*.
>
> (p. 1379, italics added)

Emotions are continually in the background of our analytic explorations and considerations. At times, they may be lost sight of as a subject in their own right, because they can be subsumed by and appear to form an almost indissoluble ensemble with "thoughts" or "ideas." Except under the most extreme conditions (psychosis and evacuative activities of the psychotic portion of the mind), when we speak of "thoughts," we understand them to be *ideas invested with emotions*. Thus, the contrast between what I (Levine, 2010b) have called "true thoughts" – that is, ideas invested with affect and meaning – and something that may superficially look and sound like thoughts, but are actually fragments, bizarre objects or other forms of "debris" that are better categorized as imitations of human speech.[1]

I think it safe to say that it is impossible to try to conceive of the development or moment-to-moment functioning of the psyche without taking note of its connection to the body, one's own and that of one's objects.

## The primal

Shakespeare famously asked, "What's in a word?" He also said, "A rose by any other *name* smells as sweet." Freud (1915a) said that words ("word

---

1  See, for example, Paul (1977) and Eekhoff (2019).

presentations") were essential in transforming "thing presentations" and saturating their meaning, so that what begins as vague somatic (sensorial) turbulence and disturbances (drives) can acquire ideational specificity, saturation and achieve a level of consciousness. The theory of representation (Chapter 2) links the ability to use words to name and thereby symbolize the absent or otherwise frustrating object to the capacity for thought and reality testing.

But Freud also talked about thought, which is dependent on the anchoring of words – word presentation "taming" and giving shape to thing presentation – as trial *action*. The work of Klein, Segal, Bion and others has added to our understanding of the word as thing, concrete object or symbolic equation. At this level, words may be used as an instrument of evacuation, concrete attack or other means – not of communicating, persuading, convincing or influencing – but of *doing to* one's self or objects, in fantasy or reality.

The foregoing descriptions imply the existence of psychic space and the unfolding of unconscious fantasy. But in order to consider the dual status of the word, it is necessary for us to imagine the impact of the word at a time of development prior to the creation of psychic space, before fantasy,[2] before objects have been securely recognized as separate from the self. This is the developmental epoch that Aulagnier (2015) has called *the primal*, in which experience that is registered or inscribed, even if it is caused by the external object, is felt as if it was "not of an object but of changes in bodily states… [that are taking place in] a self-referencing psyche" (Flanders, 2015, p. 1407). (In contrast, the *primary* is the next stage, in which self-object differentiation allows for recognition of the object and therefore unconscious fantasy scenarios).

At this earliest stage, "there is something much more embryonic in the unconscious than the word; …. a mixture of [bodily sensations that reflect] drive representations, memory traces and thing presentations" (Flanders, 2015, p. 1405). This is the period in which sensoriality (the somatic) first brings to life or activates the infant's psychic apparatus (Aulagnier, 2015, p. 1384).

Initially, for the infant, "the object only exists psychically by virtue of its unique power to modify the sensory (and thus somatic) response, and thereby to act on psychic experience" (Aulagnier, 2015, p. 1384). This means that in the first encounters, the induced somatic effects of that encounter stand in for and mark the place of that encounter.[3]

---

2 Traditional Kleinians may object to the idea that there might be a time "before fantasy," but this is a discussion for another occasion.
3 Could this be what Melanie Klein (1957, p. 180, fn. 1) referred to as "memories in feeling"?

> A bodily feeling occupies the place that will later be occupied by the mother: the anticipated I thus has its counterpart in an 'anticipated mother' through a bodily feeling.
>
> Aulagnier (2015, p. 1385)

Applied to words and speech, Aulagnier (2015) offers that

> "The first psychical ear does not pick up sounds and even less significations: it picks up the variations of its own state, of its own felt experience" (p. 1385) as these are influenced by the actions of its caretakers.

Expanding on this description, Patrick Miller (2015) gives us the foundations of a theory of unconscious affect transmission and inter-affectivity that is relevant throughout the life cycle:

> In the primal dimension there must be first a pleasure of hearing (*plaisir d'ouïr*) which is only connected to the sensory quality of what is audible, and not to the semantic meaning of the sounds carried by the voice. This essential cathecting to a pleasure of hearing must precede the pleasure and desire of listening, and renders them possible. The pleasure of listening belongs to the primary dimension where the psychic production is the phantasy. The sound is then a sign of the presence or absence of the object.
>
> (p. 1363)

It is only after self-object differentiation has become more secure that "there is, apres-coup, the linking [of this sensory dimension of feeling caused by interaction with the object] with word presentations in the preconscious and conscious mind" (Flanders, 2015, p. 1405). Thus, for Aulagnier, language and fantasy are separate from – and develop subsequent to – the primal. The latter appears first – or perhaps in parallel with the primary – is sensorial, of the body, and *will persist as a fundamental level of experience throughout life.*

Developmentally speaking, primal experience (sensori-motor) also precedes the creation of psychic space. Once self-object differentiation is secure and psychic space develops, then meaning can be known by its verbal, semantic and communicative referents. Prior to that, and then on-going, unconsciously throughout one's life, *meaning is conveyed and constructed affectively through the quality of shared bodily experiences within a topography implying the blurring of body boundaries.*

With this as background, let us look more closely at the singular word and what it is capable of generating.

## The generative word[4]

Each spoken word is a physical entity, *of the body*, a packet of sound waves and energy created by a physical act, concrete and thing-like, a "sound envelope in which the affective world of feelings, colours, smells and flavours is inscribed, and is put across since the earliest communications" (Panizza, 2016, p. 12). As conveyor of affect, or as act or action, the spoken word may function as an enigmatic signifier, an irritant in need of translation. The spoken word as physical event or presentation is capable of producing an evocative impact on the listener that may sometimes be linked to its manifest communicative content, but often reaches above and beyond its semantic meaning. This sense of the word is the flesh and blood "carrier pigeon" that holds the semantic message written on the slip of paper tied to its foot.

Thus, Panizza (2016) writes that words can produce "an emotional effect that resonates both in the speaker and listener, favoring the evocative function of language, rather than its explicative, informative or discursive aims" (p. 1). The means of doing so include the various physical qualities of speech – tone of voice, prosody, rhythm, musicality, and so on – that invest the words used over and above their semantic meaning and add affective and sensorial elements to conceptual speech.

> The singular word ... is a bridge to sensoriality and feelings. Its sound can instantly capture visual and tactile sensations and emotions such as laughter, tears, pain, compassion, as though it travelled the scale of symbolization backwards, towards sensory semiosis and emotional experience.
>
> Panizza (2016, p. 3)

Rather than causing regression, the singular word "opens up a parallel universe to the symbolic order ... where the non-verbal, the pre-verbal and emotion coexist intertwined" (Panizza, 2016, p. 3). This parallel universe, of the emergent, not yet represented and repressed, co-exists with the realm of semantic signification, sometimes reinforcing the message of the latter, sometimes contradicting it, sometimes introducing an entirely different quality or feeling to the manifest semantic meaning of the message.

As speech *act*, words originate in and reflect the physical body. They are,

> created by the vocal chords, which articulate them, the mouth openings which shape them, and the encounter with the external world and the intersubjective context, which gives them their ultimate

---

4  I am indebted to Sandro Panizza (2016) for this designation.

> meaning.... [W]ords are metabolized in the journey from body to society, and acquire their expressive, somatic and relational capacities, all together, along the way. Such an intimate blend that hinges between body, mind, and the relationship with the world, supports the hypothesis that the origin of the word is located at the border between the somatic and the psychic and points to an 'incorporated [i.e., embodied] mind'.
>
> Panizza (2016, p. 4)

The more abstract the word becomes, and the more it is strung in a conceptual chain, the further away it may seem to move from its original sensory-motor base, to reach a complex logical elaboration. However, no matter how complexly embedded in a communicative and discursive message, each word also retains and adheres to its origins as a physical entity with a direct, immediate sensorial and emotional impact. This impact, along with the *semantic meaning* of the word is responsible for its evocative function.

In analysis, in relation to the patient's free association and the analyst's internal reveries and interpretations,

> The evocative word ... releases visual images, feelings, sensations and memories of a Proustian nature ..., calls the speaker [and the listener] to the immediate present, at times almost catching him or her by surprise. The subject who meditates on the words he or she is speaking (I. Illich 1993) is inevitably placed immediately in the here and now of the session, while also calling the listener to inhabit the same present moment.
>
> Panizza (2016, p. 17)

Whereas the logical syntax of the intended interpretation usually "organizes the "state of affairs," the internal events, in a coherent shape... [and] creates a reliable and orderly syntax among the chaotic assemblage of "affairs" in the mind [establishing] unifying links ... between past experiences and their present reverberations" (Panizza, 2016, p. 1), each "singular word ... may release, within the patient, in a direct, condensed and almost analogical manner, a world of meanings, affects and sensations" (pp. 1–2). While the syntactical message of the interpretation moves toward the unwinding of diachronic linkages, the physicality (*presentation*) of the word tends toward synchronic condensation.

From the infant observational perspective, developmental research confirms the extent to which the physical and emotional qualities of parental speech, the prosody rather than the semantics, convey affective meaning that is understood and responded to by the pre-verbal infant. This is an emotional, concrete and thing-like (thing-in-itself) dimension of speech and relationship that will silently persist throughout one's life and continue to inhere in, beneath and through the more manifest lexical dimensions of all relational contact and verbal discourse.

Lyotard (1993) refers to this elusive, untranslatable core as an "affect-trace," something that lies "beneath articulation" (Kahn, 2018, p. 61) of the semantic meaning of the spoken word, a "state of the soul inhabited by something to which no answer is given" (Lyotard, 1993, p. 149).[5] Similarly, Derrida (1978) speaks of an "illegible legibility," an "energetic inscription," that is "[present] on every occasion, ... that dwells in speech while evading it" (p. 259). What both writers allude to is a mute and untranslatable energy that inheres in the very emotional essence of the speech *act* "and opposes at once the topography of translation and the notion of a dialogic message" (Kahn, 2018, p. 59).

Vivona (2019) has described how infant-directed speech[6] "has unique acoustic, affective, and linguistic qualities that facilitate infant understanding" (p. 693). She further notes that "parents use affective prosody to assist infants in regulating emotion and arousal during the first months of life" upregulating or down-regulating their infant's emotional state, signaling approval or disapproval, encouragement or disapproval, and so on (pp. 693–694).

Thus, long before infants are capable of understanding the semantic meaning of words, they are capable of understanding and have been acculturated to respond to the signal contents of emotion that is contained in and conveyed by the physical qualities of words that are directed to them by significant caretaking objects. When parents speak to infants, "the melody is the message" (Fernald, 1989, quoted in Vivona, 2019, p. 694) and we continue to "serenade" each other with these melodies as we speak throughout our lives.

To illustrate, in the early stages of the treatment of a very young 2- to 3-year-old probably autistic-psychotic boy, the analyst's cooing and sing-song interpretations that named and described what was going on in the session or potentially in the child's feelings probably did not act as lexical

---

5   For Lyotard, according to Kahn (2018), the meaning of the affect-phrase cannot be fully encompassed by what we call "emotions" or "the passions." These are later developmental accomplishments. The affect-phrase makes its presence known without representation; it "only signals to us that 'there is *something*' without us knowing 'what it is'.... [I]t is the infantile voice making itself heard, out of time" (p. 63).

6   "Relative to adult-directed speech, infant-directed speech has higher pitch, wider range of pitch, distinctive pitch contours, elongated vowel sounds, and greater articulation of vowels and consonants; speech is slower with shorter utterances and longer pauses ... Affectively, infant-directed speech typically conveys positive emotion and effectively engages infants' attention .... [Its] unique prosody infuses singing to infants as well as speaking" (Vivona, 2019, p. 693).

interpretations by virtue of the *meaning* of her words. Rather, they initially formed a "sound envelope" that offered soothing relief by upregulating and downregulating the child's emotional state and signaling the object's attention, presence and responsiveness. They helped construct a bridge to both object relations and autonomous self-soothing through the offer of a repeatedly available "soft autistic shape" (Tustin, 1992) with which the child could soothe and regulate himself. The contents of the words – the semantic meaning of the interpretation – did not yet gain "sense," but the affective, emotive (physical) presence and availability of the sound did. It is probable that the concrete physicality and emotional tone of the words rather than their meaning was building an initial bridge of relatedness to the object and to the child's own mind and feelings by offering first an autistic defense and then a nominating presence in the transitional space of their intersubjective relationship to what will eventually develop into a true object relationship.

## Summary

"Psychoanalysis has consistently maintained the centrality of the body in the development of mental functioning" (Lombardi, 2008, p. 91). There is a fundamental connection and rootedness of the mind in the body. Winnicott (1964) believed that there is an "inherited tendency of each individual to achieve a unity of the psyche and soma" (p. 112) and Press (2016) offered a similar argument: "[T]he psychesoma is at one and the same time a given – we are born with it – and the product of a construction that takes place in the course of development" (p. 93). It does not make sense for us to try to conceive of thought as an abstract entity, removed from physical and affective reality, except in the most developmentally askew conditions of hyper-intellectualization.

Freud viewed the drives as the lynchpin between body and mind and described the arc of the process of achieving representation through which somatic disturbance becomes the stimulus for representation and the foundation for the emergence of thought. Bion (1962b) viewed the somatic, sensory realm (sense impressions; beta-elements) as the origin of all abstract manifestation of thought (based on alpha elements) and later described "the body as the repository of a germinal element that can give rise to new thought which has never been thought before" (Lombardi, 2008, p. 92).

I have tried to describe and elaborate on these formulations, emphasizing the central role of affect and emotion in tying together the psychic and somatic and further illustrating the inexorable connection between mind and body by describing the dual status of the word as physical, corporeal entity and conveyer of semantic meaning.

# Chapter 10

# Psychosomatics and unrepresented states

> There are no psychosomatic illnesses: the human being, by definition, is a psychosomatic unity.
>
> Aisenstein (2017, p. 76)

## I

Psychosomatics offers psychoanalysts a rich opportunity for a deeply thoughtful explication of the vicissitudes of the processes and failures of psychic transformation, representation, symbolization, recollection, memory and subjectivization. It is a perspective from which to view the emergence and evolution of psychic regulatory processes, the formation of the self and the difficulties of development caused by trauma and environmental (object-relational) mis-attunement and failure. While psychosomatics is a worthy object of exploration in its own right, like autism and autistic defenses,[1] much of what it can reveal will have implications for the understanding and treatment of the entire range of non-neurotic pathologies that lie "beyond the pleasure principle" at the limits of analyzability.

Despite these potential opportunities, psychoanalytic psychosomatics in North America has had a problematic history and in many places seems to have fallen into disrepute. Following Freud's (1895b) initial discovery that seemingly somatic, hysterical symptoms had symbolic, psychic, unconscious meaning, a discovery whose significance and impact we cannot underestimate, an overly optimistic expectation grew in many quarters that many, if not all, somatic disorders, or at least those that became identified as the "classic psychosomatic" illnesses, such as high blood pressure, hyperthyroidism, migraine headaches, asthma, ulcerative colitis, gastric ulcers, and certain dermatological conditions, would be found to have an underlying primary, symbolic, conflictual basis and meaning.

---

1 Chapter 8.

This line of reasoning, often referred to as *primary symbolism,* was central to Ferenczi's hypotheses (1926) about a group of disorders he termed the *organ neuroses*:

> Many frequently occurring illnesses are mentally determined though they consist of real disturbances of the normal functioning of one or more physical organs. They are called organ neuroses. The fact that they involve objective as well as subjective disturbances differentiates them from hysteria, though it is not possible to draw a sharp dividing line between them and hysteria on the one hand and a number of organic diseases on the other.
>
> (p. 22)

The disturbances that Ferenczi referred to could be functional (e.g., various forms of dysregulation, as in bowel or bronchial spasms or excess secretion of gastric juices) or could extend to produce or involve actual tissue pathology (e.g., ulcerations, fibrosis). While there has been considerable debate over the years about the extent to which these disorders might potentially be reversed with successful analytic treatment – the functional disorders sometimes being seen as more amenable to analytic address than the others – as with the purely psychogenic hysterias, both categories of illness were often *initially* assumed to be amenable to analytic exploration, interpretation and treatment in a process analogous to the analysis of dreams.

In the background of Ferenczi's hypothesis was Freud's notion of the *actual neuroses*.[2] This was the basis for a second related line of psychosomatic reasoning, that of Franz Alexander (1950) and the Chicago School, which was prominent in the middle of the last century, a period that in retrospect might be call the overly optimistic heyday of psychosomatics in North America.

Alexander proposed that the central pathogenic mechanism behind the psychosomatic disorders was a disruption or dysfunction in the pathway of transformation and discharge of an emotion or group of emotions. Chronic arousal without "proper" discharge was assumed to produce "organ neuroses." The latter were believed to be conditions akin to a "damming up" or retrograde flow of emotion – or the energy or tension that underlies or accompanies emotion – into the autonomic nervous system resulting in a discharge into internal organs along either sympathetic or parasympathetic pathways. Since the organs of the sympathetic nervous system prepare us

---

2   Smadja (2010) offers a contemporary definition of the latter as "a psychical organization … accompanied clinically by disturbances of a depressive and anxious nature and by diverse somatic disturbances affecting different organs, which are akin to what doctors refer to as functional disorders" (p. 149).

for fight or flight, it was proposed that they would be affected by failure to properly regulate and discharge the emotions that followed from hostile and aggressive emotions. Similarly, discharge into the organs involved in the parasympathetic pathways were assumed to be associated with emotions and conflicts related to dependency and the search for security and attachment.[3]

While Alexander's theory made no claim for a specific symbolic meaning to the somatic symptom or dysfunctional somatic state (Taylor, 2010, p. 183), his attempt to link each general category of these somatic disorders to an a priori designated constellation of emotions, such as hostile-aggressive or dependent security-seeking, led to an implication if not an expectation that conflicts within these broad subgroups would be discovered in every patient who presented with one of the associated physical disturbances. This opened up the potential to search for and expect to discover a kind of one-to-one correspondence or informal "universal symbolism" associated with each category of disorder. Thus, asthma, for example, was often spoken of as "the body's expression of the stifled cry and tears of the infant for the mother" (Peter Knapp, 1974, personal communication).

A complicating factor that Alexander's theory failed to take sufficiently into consideration was that "bodily symptoms can become secondarily linked with fantasies and affects and, therefore, appear to give a somatic disease symbolic meaning" (Taylor, 2010, p. 183). Another was the possible existence of "mixed neuroses," a concept first proposed by Freud (1895a) in the Project and elaborated by Rappaport de Aisemberg (2010):

> the concept of mixed neurosis. [...] refers to the simultaneous presence of two diverse functionings: one is associated with somatic sexual excitation, as in anxiety neurosis, while the other refers to psychic excitation, as in hysteria. So, there coexists in the same subject a psychoneurotic organization and a somatic one, with a deficit in the psychic linkage [between the two.]
> 
> (p. 115)

These hybrid situations only added to confusion about the etiology and underlying structure of psychosomatic conditions and to the eventual disillusionment that followed from the inability of analysts to understand and effectively treat these disorders. By the 1970s and 1980s, the latter had become so much the case in the United States that psychosomatics became relatively marginalized and neglected in our training programs and as a subject of analytic study. My exploration of representation and its vicissitudes have allowed me to clinically reintegrate psychosomatics and somatization for myself – and perhaps for others – into a more consistent and clinically effective psychoanalytic perspective.

---

3 For more detailed discussion, see Smadja (2010), especially pp. 149–151, and Taylor (2010), pp. 182–183.

## II

Throughout this book, we have been concerned with the movement – or failure of movement – from soma to psyche, from pure force (drive) to meaning, from proto-psychic to psychic and from unrepresented to represented states. In Chapter 9, I have argued in favor of a psychosomatic unity that is reflected in the unifying force of affect and emotion. In this sense, the very field of psychoanalysis is inherently 'psychosomatic.'

This is a theme that runs, often silently, throughout the work of Freud. Despite revisions to his metapsychology, he maintained the view that working through (*Durcharbeiten*), in development and in the analytic process, involves "the transformation of somatic energy into a psychic quality" (Aisenstein, 2017, p. 24) followed by the elaborative growth of associative pathways. This transformation and growth are at the heart of the demand for work made on the mind by the drives.[4] Drives originate in the soma and reach the psyche, where they are the source of the "chaos full of energy … without organization or general willing" (Aisenstein, 2017, p. 59) that constitutes the deepest strata of the id (Freud, 1923).

As derivatives of the drive become psychic, they may assume one of three different forms: ideas (representations), affects (emotions) or impulses toward action (Green, 1975, 2005a). It is a matter of definition whether or not one adds somatic discharge as a fourth category of expression or consigns somatization to being a secondary derivative of affect and action that moves away from psychic containment and expression by ideational representation. It is also an open question – although one of great clinical importance – as to whether in any given instance somatic discharge is assumed to have symbolic or semiotic significance or is seen as a blind evacuation and "economic" overflow phenomenon. Still other possibilities are that somatization reflects an attempt to seek a non-psychical "place" of containment for an explosive, annihilating, infinitizing pressure or a protection against a psychotic collapse.

This spectrum of possibilities defines both the conceptual problematics and the potential clinical richness of studying somatic discharge and psychosomatic disease. Is somatic illness a manifestation of the "speechless mind" or the "communicating body?" Does it have inherent symbolic or semiological meaning or does it arise from an impoverishment of the psyche? To what extent is it a form of communication through or by the body?[5] When meanings of somatic symptoms arise in the course of anal-

---

4   To this, Bion (1962b, 1970) added the need to perform the work of transformation (alpha function) and elaboration (container/contained; apparatus for thinking thoughts) on the raw sensorial facts of perception and existence, so as to create personal meaning and furnish the building blocks of one's unique subjective idiom and identity.
5   For extended discussions of these and other related questions, see Press et al. (2019).

ysis, are they uncovered or constructed? And if constructed, to whom do they belong? Analyst? Patient? The Field?

How we conceptualize and understand somatization will influence the direction of our clinical attitudes and interventions. The Paris School (e.g., Marty, Fain, de M'Uzan, Aisenberg, Smadja) assumes that the somatic symptom is "dumb" and initially neither symbolizes nor possesses a symbolic value, although it may acquire one secondarily, *après coup*. In contrast, Kleinians (e.g., C. Bronstein, N. Temple) view somatic illness as a projection of primitive phantasies into the physical body. McDougall (1989) argued that somatic symptoms were a kind of archaic hysteria, and possessed an inherent meaning related to psychic survival of the self rather than to sexuality. Mitscherlich (1966) suggested somatic illness resulted from a process of repression that took place in two phases: from the conscious to the unconscious and then from the unconscious to the soma (pp. 2–3). In the terms that we have been using, the latter might be restated as a move from the dynamic to the unstructured unconscious.

Another possibility, offered by Winnicott (1964) is that somatic dysfunction is a last ditch, desperate "defence organization that splits environmental provision separating physical care from intellectual understanding and "psyche-care from soma-care" (p. 103). For Winnicott, "the illness in psycho-somatic disorder is not the clinical state expressed in terms of somatic pathology or pathological functioning (colitis, asthma, chronic eczema). It is the persistence of a split in the patients' ego-organisation, or of multiple dissociations" (p. 103).

Looked at from still another perspective, "Somatic outcomes are … attempts – presumably last ditch attempts – to mobilize a reparative aim in 'another', whose value as an object is at the relevant time imperceptible and uncertain" (Aisenstein, 2017 p. 90). Although this formulation does not directly reference Bion (1962b, 1970), it is very much in line with the logical conclusion of his formulations of the communicative aspect of projective identification and the mode of unconscious appeal and communication – that is, the induction of emotion in the object – employed in the presence of beta screens by the psychotic part of the mind.[6]

Psychosomatic patients often suffer from what Marty and de M'Uzan (1963) called "essential depression." In contrast to melancholia, this is a depression without pain, without conflict, without guilt. It is marked by a generalized lowering of vitality and libidinal drive often accompanied by fatigue or over-activity of a kind that does not enhance self-esteem. Patients may present with the seemingly paradoxical picture of affect suppression along with emotional excess and little qualification or

---

6 See also Roussillon's (2011) description of the signal function of the drive and my description of the Representational Imperative (Levine, 2012).

differentiation of sensorial pain into specific, object and fantasy related affect states linked to verbalizable psychic conflicts. It is often in the subjectivity and counter-transference of the analyst that differentiated affects and plausibly related fantasies are apt to first appear.

The quality of the anxiety of psychosomatic patients may be different from that of patients with a neurotic psychic organization. Force, discharge and evacuation take precedence over meaning and psychic elaboration. Anxiety is often diffuse, empty, devoid of or disconnected from ideational representation or associative connections. Thus, the sensations produced by the raw impulse of drive derivative discharge must be distinguished from the satisfaction of the neurotic patient's more organized and developed capacity for desire.

In assessing and engaging somatic discharge, it is important to note that somatizing patients may be able to *sensorially* feel things in their body, but may have no – or limited – words with which to *emotionally* describe and express what they feel (alexithymia). The somatic sensations that they do take note of may not be enriched with meaning by virtue of carrying intrinsic symbolic value or being associatively linked to chains of ideas or other feeling states. The discourse of these patients is often concrete, factual (hyper-cathexis of reality) and without metaphors or ties to fantasy activity or symbolization (Aisenstein, 2017, p. 128).

In regard to the analytic process, these patients lack the capacity for *transference onto words* (Green, 2000b, 2005b) and their "conversion of the psychic apparatus towards language cannot be taken for granted" (Aisenstein, 2017, p. 69). "It is only after the transposition into language that the space of polysemy … [and symbolic connection between word and wish and bodily sensation] can open up" (ibid., p.68). Prior to that development, lifeless, empty and two-dimensional speech may evoke a rather flat and uncreative counter-response in the mind and emotions of the analyst.[7] Consequently, attending to a patient's discourse as symbolically linked free associations and commenting on its presumed meanings as one would in the treatment of a neurotic patient often proves futile.

Rather than free associations that are unconsciously and associatively linked, the discourse of psychosomatic patients is often an imitative, pseudo-speech, an evacuative discharge of word fragments and bizarre objects (Bion, 1970) that lacks the connections and symbolic underpinnings that give evocative resonance, emotional meaning and access to a lively unconscious and

---

7 "When faced with exiguous and arid material which evokes little response in us but induces us to associate for two people, to elaborate from the signal anxiety aroused in the analyst and to construct theories and tell ourselves stories, the only course is to wait and see, listening in a manner in tune with the "anticipatory illusion" (Aisenstein, 2017, p. 92).

subjective inner life. Such a discourse is often a massive, phobic avoidance of potential emotions. And yet, paradoxically, at the same time, somatization may be an unconscious, mute call for intersubjective help in resolving the psychic regulatory problems with which these patients struggle.

Although there is general agreement that the genesis of somatic and psychosomatic illnesses is multi-factorial,[8] there seems to be a convergence of thinking around the view that early trauma, failure of maternal receptivity or other forms of impingement and mis-attunement beginning in the pre-verbal period of infancy and continuing ongoing, may prove to be predisposing or associated factors. These tend to disrupt the formation and development of the mechanisms governing psychosomatic equilibrium.

Traumatic maternal failure leads to obligatory self-holding maneuvers, compulsive hyperactivity enforced by an unappeasable super-ego and "persistence of an omnipotent self that does not allow independent objects to exist" (Press et al., 2019, p. 53). Such patients may live under the constant pressure of the need to escape from a "dead" or "empty" object and/or disentangle themselves from an intrusive maternal imago, while simultaneously unconsciously seeking and defending against a fusional symbiosis (Press et al, 2019). They may struggle with the unconscious internal threat and fear of breakdown (Winnicott, 1974) "that goes back to infancy, and because the patient has been unable to construct a reliable internal object to lean upon" (Press et al., 2019, p. 39).

At the heart of the analytic treatment of psychosomatic patients lies the inevitable encounter with the vicissitudes of the processes and failures of psychic representation, mentalization, symbolization, and subjectivization, processes through which the self (and the subjective meaning and meaningfulness of one's personal existence) may either be constructed or have its creation and development impeded by trauma and environmental (object-related) failure. This impoverishment is not the consequence of repression or other, more familiar neurotic defense mechanisms, but reflects instead a failure, weakness, or destruction of representation, symbolization, and psychic organization. The classic conditions for neurotic conflict cannot develop and do not obtain.

As Rappoport de Aisemberg (2010) reminds us,

> psychoneurotic functioning is built out of the memory traces left by the experience of satisfaction with the primary object, whereas the

---

8   Aisenstein (2017) writes,

> there is no such thing as a psychogenetic somatic illness. Whether it is serious or benign, an illness is the result of an infinite number of factors, hereditary, genetic, organic, environmental , and psychic, but it occurs at a given moment in a subject's life.
> (p. 76)

non-neurotic ... [functioning] derives from the sensorial traces left by the experience of pain which have not been transformed into psychic tissue.

(p. 113)

In contrast to classical neurotic patients, in whom desire and the capacity for psychic elaboration coexist from the outset of treatment, patients with psychosomatic or "mechanical" functioning, organize their psychic life "against desire," thereby defending themselves against the very objects on whom they must depend to help reinstate psychic development.

One further feature of the work with somatizing patients that must be mentioned is that of their entrapment in what can seem to be an inescapable compulsion to repeat. To what extent does this repetitive action reflect attempts to circumvent or institute psychic elaboration? Following the reasoning of Winnicott (1974), de Senarclens (2019) writes,

> It seems as if traces of the past had been felt and preserved, but not psychically integrated. The subject is trying to escape through any means the extreme pain that is hidden in them, but it appears that these poorly organized sensations and perceptions – which paradoxically seem as unforgettable as they are impossible to remember – are *knocking on the door* in search of visibility and integration at last. Sometimes it looks as if the compulsion to repeat contains some unconscious intentionality and acts like a 'tool' to elaborate and master what had overwhelmed the capacities of the primitive ego.
>
> In Press et al. (2019, p. 61)

Aisenstein (2017) puts this search for resolution in dramatic terms: "There is acting out. Circulating between the two protagonists in the framework of the session, the quantum of affect becomes a "headhunter of representations" (p. 199).

The potential signal function of the somatic symptom within the context of the analytic relationship puts greater stress on the analyst's receptivity (countertransference) and willingness to imagine – help dream undreamt dreams of the patient (Cassorla, 2013; Ogden, 2007, 2017) – that physical symptoms embody cries for help and miscarried or proto-attempts to find an object to help create a symbol (representation) to contain and therefore "defuse" the pressure of some unbound, excessive and disturbing excitation.

One is hesitant to call this form of repetition "transference" in the classical sense of the term. Although there may be continual repetition within the analytic relationship, there is a paucity of even unconscious ideational memory formation (representation) and no access to recall. As Green (2000b) noted,

> when trauma occurs prior to the acquisition of language, recollection is quite impossible.... Transference, in certain cases, ... means bringing

up-to-date rather than recollection, for the analysand does not see in it a return of the past; he refuses to confer to what he has lived the quality of repetition. Rather, he sees it as a new phenomenon that can be explained in and of itself, without needing to think of it as a return to the past. We might as well call this phenomenon an amnesiac recollection outside the field of conscious and unconscious memories.

(p. 108)

Faced with the impossibility of memory,

> the challenge in our clinical work consists in producing constructions that transform ... [unprocessed sensorial traces] into psychic tissue. [...] Such traces, once invested, come into the scene and become the object of exploration in contemporary psychoanalysis, thus enabling us to create something new between patient and analyst.
> Rappoport de Aisemberg (in Aisenstein and Rappaport de Aisenberg, 2010, p. 114)

## A clinical case

Walter was a 30 something single physician, who came to see me in great distress about his failure to work out a suitable love relationship with a woman and his great uncertainty about the professional niche he was in. He struck me as particularly anxious, even agitated – sitting restlessly with leg shaking or moving constantly in his chair – a bit depressed and, although "mild mannered," always seemed to be on the verge of some kind of eruption. He was a consummate and compulsive athlete, who trained long hours for triathalons and had a long history of inflammatory bowel disease. Years earlier, he had had an explosive rupture of his large bowel secondary to toxic megacolon. This required a bowel resection and a temporary ileostomy, which was then re-anastomosed after 8–10 months of intense agony and shame. When he first consulted me, he was having ten or more loose bowel movements per day, occasional soiling at night and was mortified at the thought of exposing his problems to any new woman that he might begin to date and sleep with.

He had had an analysis as a latency age child – four times per week for several years, into his early teens –, which I slowly learned was for explosive temper tantrums, fighting with his parents, extreme shyness, phobias and depression. The treatment had from one perspective been quite successful, as his outbursts at home became mitigated, he made friends, began to do exceptionally well at school and went on to a very fine university and into medical training. He remembered very little of the treatment, had what seemed to me to be a shameful angry feeling about having to have been in treatment and was adamant about not wanting to come to see me more than once a week. It was unclear at what age his bowel symptoms started, but they had already been present in some form (irritable bowel syndrome) prior to his beginning his previous analysis.

As the story of his life slowly unfolded, in addition to the recent breakup with a girlfriend that precipitated his consulting me, I learned that he was very closely involved, despite the geographic distance, with his family of origin. Although he clung to a view that he and his parents and younger sister were "very close" and "loving," his description of the family indicated that there quite likely was a good deal of pathology: his father sounded grandiose, hypercritical and very self-involved; his mother was chronically anxious, emotionally fragile, depressed and severely dysfunctional; his sister was unable to finish college or hold a job. Phone calls or visits home resulted in escalating frustration and angry outbursts for all concerned, followed by guilt and parental accusations that Walter was insensitive or "narcissistic" if he didn't go along with whatever idiosyncratic position or scheme that the others proposed.

This was a family in which grudges against parents, sibs and cousins were held for years, without talking or any attempt at self-examination or reconciliation. The point that I am trying to emphasize is that *in my mind*, there grew a plausible connection between Walter and (emotional) explosions mirrored by his unfortunate exploding megacolon and subsequent eruptive (gaseous) expulsions of liquid stool.

Treatment proceeded once a week, sitting up, but with a firm sense of the traditional analytic setting *inside the analyst*, held to as an internal reference against which to measure the actuality of what was being lived out within the sessions. The therapeutic action proceeded on multiple fronts:

- Walter's anger and shame at the fact of his past ileostomy, which was projected onto his previous gastroenterologist and prevented him from seeking further help with his frequent bowel movements, was confronted and worked through, so that he was able to seek and find new medicine to reduce his bowel movements to a more reasonable number per day and dramatically reduce the risks of nighttime soiling.
- His anger at and over involvement with his parents and sister were addressed and partially worked through. This allowed him to establish a bit more emotional distance from them and reduced the frequency and intensity of cycles of tension build-up and explosion of frustrated irritation and anger.
- In addition to the clarifications and interpretations, mostly having to do with helping him name, recognize, think about and tolerate his anger, frustration and fears, the steady focus and presence of the analyst, the almost "bodily emotional titration" in the sessions of his distress offered by my soothing presence, served as a silent regulator and support for his easily overwhelmed emotional regulatory capacities.

- I slowly and persistently pointed out to him his agitation or noted the point at which he needed to interrupt the session to use the bathroom, and asked him to try to notice and reflect on the internal emotional context of each incident.

I believe that the object relational presence of the analyst, my role in helping him recognize, name, think and talk about the build-up of tension, helped him to defuse his agitation, to better regulate his bowel function and to begin to *mentalize* that which he had presumptively only been able to manage physically (agitation, perhaps bowel frequency?). The result was that his capacity to talk and feel more *psychically*, was associated with a decrease in the urgency and intensity of his physical symptoms.

In presenting this brief sketch, I realize that I am raising many more questions than I am able to answer. This is not just a matter of limited space for my presentation, but more that relational elements, the neurotic infra- and or supra-structure and the underlying psychosomatic elements are all so deeply and inextricably intertwined, that it is impossible to separate out the various strands. Also, the once per week, sitting up setting is a potentially powerful limitation on what can be discovered, as it sets the analyst, in some ways, at a remove from much of the internal life of the patient. (Of course, there were many unconsciously determined, neurotic, defensive reasons for W's wishing and needing to reduce the frequency of our contact and, to the extent possible, these were explored and discussed.) And yet therapeutic progress, as measured by symptom reduction, increased distance from enmeshment in chaotic family interactions, closer relations with new libidinal objects all speak to something salutary that has gone on. What I have tried to indicate is that in addition to attempting to deal with conflicts based on internalized, formed unconscious phantasies, I have also – and at the same time – functioned as an auxiliary ego and "similar other" (Green, 2005a) offering the presence and capacity of my psychic regulatory potential to Walter through my receptivity, containment and interventions.

We must remain agnostic about the etiology of his "explosive" bowel pattern and its relation to his "explosive character" and "explosive" family dynamics and patterning. And yet there has come to be, at least in my mind, a rough connection between all of this explosiveness and the numerous "explosions" of his bowels. Does some psychic structure precede and underlie the metaphor I have offered or does the metaphor act as a construction, prosthesis or patch that bridges a gap or holds something together, *après coup*? That is the question and that may be impossible to ever know in any patient. It is the mystery of the psychosomatic, and yet I would argue that Walter is better off – physically and emotionally – for having had the treatment and that is something to be noted.

# References

Abensour, L. (2013). *The Psychotic Temptation*. Hove, UK and New York: Routledge.
Aisenstein, M. (2017). *An Analytic Journey*. London: Karnac.
Alexander, F. (1950). *Psychosomatic Medicine*. New York: Norton.
Alvarez, A. (2010). Levels of analytic work and levels of pathology: The work of calibration. *Int. J. Psychoanal.* 91: 859–878.
Alvarez, A. (2012). *The Thinking Heart*. London and New York: Routledge.
Alvarez, A. (2019). Extending the boundaries of psychopathology and of its psychoanalytic treatment: A review of *Engaging Primitive Anxieties of the Emerging Self: The Legacy of Frances Tustin* edited by H.B. Levine and D.G. Power. *Psychoanal. Quart.* 88: 867–882.
Aulagnier, P. (2015). Birth of a body, origin of a history. *Int. J. Psychoanal.* 96: 1371–1401.
Avzaradel, J.R. (2015). *A Propósito de um Aparelho de Linguagem*. In: Candi, T.S., ed., *Dialogos Psicanaliticos Contemporâneos*. Sao Paulo: Kultur (Collection), Editora Escuta, pp. 39–63.
Baranger, M., Baranger, W. and Mom, J. (1983). Process and non-process in analytic work. *Int. J. Psychoanal.* 64: 1–16.
Baranger, M., Baranger, W. and Mom, J. (1988). The infantile psychic trauma from us to Freud: pure trauma, retroactivity and reconstruction. *Int. J. Psychoanal.* 69: 113–128.
Bergstein, A. (2019). *Bion and Meltzers' Expedition Into Unmapped Mental Life*. London and New York: Routledge.
Bianchedi, E.T. de (1991). Psychic change: The 'becoming' of an inquiry. *Int. J. Psychoanal.* 72: 6–15.
Bion, F. (1995). The days of our years. In: Mawson, C., ed., *The Complete Works of W.R. Bion*, Volume XV, Appendix A. London: Karnac, 2014, pp. 91–111.
Bion, W.R. (1958). On arrogance. *Int. J. Psychoanal.* 39: 144–146.
Bion, W.R. (1959). Attacks on linking. *Int. J. Psychoanal.* 40: 308–315.
Bion, W.R. (1962a). A theory of thinking. In: *Second Thoughts: Selected Papers on Psycho-Analysis*. London: Karnac, 1967, pp. 110–119.
Bion, W.R. (1962b). *Learning from Experience*. London: Heinemann.
Bion, W.R. (1963). *Elements of Psychoanalysis*. London: Heinemann.
Bion, W.R. (1965). *Transformations*. London: Heinemann.
Bion, W.R. (1967). Notes on memory and desire. In: Spillius, E.B., ed., *Melanie Klein Today*, Vol. 2. London: Routledge, 1988, pp. 17–21.
Bion, W.R. (1970). *Attention and Interpretation*. New York: Basic Books.

Bion, W.R. (1976). Evidence. In: Bion, F., ed., *Clinical Seminars and Four Papers*. Abingdon, UK: Fleetwood Press, 1987, pp. 239–246.

Bion, W.R. (1979). Making the best of a bad job. In: Bion, F., ed., *Clinical Seminars and Other Works*. London: Karnac, 1994, pp. 321–331.

Bion, W.R. (1980). *Bion in New York and São Paulo*. Perthshire, Scotland: Clunie Press.

Bion, W.R. (1992). *Cogitations*. London: Karnac.

Bion, W.R. (2005a). *Tavistock Seminars*. London: Karnac.

Bion, W.R. (2005b). *Italian Seminars*. London: Karnac

Boris, H. (1972). Personal communication.

Botella, C. (2014). On remembering: The notion of memory without recollection. *Int. J. Psychoanal.* 95: 911–936.

Botella, C. and Botella, S. (2005). *The Work of Psychic Figurability*. London: Routledge.

Botella, C. and Botella, S. (2013). Psychic figurability and unrepresented states. In: Levine, H.B., Reed, G.S. and Scarfone, D., eds., *Unrepresented States and the Construction of Meaning*. London: Karnac/Int. Psychoanal. Assn., pp. 95–121.

Brito, G. (2015). Personal communication.

Brown, L.J. (2012). Bion's discovery of alpha function: Thinking under fire on the battlefield and in the consulting room. *Int. J. Psychoanal.* 93: 1191–1214.

Capello, F. (2016). The buried harbor of dreaming, psycho-analysis, and literature: Towards a Bionian non-archeological approach. In: Levine, H.B. and Civitarese, G., eds., *The Wilfred Bion Tradition*. London: Karnac, pp. 467–488.

Cassorla, R. (2013). Reflections on non-dreams-for-two, enactment and the analyst's implicit alpha-function. In: Levine, H. and Brown, L., eds., *Growth and Turbulence in the Container/Contained*. Hove, UK and New York: Brunner-Routledge.

Chervet, B. (2013). *Foreword to Abensour, L. (2013). The Psychotic Temptation*. Hove, UK and New York: Routledge, pp. xi–xxi.

Chetrit-Vatine, V. (2004). Primal seduction, matricial space and asymmetry in the analytic encounter. *Int. J. Psychoanal.* 8: 841–856.

Chianese, D. (2007). *Constructions and the Analytic Field. History, Scenes and Destiny*. London and New York: Routledge.

Cohen, L. (1970). *Leonard Cohen, Selected Poems, 1956–1968*. New York: Viking press.

Collins, S. (2011). On authenticity: The question of truth in construction and autobiography. *Int. J. Psychoanal.* 92: 1391–1409.

Comte, A. (1974). *The Positive Philosophy of Auguste Comte*. Translated and condensed by Harriet Martineau. New York: AMS Press (Original work published in 1855, New York: Calvin Blanchard).

De Masi, F. (2020). *A Psychoanalytic Approach to Treating Psychosis*. Abingdon and New York: Routledge.

Donnet, J.-L. (2009). *The Analyzing Situation*. Translated by Andrew Weller. London: Karnac Books.

Donnet, J.-L. (2010). Personal communication.

Derrida, J. (1978). *Writing and Difference*. Translated by A. Bass. London: Routledge.

Eaton, J. (2011). *A Fruitful Harvest: Essays After Bion*. Seattle: The Alliance Press.

Edelman, G. (1989). *The Remembered Present. A Biological Theory of Consciousness*. New York: Basic Books.

Eekhoff, J. (2019). *Trauma and Primitive Mental States, an Object Relations Perspective*. London and New York: Routledge.

Eliot, T.S. (1963). *Collected Poems, 1909–1962*. New York: Harcourt, Brace & World.

Eshel, O. (2017). From extension to revolutionary change in clinical psychoanalysis: The radical influence of Bion and Winnicott. *Psychoanal. Quart.* 86: 753–794.
Ferenczi, S. (1926). *Final Contributions to the Problems and Methods of Psycho-Analysis.* London: Karnac Books, 1994.
Fernald, A. (1989). Intonation and communicative intent in mother's speech to infants: Is the melody the message? *Child. Dev.* 60: 1497–1510.
Ferro, A. (2002). *In the Analyst's Consulting Room.* London: Routledge.
Ferro, A. (2005). *Seeds of Illness, Seeds of Recovery. The Genesis of Suffering and the Role of Psychoanalysis.* Translated by Philip Slotkin. Hove and New York: Brunner-Routledge.
Ferro, A. (2015). A response that raises many questions. *Psychoanal. Inquiry* 35: 512–525.
Flanders, S. (2015). On Piera Auglanier's 'Birth of a body, origin of a history.' *Int. J. Psychoanal.* 96: 1403–1415.
Freud, A. (1967). Comments on trauma. In: Furst, S., ed., *Psychic Trauma.* New York and London: Basic Books, pp. 235–246.
Freud, S. (1895a). *Project for a Scientific Psychology, Part II. S.E. 1: 347–387.* London: Hogarth Press, 1966.
Freud, S. (1895b). *Studies in Hysteria. S.E. 2.* London: Hogarth Press, 1955.
Freud, S. (1897). Extracts from the Fliess papers. Letter 69 to Wilhelm Fliess dated Vienna, September 21, 1897. In: Freud, S. (1892–1899). *Extracts form the Fliess papers. S.E. 1:73–280.* London: Hogarth Press, 1974.
Freud, S. (1899). *Screen Memories. S.E. 3:301–322.* London: Hogarth Press.
Freud, S. (1900). *The Interpretation of Dreams. S.E 4–5.* London: Hogarth Press.
Freud, S. (1905a). *On psychotherapy. S.E. 7: 257–270.* London: Hogarth Press.
Freud, S. (1905b). *Psychical (or Mental) Treatment. S.E. 7: 283–304.* London: Hogarth Press.
Freud, S. (1905c). *Fragment of an Analysis of a Case of Hysteria. S.E. 7: 3–124.* London: Hogarth Press.
Freud, S. (1911a). *Formulations on the Two Principles of Mental Functioning. S.E. 12: 213–226.* London: Hogarth Press.
Freud, S. (1911b). *The Case of Schreber. S.E. 12: 1–82.* London: Hogarth Press.
Freud, S. (1912). *The Dynamics of Transference. S.E. 12: 97–108.* London: Hogarth Press.
Freud, S. (1913). *The Disposition to Obsessional Neurosis. S.E. 12:311–326.* London: Hogarth Press.
Freud, S. (1914). *Remembering, Repeating and Working-Through. S.E. 12: 145–156.* London: Hogarth Press.
Freud, S. (1915a). *The Unconscious. S.E. 14: 159–215.* London: Hogarth Press.
Freud, S. (1915b). *Instincts and their Vicissitudes. S.E. 14: 109–140.* London: Hogarth.
Freud, S. (1915–1917). *Introductory Lectures on Psycho-Analysis. S.E. 15–16.* London: Hogarth Press.
Freud, S. (1917). *Mourning and Melancholia. S.E. 14: 237–260.* London: Hogarth Press.
Freud, S. (1918). *From the History of an Infantile Neurosis. S.E. 17: 1–124.* London: Hogarth Press.
Freud, S. (1919). *Introduction to Psycho-analysis and the War Neuroses. S.E. 17: 205–210.* London: Hogarth Press.
Freud, S. (1920). *Beyond the Pleasure Principle. S.E. 18: 3–64.* London: Hogarth Press.
Freud, S. (1923). *The Ego and the Id. S.E. 19: 1–66.* London: Hogarth Press, 1959.
Freud, S. (1925). *On Negation. S.E. 19: 235–239.* London: Hogarth Press.

Freud, S. (1925a). An autobiographical study. S.E. 20, pp. 3–76.
Freud, S. (1930). *Civilization and Its Discontents*. S.E. *21: 57–146*. London: Hogarth Press.
Freud, S. (1933). *New Introductory Lectures On Psychoanalysis*. S.E. *12: 1–182*. London: Hogarth Press.
Freud, S. (1937). *Constructions in Analysis*. S.E. *23: 255–270*. London: Hogarth Press.
Freud, S. (1939). *Moses and Monotheism*. S.E. *23: 1–138*. London: Hogarth Press.
Furst, S., ed. (1967). *Psychic Trauma*. New York and London: Basic Books.
Green, A. (1975). The analyst, symbolization and absence in the analytic setting (on changes in analytic practice and analytic experience)—In memory of D.W. Winnicott. *Int. J. Psychoanal.* 56: 1–22.
Green, A. (1977). Conceptions of affect. In: Green, A. ed., *On Private Madness*. London: Karnac, pp. 174–213.
Green, A. (1980). The dead mother. In: Green, A. (1997). *On Private Madness*. London: Karnac, pp. 142–173.
Green, A. (1995). *La Causalité Psychique: Entre Nature et Culture*. Paris: O. Jacob.
Green, A. (1997). *On Private Madness*. London: Karnac.
Green, A. (1998). The primordial mind and the work of the negative. *Int. J. Psychoanal.* 79: 649–665.
Green, A. (2000a). The central phobic position. *Int. J. Psychoanal.* 81: 429–451.
Green, A. (2000b). Transfert, repetition, liaison. In: Green, A., *Les Temps Éclaté*. Paris: Minuit.
Green, A. (2005a). *Key Ideas for a Contemporary Psychoanalysis. Misrecognition and Recognition of the Unconscious*. Translated by A. Weller. London and New York: Routledge.
Green, A. (2005b). *Psychoanalysis. A Paradigm for Clinical Thinking*. Translated by A. Weller. London: Free Association.
Greenberg, J. (2019). Trauma, and the metaphor of oppression. *Int. J. Psychoanal.* 100: 1144–1153.
Grinberg, L., Sor, D. and Bianchedi, E. T. (1977). *Introduction to the Work of Bion*. New York: Jason Aronson.
Hartke, R. (2013). Psychological turbulence in the analytic situation. In: Levine, H.B. and Brown, L.J., eds., *Growth and Turbulence in the Container/Contained*. New York: Routledge, pp. 131–148.
Heimann, P. (1950). On countertransference. *Int. J. Psychoanal.* 31: 81–84.
Herzog, W. (2016). On the absolute, the sublime, and ecstatic truth. *Arion: A Journal of Humanities and the Classics* (Boston University). http://www.bu.edu/arion/on-the-absolute-the-sublime-and-ecstatic-truth/
Illich, I. (1993). *In the Vineyard of the Text: A Commentary to Hugh's Didascalicon*. Chicago, IL: University of Chicago Press.
Kahn, L. (2018). *Psychoanalysis, Apathy and the Postmodern Patient*. Abingdon and New York: Routledge.
Khan, M. (1963). The concept of cumulative trauma. *Psychoanal. Study Child* 18: 286–306. New York: International Universities Press.
Killingmo, B. (2006). A plea for affirmation relating to states of unmentalised affects. *Scand. Psychoanal. Rev.* 29: 13–21.
Klein, M. (1957). Envy and gratitude. In: Klein, M. (1975). *Envy and Gratitude and Other Works 1946–1963*. New York: Delacorte Press/Seymour Lawrence.
Klein, S. (1980). Autistic phenomena in neurotic patients. *Int. J. Psychoanal.* 61(3): 395–401.

Knapp, P. (1974). Personal communication.
Kris, E. (1952). *Psychoanalytic Explorations in Art*. New York: International Universities Press.
Kris, E. (1956). The recovery of childhood memories. *Psychoanal. Study Child* 11: 54–88. New York: International Universities Press.
Laplanche, J. (1987). *New Foundations for Psychoanalysis*. Translated by David Macey. Oxford: Basil Blackwell, 1989.
Laplanche, J. (1994). Psychoanalysis as anti-hermeneutics. In: Laplanche, J. *Between Seduction and Inspiration: Man*. New York: The Unconscious in Translation, 2015, pp. 203–218.
Laplanche, J. (1998). Narrativity and hermeneutics: A few propositions. In: Laplanche, J., *Between Seduction and Inspiration: Man*. New York: The Unconscious in Translation, 2015, pp. 245–251.
Laplanche, J. and Pontalis, J.B. (1973). *The Language of Psychoanalysis*. New York and London: Norton.
Levine, H. B., ed. (1990). *Adult Analysis and Childhood Sexual Abuse*. Hillsdale, NJ: The Analytic Press.
Levine, H.B. (1994). The analyst's participation in the analytic process. *Int. J. Psychoanal.* 75: 665–676.
Levine, H.B. (1997a). The capacity for countertransference. *Psychoanal. Inquiry* 17: 44–68.
Levine, H.B. (1997b). Book review of: How Freud worked: First-hand accounts of patients by Paul Roazen. *J. Am. Psychoanal. Assoc.* 45: 1314–1318.
Levine, H.B. (2010a). Creating analysts, creating analytic patients. *Int. J. Psychoanal.* 91: 1385–1404.
Levine, H.B. (2010b). 'The consolation which is drawn from truth': The analysis of a patient unable to suffer experience. In: Mawson, C., ed., *Bion Today*. London: Routledge, pp. 188–211.
Levine, H.B. (2011a). Construction then and now. In: Lewkowicz, S., Bokanowski, T. with Pragier, G., eds., *On Freud's "Constructions in Analysis."* London: Karnac, pp. 87–100.
Levine, H.B. (2011b). Book review: Feldman, M. (2010). *Doubt, Conviction and the Analytic Process. Selected Papers of Michael Feldman*. *Int. J. Psychoanal.* 91: 235–240.
Levine, H.B. (2012). The colourless canvas: Representation, therapeutic action and the creation of mind. *Int. J. Psychoanal.* 93: 607–629.
Levine, H. B. (2014). Beyond neurosis: Unrepresented states and the construction of mind. *Revista Psicoanalisi* 60: 277–294.
Levine, H.B. (2016a). Myth. In: Levine, H.B. and Civitarese, G., eds., *The WR Bion Tradition*. London: Karnac, 2015, pp. 307–314.
Levine, H.B. (2016b). Is O necessary for psychoanalysis? In: Levine, H.B. and Civitarese, G., eds., *The W.R. Bion Tradition*. London: Karnac, pp. 377–386.
Levine, H.B. (2020). Reflections on therapeutic action and the origins of psychic life. *J. Am. Psychoanal. Assoc.* 68: 9–25.
Levine, H. and Friedman, R.J. (2000). Intersubjectivity and interaction in the analytic process: A mainstream view. *Psychoanal. Quar.* 69: 63–92.
Levine, H.B., Reed, G. and Scarfone, D., eds. (2013). *Unrepresented States and the Creation of Meaning*. London: Karnac/IPA.
Lombardi, R. (2008). The body in the analytic session. *Int. J. Psychoanal.* 89: 89–110.

Lombardi, R. (2017). *Body-Mind Dissociation in Psychoanalysis. Development After Bion*. Abingdon, Oxon and New York: Routledge.

Lyotard, J.-F. (1993). Harvey, R. and Roberts, M., eds., *Toward the Postmodern*. Boston: Brill Puyblishers.

Maetzener, C. (2015). Diary of an analysis with Freud. *J. Am. Psychoanal. Assoc.* 63: 337–350.

Mahler, M.S., Pine, F. and Bergman, A. (1975). *The Psychological Birth of the Human Infant*. New York: Basic Books.

Marty, P. (1976). *Mouvements Individuels de vie et de mort*. Paris: Payot.

Marty, P. (1980). *L'ordre Psychosomatique*. Paris; Payot.

Marty, P. and de M'Uzan, M. (1963). La pensée opératoire. *Revue Francaise Psychanalyse* 27: 345–356.

Marty, P., de M'Uzan, M. and David, C. (1962). *L'investigation Psychosomatique*. Paris: Presses Universitaires de France.

Marucco, N.C. (2007). Between memory and destiny: Repetition. *Int. J. Psychoanal.* 88: 309–328.

McDougall, J. (1978). *A Plea for a Measure of Abnormality*. New York: International Universities Press.

McDougall, J. (1985). *Theatres of the Mind*. New York: Basic Books.

McDougall, J. (1989). *Theatres of the Body*. New York: Norton.

*Merriam-Webster Dictionary*. (1913). http://www.webster-dictionary.net/definition/truth

Miller, P. (2015). Piera Aulagnier, an introduction: Some elements of her intellectual biography. *Int. J. Psychoanal.* 96: 1355–1369.

Mitrani, J.L. (1995). Toward an understanding of unmentalized experience. *Psychoanal. Quart.* 64: 68–112.

Mitscherlich, A. (1966). *Die Krankheit Als Konflikt*. Frankfurt: Suhrkampf Verlag.

M'Uzan, M. de (1984). Slaves of quantity. *Psychoanal. Quart.* 72: 711–725, 2003 trans. By Richard Simpson.

OED. (1971). *The Compact Edition of the Oxford English Dictionary*. New York: Oxford University Press.

Ogden, T.H. (2003). What's true and whose idea was it? *Int. J. Psychoanal.* 84: 593–606.

Ogden, T.H. (2004). This art of psychoanalysis: Dreaming undreamt dreams and interrupted cries. *Int. J. Psychoanal.* 85(4): 857–877.

Ogden, T.H. (2007). On talking-as-dreaming. *Int. J. Psychoanal.* 88: 575–589.

Ogden, T. (2015). Intuiting the truth of what's happening: On Bion's "Notes on memory and desire." *Psychoanal. Quart.* 84: 285–306.

Ogden, T.H. (2017). Dreaming the analytic session: A clinical essay. *Psychoanal. Quart.* 86: 1–20.

Panizza, S. (2016). The generative word. Unpublished paper. (A related version of this paper appears in Chapter 10, pp. 88–100, in Italian in Panizza, S., *L'Interpretazione Nella Psicoanalisi Contemporanea: L'Efficacia*. Milano: FrancoAngeli, 2016).

Parsons, M. (1992). The refinding of theory in clinical practice. *Int. J. Psychoanal.* 73: 103–115.

Paul, M.P. (1997). *Before We Were Young: An Exploration of Primordial States of Mind*. Binghamton, NY: ESF Publishers.

Pirandello, L. (1998). *Six Characters in Search of an Author*. Translated and Introduction by Eric Bentley. New York: Signet Classics.

Potamianou, A. (2015). Amniotic traces: Traumatic after-effects. *Int. J. Psychoanal.* 96: 945–966.
Power, D.G. (2017). Introduction. In: Levine, H.B. and Power, D.G., eds., *Engaging Primitive Anxieties of the Emerging Self: The Legacy of Frances Tustin*. London: Karnac, pp. xv–xxx.
Press, J. (2016). Metapsychological and clinical issues in psychosomatic research. *Int. J. Psychoanal.* 97: 89–113.
Press, J. et al. (2019). *Experiencing the Body. A Psychoanalytic Dialogue on Psychosomatics*. Abingdon, Oxon and New York: Routledge.
Racker, H. (1968). *Transference and Countertransference*. London: Karnac Books.
Rappaport de Aisemberg. (2010). Psychosomatic conditions in contemporary psychoanalysis. In: Aisenstein, M. and Rappoport de Aisemberg, E., eds., *Psychosomatics Today: A Psychoanalytic Perspective*. London: Karnac Books, pp. 111–130.
Reed, G.S. (2009). An empty mirror: Reflections on non-representation. *Psychoanal. Quart.* 88: 1–26.
Reed, G.S. and Levine, H.B., eds. (2015). *On Freud's Screen Memories Paper*.
Renik, O. (1993). Countertransference enactment and the psychoanalytic process. In: Horowitz, M., et al., eds., *Psychic Structure and Psychic Change. Essays in Honor of Robert S. Wallerstein, M.D.* New York: International Universities Press.
Renik, O. (1998). Getting real in analysis. *Psychoanal. Quart.* 67: 566–593.
Roazen, P. (1995). *How Freud Worked: First-Hand Accounts of Patients*. Northvale, NJ and London: Jason Aronson.
Rolland, J.-C. (1998). *Guérir Du Mal D'Aimer*. Paris: Gallimard.
Roussillon, R. (2011). *Primitive Agonies and Symbolization*. London: Karnac/Int. Psychoanal. Assn.
Roussillon, R. (2014). Remarks made during a panel discussion at the $74^{th}$ French Language Congress (CPLF), Montreal, Canada, June 30.
Sandler, J. (1967). Trauma, strain and development. In: Furst, S., ed., *Psychic Trauma*. New York and London: Basic Books, pp. 154–174.
Scarfone, D. (2005). Personal communication.
Scarfone, D. (2015). *The Unpast*. New York: The Unconscious in Translation.
Scarfone, D. (2017). Ten short essays on how trauma is inextricably woven into psychic life. *Psychoanal. Quart.* 86: 21–44.
Sechaud, E. (2008). The Handling of the Transference in French Psychoanalysis. *Int. J. Psycho-Anal.*, 89(5): 1011–1028.
Semrad, E. (1973). Personal communication.
Senarclens, B. de (2019). Somatic and borderline states. In: Press et al., *Experiencing the Body*. Abingdon and New York: Routledge, pp. 59–64.
Shapiro, L. (1972). Personal communication.
Souter, K. (2009). *The War Memoirs*: Some origins of the thought of W.R. Bion. *Int. J. Psychoanal.* 90: 795–808.
Smadja, C. (2010). The place of affect in the psychosomatic economy. In: Aisenstein, M. and Rappoport de Aisemberg, E., eds., *Psychosomatics Today: A Psychoanalytic Perspective*. London: Karnac Books, pp. 145–162.
*Stanford Encyclopedia of Philosophy*. (2013). http://plato.stanford.edu/entries/truth. Revised January 22.
Stanicke, E., Zachrisson, A. and Vetlesen, A.J. (2020). The epistemological stance of psychoanalysis: Revisiting the Kantian legacy. *Psychoanal. Quart.* 89: 281–304.
Stein, G. (1990). *The Autobiography of Alice B. Toklas*. New York: Vintage.

Sterba, R. (1934). The fate of the ego in analytic therapy. *Int. J. Psychoanal.* 15: 117–126.

Szykierski, D. (2010). The traumatic roots of containment: The evolution of Bion's metapsychology. *Psychoanal. Quart.* 79: 935–968.

Tarantelli, C.B. (2016). "I shall be blown to bits": towards Bion's theory of catastrophic trauma. In: Levine, H.B. and Civitarese, G., eds., *The W.R. Bion Tradition*. London: Karnac, pp. 47–66.

Taylor, G. (2010). Symbolism, symbolization and trauma in psychosomatic theory. In: Aisenstein, M. and Rappoport de Aisemberg, E., eds., *Psychosomatics Today: A Psychoanalytic Perspective*. London: Karnac Books, pp. 181–200.

Tustin, F. (1986). *Autistic Barriers in Neurotic Patients*. New Haven and London: Yale University Press.

Tustin, F.(1992). *Autistic States in Children* (revised edition) London: Routledge.

Tustin, F. (1993). On psychogenic autism. *Psychoanal. Inquiry* 13: 34–41.

Urribarri, F. (2017). On clinical thinking: The extension of the psychoanalytic field towards a new contemporary paradigm. In: Perelberg, R. and Kohon, G., eds., *The Greening of Psychoanalysis. Andre Green's New Paradigm in Contemporary Theory and Practice*. London: Karnac, pp. 133–150.

Urribarri, F. (2018). The negative and its vicissitudes: A new contemporary paradigm for psychoanalysis. In: Reed, G. and Levine, H.B., eds., *Andre Green Revisited Representation and the Work of the Negative*. Abingdon and New York: Routledge, pp. 65–86.

Vann, D. (2010). *Legends of a Suicide*. New York: Harper Perennial.

Vivona, J. (2019). The interpersonal word of the infant. *Psychoanal. Quart.* 88: 685–726.

Winnicott, D.W. (1949). Mind and its relation to the psyche-soma. In: Winnicott, D.W., *Collected Papers. Through Paediatrics to Psycho-Analysis*. London: Tavistock, 1958, pp. 243–254.

Winnicott, D.W. (1960a). The theory of the parent–infant relationship. In: Winnicott, D.W., *The Maturational Processes and the Facilitating Environment*. New York: International Universities Press, 1965, pp. 37–55.

Winnicott, D.W. (1960b). Ego distortion in terms of true and false self. In: Winnicott, D.W., *The Maturational Processes and the Facilitating Environment*. New York: International Universities Press, 1965, pp. 140–152.

Winnicott, D.W. (1962). The aims of psycho-analytical treatment. In: Winnicott, D.W., *The Maturational Processes and the Facilitating Environment*. New York: International Universities Press, 1965, pp. 166–170.

Winnicott, D.W. (1964). Psycho-somatic disorder. In: Winnicott, C., Shepherd, R. and Davis, M., eds., *Psychoanalytic explorations*. Cambridge, MA: Harvard University Press, 1989, pp. 103–118.

Winnicott, D.W. (1963). From dependence towards independence in the development of the individual. In: Winnicott, D.W. *The Maturational Processes and the Facilitating Environment*. New York: International Universities Press, 1965, pp. 83–92.

Winnicott, D.W. (1971). *Playing and Reality*. New York: Basic Books.

Winnicott, D.W. (1974). Fear of breakdown. *IRPA* 1: 103–107.

Winncott, D.W. (1965). The Psychology of Madness. In: Winnicott, C., Shepherd, R. and Davis, M., eds., *The Psychology of Madness*. Cambridge, MA: Harvard University Press, 1989, pp. 119–129.

Yeats, W.B. (1919). In Memory of Major Robert Gregory. In: *The Collected Poems of W.B. Yeats*. New York: Macmillan, 1966, pp. 130–133.

# Index

Note: Page numbers followed by "n" denote endnotes.

Abensour, L. 44
actual neurosis 8, 28, 97–98, 133
addictions 107, 124
Aisenstein, M. 138n8
Alexander, F. 133, 134
alexithymia 137
alpha function 2, 20, 55, 73, 81, 99, 108, 121
Alvarez, A. 103–104, 107, 110, 112–114, 117
analyst: construction 26, 62, 78, 79, 101; mode of functioning 17; and patient 45; subjectivity 6, 13, 56; unconscious 23
analytic: meaning 118; process 2, 3, 6, 12–17, 23, 40, 48, 50, 56, 62, 72–76, 80, 84–90, 92, 94, 99, 116, 135, 137; remediation and repair 101; technique 21–24, 65, 79, 80, 93, 100, 110
annihilation 3, 10, 33, 47, 90, 102, 107, 111
anxiety 3, 4, 10, 21, 38, 39, 43, 47, 90, 95, 96, 105, 119, 134, 137, 137n7
archeological analysis 20, 57–62
ASD 107, 108, 110, 113
Aulagnier, P. 124–127
autism 107, 110, 112, 114, 132
autistic: disturbances 119; maneuvers and defenses 111, 132; objects 112; shapes 112, 131
Avzaradel, J.R. 54–55

Baranger, M. 17, 92
Bergstein, A. 40–41, 101, 102
beta-element 25n10, 124

Bion, F. 16–17, 39n6, 51n3, 66, 74; alpha function 2, 20, 55, 73, 81, 99, 108, 121, 135n4; assertion 65, 67, 102; attacks on linking 44, 66; beta-element/bizarre object 25n10, 108, 124; communication level 23–24; container/contained 2, 16, 20, 39, 88, 99, 108, 121; experience 51–53; hearsay evidence 46; *Learning From Experience* 119–120, 124; necessary dimension 42; Notes on Memory and Desire 67; obscurity 65–66; perception and thinking 98–99; proto-mental matrix 122; psychic apparatus 1; psychic reality 51–53; psychic states and emotions 37; sense 51–53; Tavistock Seminars 74–75; theory of thinking 108; Thomas case 115–121; *Transformations* 65–66; truth 51–53; ultimate reality 71, 72
black holes 25, 100, 111
body: and mind 122–125, 131; physical 51, 59, 128, 136; subject and object 125
borderline 3, 8, 15, 43, 44, 50, 80, 86, 89, 113
Boris, H. 72
Botella, C. 20, 49, 73n10, 98, 99
Botella, S. 20, 73n10
brain 123, 124
bridge building 101

Capello, F. 74
capital E Experience 22n6, 42n14, 53, 57, 71

Cassorla, R. 26
Chervet, B. 45
childhood memories 20, 22, 40, 55, 78, 109
classic psychosomatic illnesses 132
compliance 27, 64, 69, 72, 77, 78, 82
Comte, A. 38
conditional truth 69
conflict theory 13, 19
container/contained 2, 16, 20, 39, 88, 99, 109, 121
conviction 5, 7, 41, 78, 79, 101
correspondence theory 67

defenses 13, 15, 16, 20, 21, 30, 49, 88, 96, 98, 107, 110, 111, 113–115, 132, 138
De Masi, F. 39n6
depression 58, 89, 136, 140
derivatives of the drive 108, 135
Derrida, J. 130
descriptive level 113
dialectics 1, 6, 9, 68, 82
dialects 10, 71, 76n9
discourse 2, 8, 15, 16, 24, 29, 39, 44, 46, 47, 106, 116, 123, 137
disorder: functional 133; organ neuroses 133; primitive personality 27; psychosomatic 133, 134, 136
distress 3, 10, 11, 24, 30, 59, 119, 122, 140, 141
Donnet, J. -L. 82–83
dream undreamt dreams 49, 139
drive *(treib)* 2
drive-frustration-desire-satisfaction 7

Edelman, G. 55
effacement 42, 44, 46, 50, 89
ego 107; defenses 29, 105; need 88; psychology 7, 13, 14, 19, 85
elementary traumatic neurosis 98
emergent truth 71–75
emotion: and affect 124–125, 131, 135; equilibrium 105; experience 10, 73, 128; homeostasis 105; loss 7; positive 118, 130n6; quality and significance 3; states 23; stem cell 81
emotional life 28, 30, 44
engagement 81, 104, 118
endogenous autosensuousness 120
essential depression 136
explanatory level 113

Ferenczi, S. 133
Ferro, A. 17, 20n2, 71n9, 74
field theory 17, 20, 71n9
Freud, A. 92
Freudian matrix 49
Freud, S.: archeological metaphor 57, 64–65, 71; archeological model 20; assertion 4, 22n7, 83, 98; *Beyond the Pleasure Principle* 22, 96, 107, 132; *Constructions in Analysis* 5, 27, 28, 40–48, 50, 72, 78–80; dynamic unconscious 72; *Ego and the Id, The* 96; Ellen case 28–35; epistemology 4–5, 49n1; frontier concept 54; infantile psychic trauma 92; interpretive interventions 65; *Moses and Monotheism* 96; *Mourning and Melancholia* 56; neurotica 64; *New Introductory Lectures* 54; pessimistic assumption 94; *Project for a Scientific Psychology* 123; psychic experience 80; reconstructions 41, 58, 65; *Remembering, Repeating and Working-Through* 21; representations of reality 43; repression 21, 23, 43, 58, 72, 98, 115, 136, 138; *Screen Memories* 4, 22, 54; structural theory 1, 10, 14, 17, 39, 107; *Studies in Hysteria* 123; topographic theory 1, 8, 10, 21, 39, 106, 108; trauma 95–96
functional capacity 8, 89
fundamental anthropological situation 109
fundamental epistemological situation 53–57, 62, 63

Green, A. 1, 8, 39, 45, 46, 75, 85, 139; construction 42; dead mother 50, 123; de-cathexis 30, 45–47, 95, 100; framing structure 89; psychoanalysis 49; repression 43; sharing of experience 50
Greenberg, J. 93
Grinberg, L. 66

Hartke, R. 46
Heimann, P. 16
Herzog, W. 70
homeostasis 1, 12, 99, 105, 110
homeostatic process 3, 42, 95, 100
hypnotic suggestion 77
hysteria 91, 123, 133–136

id 3, 8, 10, 22, 42, 47, 54, 74, 96, 107, 135
infancy 4, 4n2, 6, 19, 50, 51, 138
infans 9
infant 30, 39n6, 50, 81, 87, 89, 104, 105, 108, 110, 111, 126, 129, 130
infant-directed speech 130, 130n6
infantile psychic functioning 47n6
infantile psychic trauma 92
influence 3, 25, 53, 68, 77, 79, 136
instructional intervention 90
internal acts 26
interpretation 57, 74, 81, 103, 129, 130; analytic 67, 73; genetic 45; transference 102; truth-value of 40, 46
intersubjective assistance 100, 101
intersubjectivity 12, 73, 76
intervention 34, 57, 65, 73, 74, 79, 81, 90, 100, 103, 113, 116–118, 142
intuition 4, 37, 41–42, 52, 57, 59, 65, 66, 67, 72, 81, 85, 88, 102, 119
irreducible subjectivity 17

Kahn, L. 4n2, 36, 37, 51, 130n5
Klein, S. 16, 17, 19, 85, 126n2
knowable experience 56, 121

Laplanche, J. 28, 83, 109
*Learning From Experience* (Bion) 119–120
Lyotard, J.-F. 130, 130n5

McDougall, J. 25, 136
Marty, P. 109, 124, 136
Marucco, N.C. 47
melancholia 83, 136
memory: impossibility of 140; and remembering 23; save 44; speech and 123
metapsychology 13, 20, 45, 64, 72, 90, 94, 123, 135
Miller, P. 118, 127
missing other 10–12
Mitscherlich, A. 136
mixed neurosis 134
de M'Uzan, M. 109, 136
myth making 26

narcissistic neuroses 8, 94
neurosis 20n2, 106; actual 8, 28, 98, 133; limits of 9; mixed 134; relation to 20–21; and unconscious 24

neurotic 10, 50, 85; conflict 97, 138; patients 7–9, 15, 44, 65, 137; treatment 85
non-neurotic patient 5, 8–9, 11, 15, 17, 22, 23, 40, 43, 46, 50, 73, 80, 94, 107, 114, 119, 132, 139
noumena 36, 63

object relationship 3, 7, 14, 30, 83, 100, 112, 118, 131
obscurity 66
Ogden, T.H. 49, 67–69
organ neuroses 133
other character disorders 25

panic disorders 1, 33–34
Panizza, S. 128, 129
perversions 107, 113, 124
phenomena 8, 29–30, 36, 100; intrapsychic 13; overload 19, 109; psychological 123
physical nourishment 51
Pirandello, L. 64
plausible conjecture 5, 78
post-traumatic 94
Potamianou, A. 101
Power, D.G. 111, 119
precious ambiguities 82
premature 78, 111, 111n4
Press, J. 125, 131, 139
primal 2, 46, 65, 125–127
primary symbolism 133
primitive narcissistic 15, 79, 94, 141
projective identification, communicative dimension of 5, 17, 23–24, 23n8, 39, 66, 136
proper technique 13
psyche 25, 39n6, 47, 66, 73, 81–82, 84, 95–96, 104, 107, 120, 123–126, 131
psychesoma 131
psychic: apparatus 1–3, 66, 97, 107, 110, 121, 126, 137; capacity 20, 109, 110, 120; deficits 108; elements 4, 24, 48, 80, 81, 124; experience 80, 124, 126; organization 8, 19, 22, 23, 59, 90, 98, 137, 138; reality 3, 7, 12, 21, 23, 36–40, 52, 53, 63, 64, 67–71, 76, 120; regulatory 1–3, 11, 16, 17, 23n8, 24, 27, 90, 105, 108, 109, 132, 138, 142; representations 7, 15, 46, 54, 92, 107–109, 118, 138; space 39, 50, 87–89, 126, 127; voids 43, 48, 50, 95, 100, 107, 119, 123

psychoanalysis 6–7, 9, 37, 38, 40, 40n7, 49, 52, 58, 75, 90, 94, 130–131; art of 17; classical 24; contemporary 108, 110, 119; development of 10; history of 77; truth 63–67, 70
psychoanalyst 6, 17, 37, 52, 55, 65, 68, 75, 84, 90, 132
psychoanalytic: inquiry 21n4, 45, 52, 107; process 12, 17, 58, 65, 88, 104, 120; theory 7, 10, 12, 13, 20, 38, 91, 97, 120; truth 67, 68, 71–73; vertex 66, 124
psychoneurotic functioning 138
psychopathology 10, 13, 64, 65, 92, 97, 105, 110
psychosis 39n6, 125
psycho-somatic disorder 136
psychosomatics 15, 19, 92, 132–139, 142

Racker, H. 16
radical discontinuity 8
Rappoport de Aisemberg, E. 134, 138
reclamation 103, 113, 120
remembering 22–23, 49
representation 1–5; capacity for 20; ideational 43, 107, 135, 137; imperative 23n8; insufficiency 105; and neurosis 22; psychic 7, 15, 46, 54, 92, 107–109, 118, 138
representational imperative 2, 23n8, 99
repression 21, 23, 43, 58, 72, 98, 115, 136, 138
Roazen, P. 79
Roussillon, R. 55–58, 74, 83

Scarfone, D. 50, 96, 98
seduction 10, 41n9, 64, 82, 91, 99
self: false 83, 123; infantile 102, 109; and object 2, 7, 8, 12, 76, 126, 127
Semrad, E. 85
Senarclens, B. de 139
sexuality 28, 136
Shapiro, L. 13
slaves of quantity (M'Uzan) 109
Smadja, C. 133n2
small e experience 22n6, 53, 56
soma 2, 19, 21, 22n7, 54, 122–125, 135, 136
somatic: discharge 3, 44, 107, 108, 135, 136; disorders 132–134, 136; illness 19, 132, 136, 138, 148n8; metaphor 123; sensation 53, 57, 137; symptom 109, 123, 124, 134, 135, 136, 139
soul 123, 130
sound envelope 128, 131
speech 11, 24, 104; act 129, 130; conceptual 128; human 125; and memory 123–124; parental 129; words and 128
*Stanford Encyclopedia of Philosophy* 70
Stein, G. 57, 70
structural theory 1, 10, 14, 17, 39, 107
subjectivity 6, 12–14, 17, 26, 56, 81, 82, 104, 120, 138
suggestion 64, 69, 72, 77–80, 82, 89, 90, 121
superego 4, 16, 39, 43
symptomatic distress 10

therapeutic split 14
thing presentation 3, 8, 24, 44, 53, 54, 57, 104, 126
topographic theory 1, 7–8, 10, 22, 38–39, 106, 108
transference interpretation 102
transference neuroses 8
transformational analysis 20, 57–62
*Transformations* (Bion) 65–66
trauma 2, 22, 64n3, 88, 99, 108, 139; childhood 32, 40, 77; definitions of 91, 95; developmental 93; disappointment 88; failure 95, 138; macro 105; massive 11, 48, 100, 103, 107; micro 98, 102, 105, 109; neurosis 97, 98; problems 92–93; process of 97; psychic 11, 46, 92
true thoughts 34, 87, 125
truth 6, 51–53, 84; definitions of 66–69; distortion of 16; historical 15, 21–23, 46, 56, 80, 81; in philosophy 70–71; in psychoanalysis 63–67; psychoanalytic 71–73; suggestion and compliance 73–75
Tustin, F. 110–112

unconscious 10, 13–14, 21, 37; communication 14, 26, 35, 39; conscious and 1, 37, 38, 53, 140; dynamic 4, 27, 39, 43, 50, 57, 72, 96, 100, 107; fantasy 19, 30, 35, 59, 104, 106, 126; repressed 21, 25, 47, 72;

unstructured 4, 5, 39, 39n6, 41, 66, 100, 136
unrepresented states 5, 28, 71, 98, 107, 110, 113, 123, 124

Vann, D. 71
vitality 1, 31, 59–61, 75, 110, 113, 118, 120, 136
Vivona, J. 130
voids 19, 20, 25, 43, 50, 95, 100, 102, 107, 110, 111, 119

Walter case 140–142
Winnicott, D.W. 17, 25, 30, 50–51, 81, 87, 102, 105, 108, 109, 112, 122, 123, 131, 139; false self 27, 83, 123; *Fear of Breakdown* 102, 109, 138; somatic dysfunction 136
words: evocative 129; generative 128–131; presentation 3, 8, 54, 57, 126, 127; semantic meaning 129; singular 128; and speech 127; spoken 4, 123, 128, 130

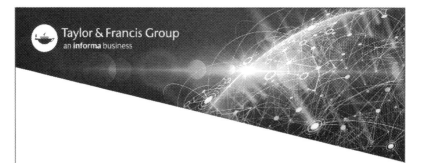

Printed in the United States
by Baker & Taylor Publisher Services